WITHDRAWN
NDSU

DEMOCRACY IN FRANCE

The Royal Institute of International Affairs is an unofficial and non-political body, founded in 1920 to encourage and facilitate the scientific study of international questions.

The Institute, as such, is precluded by its Royal Charter from expressing an opinion on any aspect of international affairs. Opinions expressed in this book are, therefore, purely individual.

Democracy in France

The Third and Fourth Republics

DAVID THOMSON, M.A., Ph.D.
Master of Sidney Sussex College, Cambridge

Third Edition

*Issued under the auspices of the
Royal Institute of International Affairs*

OXFORD UNIVERSITY PRESS
LONDON   NEW YORK   TORONTO

Oxford University Press, Amen House, London E.C.4

GLASGOW NEW YORK TORONTO MELBOURNE WELLINGTON
BOMBAY CALCUTTA MADRAS KARACHI KUALA LUMPUR
CAPE TOWN IBADAN NAIROBI ACCRA

© *Royal Institute of International Affairs 1958*

First edition	1946
Second edition	1952
Third edition	1958
Reprinted	1960

DC
340
T5
1958

PRINTED IN GREAT BRITAIN

PREFACE TO THE FIRST EDITION

This is not a history of the Third Republic in France. In conformity with the series of studies planned by the Royal Institute of International Affairs, it is an inquiry into the working of democratic ideals and institutions in France during the Third Republic. The arrangement is therefore primarily logical and not chronological. But since time-sequence and the order of development are themselves often of significance in such a study, a loose chronological treatment has seemed desirable in certain chapters—particularly in the last three. Also, since the origins of the Third Republic are at once so important and so unfamiliar in English-speaking countries, Chapter III includes a description of the curious series of events by which the Republic came into existence.

The *élan* of French recovery since 1943, when this study was begun, should in itself refute any notion that this is a *post mortem* on France. It remains all the more, since the emergence of the Fourth Republic, something of a *post mortem* on the Third Republic. If the analysis here offered should help in any way to clarify the tasks of building a better democratic order in France the work will not have been in vain.

The author wishes to thank the authorities of Chatham House for their invitation to undertake a task which has given him so much pleasure; and the Master of Balliol for his helpful interest and kindness at every stage.

D.T.

Sidney Sussex College, Cambridge
January 1946

NOTE ON THE THIRD EDITION

THE former concluding Chapter (VI) has been replaced by two new Chapters (VI and VII). One deals more fully with the phase of the Vichy Governments and the Provisional Governments between 1940 and 1946, when 'The Open Schism' in French national life, long endemic in the Third Republic, appeared with dramatic clarity. The other deals with the Fourth Republic as it has developed since 1946. In both attention has been focused on the continuities and recurrent features of events since 1940 so far as these further illuminate the special meaning and character of democracy in France. The Bibliography has been revised and brought up to date. The English version of the Constitution of 1946, included in Appendix I (J), has been completely revised by the author, and the Index has been amended.

D.T.

June 1958

To
ROBERT JAMES
A contemporary of the Fourth Republic

CONTENTS

PREFACE TO THE FIRST EDITION	*page* 5
NOTE ON THE THIRD EDITION	5
I. THE REVOLUTIONARY TRADITION	9
The Political Strand	9
The Socialist Strand	18
The Forces of Opposition	27
The Climax	35
II. THE SOCIAL BASES	39
The Peasants	39
The Industrial Workers	45
The Middle Classes	53
The Aristocracy and Gentry	64
The Oligarchy	66
Two Generations	72
III. THE DEMOCRATIC INSTRUMENT	75
The Birth of the Republic	75
The Principles and Institutions	91
How the Constitution Worked	101
IV. THE NATIONAL VISION	116
The Democratic Ideal	116
The New Europe of 1870	134
The Church	139
National Security	147
Colonial Development	163

CONTENTS

V. THE MODERN CHALLENGE — page 170
- Has Democracy Failed? — 170
- The Challenge of the Positive State — 173
- The Impact of War — 179
- Political Problems, 1918-40 — 184
- Economic and Social Problems, 1918-40 — 192
- The International Position of France, 1918-40 — 200

VI. THE OPEN SCHISM — 211
- The Armistice of 1940 — 211
- The Vichy Governments — 216
- The 'National Revolution' — 219
- The Legacy of Laval — 225
- The Provisional Governments — 230

VII. THE FOURTH REPUBLIC — 237
- The Constitution — 237
- The Political System — 244
- The Social Balance — 247
- Conclusion — 255

APPENDICES
- I Constitutional Laws — 261
- II Party Programmes — 292
- III The Franco-German Armistice Convention 1940 — 302

BIBLIOGRAPHY — 309

INDEX — 319

I

THE REVOLUTIONARY TRADITION

The Political Strand

ON 15 May 1940 the German armies broke through the defences of the Meuse and enveloped Sedan. Within two months this military defeat led to the capitulation of France, and this in turn led to the overthrow of the Third French Republic. Seventy years before, on 1 September 1870, the German armies of Bismarck had also broken through at Sedan and the capitulation of the Emperor Napoleon III had led to the overthrow of the Second French Empire. Between these two dates the history of France is the story of the Third Republic, the most prolonged experiment in parliamentary democracy that France has ever made. It was an experiment which began and ended amid the sound of gunfire dying away round Sedan. There is a rounded completeness about it which had no need to be adorned by such carefully staged performances as Hitler's dictation of the armistice terms in Foch's railway-carriage in the forest of Compiègne. The story of the Republic in the intervening seventy years is dominated by certain constant forces which, in their persistence and fatality, give an atmosphere of doom and dramatic unity reminiscent of the highest tragedy.

This book is an attempt to analyse and describe these forces, and to examine the working of democratic ideas in these particular circumstances of time and place. It is an account of why France adopted, after 1870, a system of parliamentary government; of the operative ideas on which this particular form of the modern democratic State depended; of their interaction with social conditions and political developments in France; of their successes and failures in claiming the loyalty of various sections of French public opinion. It is concerned neither to vindicate nor to condemn, but only to explain. It is a study of one particular and important example of 'the modern democratic State'.

But study of the Third Republic cannot be divorced from consideration of the whole development of modern France. Considered in historical perspective, its foundation was the climax of a century of varied and violent political experiments. The regime gained national acceptance amidst memories of the failure of all its predecessors, and was deeply influenced by the experience of these alternative systems of government. Part of its power of survival came from the lack of any widely acceptable alternative: just as part of its weakness came from the persistence of certain habits of thought and patterns of behaviour produced by the events of the previous hundred years. This historical background to the Republic may conveniently be called 'the revolutionary tradition'.

The experience and memory of the French Revolution of 1789 loomed as large over nineteenth-century France as the traditions of 1689 loomed over eighteenth-century England, or the ideas of 1776 over modern America, or the ideas of 1917 over modern Russia. These traditions took a shape as definite and as permanent as the English, American, or Russian traditions. But their coherence has been obscured by the variety of institutions and political forms in which they found expression. The English Revolution of 1689 established the sovereignty of Parliament as the central, operative principle of British democracy. The American Revolution of 1776 created, in the written Constitution of the Federal Government, the backbone of the American democratic system. The Soviets became the permanent units of political life in the U.S.S.R. But the French Revolution of 1789 asserted only that the essence of the democratic ideal is the 'sovereignty of the people'.[1] That elusive

---

[1] The French Revolution did not necessarily, however, derive the idea of 'sovereignty of the people' from Rousseau and his conception of the 'general will'. Cf. Daniel Mornet: *Les Origines Intellectuelles de la Révolution Française* (1933), and A. Cobban: *Dictatorship* (1939), pp. 50-77. The Abbé Sieyès would seem to have been the most influential theorist of the doctrine of popular sovereignty, in the sense that his *Qu'est-ce que le Tiers État?* (1788) became the text-book of the revolu-

ideal remained the core of the revolutionary tradition: but how this ideal should best be embodied in institutional form remained a matter of constant, many-sided controversy throughout the nineteenth and twentieth centuries. Its possible implications and manifestations were so many, and the social divisions created by the Revolution itself were so deep, that a profound restlessness became the most conspicuous characteristic of French political life. And the revolutionary tradition became a tradition of revolution, as well as of the Revolution.

There is paradox in a tradition derived from a revolution which was itself a revolution against traditionalism. The French monarchy of the *ancien régime* was the embodiment of traditionalism. It involved a glorification of the past, an inherent resistance to change and a constitutional incapacity to reform. The absence of a real system of common law and the survival of a tangled mass of local immunities, competing jurisdictions and embedded privileges tied the monarchy of Louis XVI to the previous three centuries. The age even of repentant monarchy was too far removed from the new, fermenting forces of western Europe to accommodate itself to them. In England parliamentary sovereignty could replace royal sovereignty because political power was already centralized in one composite authority, 'the King in his Council in his Parliament', and judicial power was already unified in the King's courts. In France, the overthrow of royal sovereignty meant the destruction of the only power which had held together the diverse, dispersed powers of Church, nobility, and *parlements*. The only theory and principle by which all could at last be fused together and centralized was that of popular sovereignty—the notion of a national 'general will', outlined by Rousseau and Sieyès and interpreted in practice by the Jacobins. This 'general will', revolting against the bonds of an outworn and antiquated political system, could function only through revolution.

tionaries. He even described the will of nations as being 'outside the social bond' and 'free and independent of all civil forms': which did not prevent his becoming the chief constitution-monger of the Revolution.

There were, however, three attempts to reconcile the revolutionary tradition and its principle of popular sovereignty with the traditional institutions of monarchy. The first was the attempt of Louis XVI and Mirabeau, and their efforts constitute the first phase of the Revolution. The summoning of the Estates-General in 1789 evoked a wave of popular support for the monarchy as a possible agency of reform. When the King's minister, Loménie de Brienne, tried to establish liberty and equality by royal decree and in 1788 attacked the powers of the *parlements*, it was they which emerged as the champions of 'freedom' against royal despotism. Their resistance made Louis dismiss Brienne; and Mirabeau remarked, 'I will never make war on the *parlements* except in the presence of the nation'. To resort, after that, to the Estates-General rather than to a National Assembly was to awaken hope of reform without creating the machinery to achieve it. It was to prepare for that split between the Estates which took place on 17 June 1789 by the Third Estate unilaterally declaring itself to be the National Assembly of France. It produced that delay and deadlock which did so much to disillusion reformers and open the doors to violence. It led, a week later, to the fusion of the Three Estates into a new National Assembly, to which nobility and clergy had been impressed against their will. Thenceforth the institution of one sovereign National Assembly hypnotized Frenchmen as the one agency through which the 'general will' and the 'sovereignty of the people' could find expression. And it was now an Assembly forced upon the King by national exigencies and by pressure from below: it was potentially a revolutionary institution, more explosive in its ingredients than the conservative local *parlements* could ever be.[1]

How far the Assembly could be reconciled with royal power depended on whether or not there should appear a minister, acceptable to both King and Assembly, and sagacious enough to guide the King towards reform and the Assembly away from revolution. Mirabeau emerged as the only likely candidate for such a task. For two years he worked to reconcile King and Assembly, tradition and reform. The task proved beyond

[1] For the later effects of this development, see Chapter III.

even his political realism and ingenuity, and his death in 1791 destroyed the last hope of reform without revolution. The next experiment in reconciliation had to wait until after the revolution had destroyed the monarchy, and after Napoleon had triumphed over the Revolution. By then reconciliation had to take new forms.

This second attempt came at the restoration. Again France was given a legitimist, traditionalist monarch, in the person of Louis XVIII. But now the return of monarchy was heralded by the issue of a Charter, setting up a Parliament of two Houses—a Chamber of Peers nominated by the King and a Chamber of Deputies elected on a narrow franchise. As a further gesture to the revolutionary tradition, the Charter was even prefaced by a declaration of rights of liberty and equality. But the whole question of ministerial responsibility—and so of the precise relation between executive and legislature—was left undefined. The vague and uneasy compromise endured only as long as Louis XVIII lived. It broke down under the more autocratic rule of his successor, Charles X, whose abdication led to the third experiment in reconciliation, the Orleanist monarchy of Louis Philippe.[1]

Again, the experiment was prefaced by a Charter of the Constitution, declaring the King to be head of the executive power and '*le chef suprême de l'État*', and stating in more detail the civil liberties of the subject. Again, the two Chambers acted as a National Assembly, expressing the general will of the people. The property qualifications for the vote were lowered. But again the question of ministerial responsibility was left undecided: and Article 47 of the Charter, giving the Chamber of Deputies the right to impeach ministers before the Peers, was an indication of how little the notion of political responsibility of ministers was appreciated. An attempt in 1835 to reach further definition failed. Still there was duality between a sovereign executive and a sovereign legislature, and the eventual deadlock could be broken only by revolution. It was—in 1848.

[1] For the texts of the Charters of 1814 and 1830, see L. Duguit, H. Monnier, and R. Bonnard: *Les Constitutions et les Principales Lois Politiques de la France depuis 1789* (5th edition, 1932).

These years which the locusts ate, between 1815 and 1848, marked the failure of France to reach any working compromise between the old order and the new, between the traditions of the *ancien régime* and the new traditions of the Revolution. There were to be a few last belated efforts between 1870 and 1877, when, encouraged by a National Assembly which included a Monarchist majority, the supporters of monarchy tried to rally their forces and promote another restoration. But the dynastic division between Legitimists and Orleanists, and the personal discord between the rival claimants, the Comte de Chambord and the Comte de Paris, frustrated all attempts at 'fusion'. These will be described later, for it was this failure which consolidated the Third Republic.[1]

Between 1848 and 1870 the revolutionary tradition gained the upper hand. Tending always to express itself in the last resort by putting up the barricades, it won its second great triumph in 1848 by the creation of the Second Republic. The victory of Republicans and Socialists behind the barricades produced a doctrinaire paper constitution which repeated most of the revolutionary idealism and most of the unpractical qualities of the First Republic. Whilst asserting Rousseau's doctrine of the indivisible and inalienable sovereignty of the people, it repeated all the familiar features of its immediate predecessors. Again it was in practice the work of a single sovereign National Assembly, and again it presupposed a dichotomy between executive and legislature. The prospect of a deadlock between government and parliament remained the one constant and permanent characteristic of all French constitutions in the nineteenth century until the Third Republic. It became customary to think of democracy and government as two separate poles in politics, too far apart for the vital spark of democratic government to flash between them.[2]

Under the short-lived Second Republic, the President as head of the executive was elected by separate popular vote for a period of four years. He was given no power to dissolve or

[1] See Chapter III, pp. 76–91.
[2] For the Constitution of 1848, see Duguit, Monnier, and Bonnard, op. cit., pp. 232-47.

prorogue the National Assembly, which was elected by universal male suffrage for a term of three years. The principle of separation of powers was applied absolutely, and again French democrats showed no appreciation of the essential problem: securing the political responsibility of ministers to parliament. The election of Louis Napoleon Bonaparte as President foredoomed the Republic, for he had already, in his exposition of the *Idées Napoléoniennes*, revealed a very positive and dynamic conception of government.

Un gouvernement n'est donc pas, comme l'a dit un économiste distingué, un ulcère nécessaire, mais c'est plutôt le moteur bienfaisant de tout organisme social.

The end of his term as President brought not his resignation but a *coup d'état* establishing a Second Empire. Homage was paid to the principle of popular sovereignty by the typical Napoleonic device of the plebiscite, and by retaining a legislative assembly of two houses. But essentially the Empire was merely a subtraction from the powers of parliament and an addition to the powers of the executive, leaving unresolved the issue of ministerial responsibility, and the fatal duality of principles. The riddle of democratic government had still not been answered in France. It was only beginning to be asked. In the last years of his reign Napoleon III fumbled belatedly with the problem. A decree of 1869 laid down that 'Ministers are dependent only on the Emperor. . . . They are responsible. They can be impeached only by the Senate. Ministers can be members of the Senate or of the Legislative Body. They have access to either House, and must be heard whenever they want to be.' But the experiment of the 'Liberal Empire' was cut short by the Franco-Prussian War.[1]

Thus by 1870 the revolutionary tradition had become associated, in the course of historical events, with certain specific ideas. It had become divorced from the ideas of constitutional monarchy because of the failures of the years between 1789 and 1848. It had become identified with republicanism. It had become dissociated completely from the traditions of the *ancien régime*, which included acceptance of the Roman Catholic

[1] Ibid., pp. 307-8.

Church as the national Church of France. It had become hostile to Bonapartism because of the experience of the Second Empire. It had become imbued with a deep-rooted distrust of a strong executive in any form, having learnt to regard strong government as the origin of Caesarism and therefore a potential enemy of democracy. The revolutionary tradition was beset with frustration, and French democrats were distinguished more by what they were against than by what they were for. They were against monarchy, against clericalism, against Bonapartism, against too powerful an executive. They were for the ideals of 1789—for Liberty, Equality, Fraternity and the Sovereignty of the People. But they remained puzzled as to how these great ideals might best be reduced to terms of practical politics and embodied in the actual machinery of government. The cycle of experiments—monarchy, republic, empire—had been tried not once but twice, and each had been found wanting.

They were haunted now by three main ideas: the need for republican institutions to secure liberty, the inevitability of a sovereign National Assembly, and recourse to the barricades as the final sanction of liberty against an over-mighty executive. That was the pattern of action laid down by the powerful 'revolutionary tradition' of nearly a century, and beyond that little was clear. Not the least important legacy of the great Revolution and of later subsidiary revolutions was undue concentration on political forms, with a corresponding neglect of social and economic realities. The question of the formal constitutional structure of the regime had assumed exaggerated importance, and obsession with the principle of separating executive from legislative power continued to obscure the central problem of making one responsible to the other without making it powerless. This problem was to raise its head repeatedly throughout the history of the Third Republic, and was never to find a completely satisfactory solution. It remained the embarrassing skeleton in the political cupboard of modern France. It not only cramped and handicapped the practical operation of parliamentary government: it also disabled the defenders of democratic principles from giving a completely

THE REVOLUTIONARY TRADITION

convincing retort to the accusation that democratic principles could not be made compatible with efficient administration. The ideal of democracy seemed more akin to anarchy in France than it ever could in Britain or in the United States of America.[1]

Nevertheless, despite so many political oscillations, there had been a certain accumulative progress in the assertion of constitutional rights and civil liberties. The Constitutional Charter of 1814 at least established the embryo machinery of representative government on the British model, and except for the Second Republic no subsequent constitution abandoned the outline of this framework of government. Its first twelve articles declared all men equal before the law and in their eligibility for political and military office; taxation was to be in proportion to wealth; personal civil and religious liberty was guaranteed; limited freedom of the Press was accepted. These rights were never again lost sight of as desirable rights. They were frequently frustrated during the next sixty years, but they could never be denied for long with impunity. The problem which was never solved was how to preserve them inviolate without recourse to the sanctions of violence and the barricades. But those sanctions were always invoked in the last resort, and the franchise was progressively widened. Even the 'personal government' of Napoleon III was forced to retain universal male suffrage and an elected assembly, although the democratic functioning of these institutions was foiled by governmental pressure and management of elections, and by the transfer of real political power to the Council of State and the Senate so that—as the Imperial Constitution accurately stated —'The Emperor governs by means of the Ministers, the Council of State, the Senate, and the Legislative Body'. But this homage even to the forms of democratic government was not without significance for the future. During the period of the 'Liberal Empire' these restrictions on the powers of the Legislative Body, on the freedom of the Press and freedom of election,

[1] For a fuller comparison of the French and British ideas of democracy, see the present writer's *The Democratic Ideal in France and England* (1940); cf. Leonard Woolf: *After the Deluge* (2 Vols. 1931-9).

were whittled down. Parliamentary institutions partially recovered their vigour, popular enthusiasm for a more democratic regime grew stronger, and men like Thiers began to demand 'the indispensable liberties'. When the Empire fell at Sedan, the Government of National Defence was a direct reversion, in theory, to the regime of the Second Republic.

The Socialist Strand

Such, then, were the character and tendencies of the main strand in the revolutionary tradition before 1870. It was not the only strand. Closely interwoven with this direct legacy of the Revolution was the strand of Socialism; itself of many shades. The original theoretical link between them is perhaps Rousseau himself, the father of French Socialism as well as of the revolutionary tradition. The notion that 'man is born free and everywhere he is in chains' involved condemning economic chains as well as political chains. The earliest example of their inter-connection in practice was perhaps Robespierre, and the experience of the Commune and the Reign of Terror. The central doctrine of Jacobinism was the omnicompetence of the State. There is little in the Jacobin wartime collectivism of the French Revolution to distinguish it in practice from the wartime Marxist Communism of the Bolshevik Revolution. Robespierre's 'despotism of liberty over tyranny' corresponds significantly to Lenin's 'dictatorship of the proletariat'.

In Jacobin theory the supremacy of the State extended over life and property alike. 'Whatever is essential to preserve life', declared Robespierre, 'is common property of society as a whole'. It took practical shape in the *levée en masse*. The decree of August 1793 announced that 'from now until the moment when all enemies shall have been driven from the territory of the Republic all Frenchmen are permanently requisitioned for military service'. It took practical shape, too, in the law of the *maximum général*, fixing a ceiling for all prices and wages: for only by an omnicompetent State, operating through an authoritarian government, could such a decree be enforced. Driven partly by the logic of their own doctrines, partly by the inherent exigencies of war and revolution, the Jacobins sought to build a society where no citizen should be too rich, and where every citizen should have enough to live. The omnicompetent State became, in practice, the agency for confiscating the property of Crown, Church, *émigrés* and all 'suspect' individuals and organizations, and for the redistribution of this wealth amongst the poor and those whose merit was to support the Revolution. The communards found themselves practitioners of an unpremeditated communism. That even this historical association of ideas was not to be broken in the revolutionary tradition was shown during the Paris Commune of 1871, which again arose during conditions of national revolution and siege.

The name which links this particular strand of the tradition with later French Socialism is the name of Babeuf. He became an important part of the tradition because of the *Conjuration des Égaux* of 1796 and because his execution by the Directory made him the first of the martyrs of French Socialism. He and his followers were that phenomenon common to all great revolutions—the frantic champions of yet one more 'final revolution', designed to complete and consolidate the 'original principles' of the First Revolution. The famous Manifesto declared:

> The French Revolution is only the fore-runner of a much greater, much more solemn revolution, which will be the last. . . . No more private property in land! . . . Begone, hideous distinctions of rich and poor, of great and small, of masters and servants, of governing and governed. . . . In the cry of equality, let the forces of justice and happiness organize themselves. The moment has come to found the Republic of Equals, that great hospice open to all men.

The Directory eliminated these embarrassing 'second-revolutionaries', just as Hitler purged the National Socialist party of their counterpart in 1934. Insistence on a further 'social revolution' is seldom welcome to those who have just consolidated their own power by a political revolution. But Babouvism lived on, as a voice of idealism and a plea for greater social equality. Guesde and Jaurès were later to speak of him with respect, and Paul Louis, the historian of French Socialism, describes the Conspiracy of Equals as 'the first great episode in the history of Socialism in this country, and indeed in the whole world'. Babouvism has the curious power and fascination of the revolution which failed. And it was in harmony with the French preference for equality rather than liberty as an operative ideal.[1]

The antithesis between the political and the social implications of revolutionary principles appears still more clearly in the thought of Saint-Simon and Fourier. The early, indigenous movement of French Socialism associated with their names is a direct offshoot of the 'revolutionary tradition'. It is distinct, both in origins and spirit, from the later Socialist movements which were produced by the industrial revolution. It is optimistic, just as Rousseau is optimistic. It believes in the essential goodness of man. It is idealistic, and tends to expect not so much a class war as a great brotherly and voluntary surrender of economic privileges, comparable with the aristocratic surrender of feudal privileges on 4 August 1789. But it is in reaction against the exaggerated importance attached to political reforms and formal democracy. It presses for the reformation of society to implement and complete the Revolutionary transformation of the State. It is Socialist in the sense that it concentrates attention on social conditions and economic life, rather than on political organization. Being also in reaction against the Jacobin development of the omnicompetent State, it is not Socialist in the sense of seeking the nationalization of wealth.

Henri de Saint-Simon and Charles Fourier are, indeed, in outlook no less than by birth, products of the eighteenth century. One was born in 1760, the other in 1772. The movements of the eighteen-twenties and the eighteen-thirties which are connected with their names are not the creation of industrialism so much as the belated development of the social principles of 1789. There is an element of delayed action about them, which perhaps explains their ineffectiveness in nineteenth-century conditions. In regarding the distribution of property and the system of production as the basic factors governing political

[1] On Babeuf see Paul Louis: *Histoire du Socialisme en France* (1925); V. Advielle: *Histoire de Gracchus Babeuf et du Babouvisme* (1884).

and social life, in subordinating politics to economics and in emphasizing the importance of scientific and technical progress, they constitute, in historical perspective, a half-way house to the more materialistic and more pessimistic doctrines of later Socialism. Their influence on later thought and developments was far-reaching but diffused. They were the prophets but not the law-givers. They stimulated thought and gave a bias to it, without determining the precise lines it was to follow or the eventual shape it was to assume. Even whilst repudiating the methods of violence and revolution, they infused a new measure of idealism and reforming enthusiasm into the 'revolutionary tradition', which was never to be completely obliterated. It is perhaps best expressed in Saint-Simon's own remark: 'The golden age lies not in the past but in the future.'[1]

There are different nuances of belief between Saint-Simon and Fourier which are relevant to our argument. If one was the heir of the Encyclopaedists—rationalist and utilitarian in temper—the other was the heir of Rousseau and the Romantics, more wayward and baroque, exalting as his ideal the small, intense community of equal individuals. Both kinds of mentality and outlook had their counterparts in later Socialist thought. But in practical effectiveness both had to yield to the more clear-cut, drastic teaching of Louis Blanc and the other pioneers of State Socialism. Just as the early revolutionaries had been submerged by the omnicompetent state of the Jacobins, so the early Socialists were soon displaced by those social reformers who looked to the State as the inevitable agency of reform.

This second great wave of Socialist ideas is the true product of industrialism. It is essentially an analysis of the new industrial society which had begun to take shape by the second quarter of the nineteenth century. Constantin Pecqueur began to contend that 'The aim is for everybody to have his own proper function within the State or, better, within his own profession, every profession being under the direct supervision of

[1] There are useful anthologies of the writings of Saint-Simon and Fourier in Albert Bayet et François Albert: *Les Écrivains Politiques du XIXe. siècle* (1935) and E. Poisson: *Fourier* (1932).

the State'. This foreshadowing of the corporative conception of the State is far removed from both the revolutionary ideal and the Socialism of Saint-Simon. Louis Blanc began to draw a sharp division between owners of capital and wage-earners, and Socialist thought advanced on the road to Marxism. Louis Blanc has the added importance of having actually held political power in 1848 and experimented in practice—albeit disastrously—with State-workshops. His contribution to the revolutionary tradition merges into the consequences which followed from the failure of the Second Republic.[1]

With this new emphasis on the place of the State in social reform and control of economic life came a new emphasis on the place of coercion and violence amongst the inevitable methods of progress. 'Not to seize power as an instrument is to find it in one's path as an obstacle,' said Louis Blanc. The spread of this belief brought Socialism down from the cloudy realm of theories and speculations, into the arena of organized politics. The movement tended to become a party. And with practicality came pessimism, for by now it was the period of the Second Empire which had many of the more oppressive elements of modern totalitarian States. France had a controlled and censored Press, knew only manipulated elections, and bore the burden of a large, rapacious bureaucracy and State-police. The bitterness of disillusion and repression was reflected in the peculiar Socialism of Proudhon.

Proudhon saw, on the one hand, the apparent failure of the French Revolution and its political tradition to secure civic freedom: on the other, the latest inroads of the industrial revolution upon social freedom and human happiness. He saw sweated labour, urban overcrowding, recurrent unemployment, and the accumulation of wealth by a few. His writings are not only

---

[1] On Constantin Pecqueur (1801-87) see G. Marcy: *Constantin Pecquer, fondateur du collectivisme d'état* (1934); on Louis Blanc (1813-82) see his *Organization du Travail* (1840—an English reprint in 1913), and his *Catéchisme des Socialistes* (1849) reprinted in Bayet et Albert: op. cit., p. 439 ff. For a critique of both see R. Soltau: *French Political Thought in the Nineteenth Century* (1931)—an invaluable work for the whole subject of this chapter.

the climax of protests against the inadequacy of revolutionary politics. They are also the first drastic demand for revolutionary economics. He, like the earlier Socialists, is important not so much because his ideas found expression in action and events, as because he became a moral influence transcending his own times.[1]

Moral fervour is perhaps his basic characteristic. Defining progress as 'the free growth of mankind in righteousness and perfection' and justice as 'the respect of human dignity, spontaneously felt and mutually guaranteed . . . whatever the risks involved in its defence', he clings through all his pessimism to a faith in moral progress. In protest even against the Socialism of his own day, he relapsed to the earlier distrust of the State and of all coercion, maintaining that all power corrupts. Reaction against the revolutionary obsession with politics could scarcely be pressed further than his famous contention that there is really only one form of government—monarchy—with 'more or less of a hierarchy, more or less concentration, more or less equilibrium, according to the laws controlling property and the division of labour'. He goes back even behind the Revolution to the Renaissance antithesis between the 'sovereign individual' and the 'sovereign State': and he denies absolutely that 'the spurious, bankrupt State can ever be reformed and become a real source of credit and of right'. He belongs to the voluntarist, anarchist side of the revolutionary tradition, just as Louis Blanc belongs to the *étatiste* side. The contrast and conflict between these two strands, deeply imprinted on French Socialist ideas by these earlier theorists, continued throughout the Socialist movements of the Third Republic. Both strands are native and indigenous to French thought, and only in the latest stages are they influenced by the teachings of Karl Marx. French thinkers reached, piecemeal, certain conclusions which tend now to be regarded as specifically Marxist in character. But they reached these conclusions within the framework and

[1] On Proudhon (1809-65) there is a vast literature, but see especially his *Théorie de la Propriété* (1866), *L'Idée Générale de la Révolution au XIXe siècle* (some excerpts of which are given in Bayet et Albert, op. cit., p. 392 ff.).

environment of the French revolutionary tradition, latterly by observation of the results of the new industrialism. From the rich profusion—and confusion—of ideas which they propounded many later Socialistic movements were to take their choice. The same trend and sequence of ideas can be found working themselves out in the later developments of Socialism in the Third Republic. But this will be dealt with later (in Chapter V).

The relevance of the whole revolutionary tradition, with all its nuances, to the operation of democratic ideas in the Third Republic takes dramatic form in the episode of the Paris Commune. The Commune of 1871 caught up, fused and projected forward into the new Republic every main strand in the revolutionary tradition as it has been analysed above. Confused and short-lived though it was, the experience of the Commune provided the lurid and violent background against which the institutions of the Republic were devised and consolidated. Seized upon by Marx and exalted, in his pamphlet, into the model pattern and classical triumph of insurrectionary proletariat over centralized nation-State, it provided the nascent Communist Party with a powerful new *mystique*. The French revolutionary tradition, in its most violent form, was thus adopted and borrowed by the most extreme Socialist movement of the Republic. This transference had considerable significance in later years: even though it rested on a confusion of *capitulards* with *capitalistes*, *communards* with *communistes*.[1]

Historically, the Commune represented neither the theory nor the work of Marxism. Nor, of course, was it distinctively proletarian. It was the product of an immensely complex interaction of national and civic humiliation, economic distress and ideological aspirations. It began on 18 March 1871—

[1] On the Paris Commune a vast amount has been written, but see especially the first-hand account by Lissagaray: *Histoire de la Commune de 1871* (1896); Frank Jellinek: *The Paris Commune of 1871* (1937) —with an excellent bibliography; D. W. Brogan: *The Development of Modern France* (1940), pp. 54-74; the novel by Paul et Victor Margueritte: *La Commune* (1903). There is a somewhat tendentious account by the Corsican journalist, Pierre Dominique: *La Commune* (1930).

THE REVOLUTIONARY TRADITION 25

after the national humiliation at Sedan, after Paris had endured four months' siege by the Germans, after Gambetta's republican Government of National Defence had failed to sustain the *guerre à outrance*, and after Bismarck's troops had marched down the Champs-Élysées. It was occasioned, but scarcely caused, by the decision of the new National Assembly at Bordeaux to move to Versailles rather than to Paris, and by the attempt of Thiers to remove the battery of guns from Montmartre. As an aftermath of the siege the population of Paris no longer included many of its more wealthy citizens, who had fled south, but it did include some 40,000 evacuees and refugees from the German-occupied provinces. The lead in the insurrection was taken by the few thousand followers of that peculiarly Parisian figure, Auguste Blanqui. His was the great name in the Paris underworld of full-time, professional revolutionaries which had grown up throughout the many changes of the nineteenth century. Blanqui's tradition was that of the barricades—he had fought behind them as early as 1827. He represents the simplest form of the revolutionary tradition, anti-parliamentarian and anarchist, and he was the idol of many young intellectuals. Perhaps he was the direct heir of Babeuf.

Closely allied with the Blanquists in precipitating the Commune were the Jacobins, led by Delescluze and Félix Pyat. They clung to the old traditions, particularly deep-rooted in Paris, of the Commune of 1793 and the Reign of Terror. They kept as their slogans Liberty, Equality, Fraternity, Sovereignty of the People, and the Republic 'one and indivisible'. They had become long skilled in the technique of resistance in the previous fifty years but had become, in the process, quixotic, doctrinaire and romantic. These were the real *Communards* —harking back to the Terror as a golden age when republican virtue really triumphed, seeing in demagogy, an inflammatory press and the barricades the true instruments of progress. The spirit of Rousseau lived on, even in their 'city-State' conception of politics; and if these neo-Jacobins admitted an omnicompetent State, it was only the State as a commune, not as a nation.

To complete this apotheosis of the revolutionary tradition there were the Socialists—followers of Saint-Simon and Fourier, Louis Blanc himself and above all the disciples of Proudhon: uniting only in their demand for social reform or revolution to complete the political revolt. The disciples of Proudhon were particularly influential because his vision of society as a community of small, self-governing groups and co-operative associations glorified the Commune as the natural unit of society. To the extreme left were the Communists, disciples of Marx and Engels, who played a considerable individual part in the history of the Commune. These included men like Édouard Vaillant, who became Minister of the Interior in the Commune: men like Leo Franckel who kept in touch with Marx himself, and with the First International which Marx had founded in 1864. As Professor Brogan has pointed out, 'Neither formally nor really had the International a leading role in the revolt, and . . . . it was not Marxism that was the animating creed of the Paris workers or their leaders.' The unanimity of the demand for 'a Commune' concealed a wide variety of different aims. 'The Commune' meant something different to each group, and provided the same sort of common rallying cry which the demand for 'a Constitution' provided in 1789, or for 'The Revolution' in Russia of 1917.

Marx, by adopting and defending the Commune in his manifesto of the International, later known as *The Civil War in France*, tried to make it the pattern for future proletarian revolutionary action. Considered historically, the Paris Commune makes sense only if it is regarded not as the hopeful model for future political action but as the somewhat forlorn climax of the old French tradition. It is an end rather than a beginning. For the next two generations, at least, the future was to lie with the big, centralized nation-State, and both political and technical developments were to militate against the success of local, spontaneous revolts. In a Europe where Germany and Italy had become political units, France too had to be a powerful centralized nation-State. In this sense Thiers ranks with Bismarck and Cavour as one of the great nationalists of modern Europe. He stood for the preservation of political and constitutional unity, just as did his contemporary Abraham Lincoln in America: and both had to fight a civil war in order

THE REVOLUTIONARY TRADITION   27

to preserve union. The Paris Commune was not the only revolt. Its example was followed by other big cities—by Lyons, Marseilles, Saint-Étienne—and local risings took place at Toulouse, Narbonne and Limoges. The events of 1871 were, in short, the greatest of all knots in the tangled skein of the revolutionary tradition in France.

France had thereafter to view that tradition through the bitter experience of these short-lived rebellions, duly suppressed with much bloodshed by the national executive. The *communards* had won for themselves something of the glamour of martyrdom claimed by Babeuf eighty years before: the Commune, too, had the fascination of the revolution which might have been. But meanwhile recourse to violence was much discredited. At first those who still sought reform were offered no clear constitutional alternative. By them the new Republic of M. Thiers was accepted at worst with positive resentment, at best with lukewarm caution. Before long their eyes were to turn to Gambetta, hero of the national defence, as the rising hope of the stern and unbending revolutionaries. His influence is the main channel through which the revolutionary tradition was finally transmitted to the politics of the Third Republic.

The relative shares of Thiers and Gambetta in establishing the Third Republic will be considered more conveniently in the next chapter. First it must be shown that the full legacy of the Revolution was something wider and more complicated than the direct tradition which has so far been analysed. The tide of revolution and of revolutionary ideas produced a certain backwash. Few historical developments are the direct and simple consequence of one movement. They are usually the result of the interaction between a movement and its backwash. And the forces opposed to the revolutionary tradition played an essential part in the establishment of the Third Republic, which was at heart an attempt to reconcile the conflicting forces of modern France.

The Forces of Opposition

It is perhaps useful to distinguish between the anti-revolutionary forces which were negative enough to want to go back to the years before 1789, and the counter-revolutionary forces, which accepted some fruits of the Revolution but reacted against certain of its historical consequences. Both these currents of opinion continued to flow throughout the life of the Third Republic, and both had their roots in the first half of the nineteenth century; but there was not always harmony between them.

The anti-revolutionary forces find most absolute expression in the writings of traditionalists like Maistre and Bonald, and in the policy pursued by Charles X. They rallied all those who believed that the Revolution was inherently wicked, and contrived to demonstrate, with immense intellectual skill and literary brilliance, that it was the product of evil. They naturally took over all the conservatism of Edmund Burke, who had first denounced the Revolution in terms which shook the Continent. But they carried his conservatism to the defence of extreme authoritarianism. Government is by its nature absolute and unlimited, and therefore the executive is complete sovereign. To be infallible authority must be Divine in origin, and therefore must ultimately be supervised by the Catholic Church. The extreme ultramontane claim of the Papacy was the logical inference which these writers drew from their conception of political society. Democracy and the Revolution, like Protestantism and dissent, are in the nature of heresy—evil things, which must be totally resisted. Maistre and Bonald are thus the logical anti-revolutionaries, opposed in detail to all that was involved in the principles of 1789. Bonald expressed the view unforgettably in his epigram, 'When God wished to punish France He took away the Bourbons from her governance'. He insisted more clearly than Maistre on legitimist monarchy as the necessary barrier to the Revolution, and he is the logical reactionary. But both champions of authority found it difficult to avoid defending any given *de facto* authority, any *status quo*: and so to argue that to endure any tyranny is better than to incur the risk of anarchy.[1]

[1] On Maistre and Bonald see Bourget et Albert, op. cit.; R. Soltau: op. cit.; H. J. Laski: *The Foundations of Sovereignty* (1921);

THE REVOLUTIONARY TRADITION 29

These conservatives *à outrance* became a fountain-head of inspiration for all later reactionary movements: most important, perhaps, to Charles Maurras and the movement of the *Action française*, which not only took an active part in mobilizing the forces of opposition to the Third Republic, but became the mainstay of the Vichy Government of Marshal Pétain after 1940. In their own day their only counterpart in practical politics was the party of the 'Ultras' which focused its hopes on Charles X. Representing the party of the *Émigrés* and the Church, they stood for a total return to the *ancien régime*. Bitterly quarrelsome and greedily opportunist, they did as much to discredit the forces of conservatism as the Catholic intellectuals had done to exalt them. By the eighteen-seventies, the Legitimist politicians were the worst enemies of Legitimism.

Under the Second Empire the anti-revolutionary writers proved a similar embarrassment to the cause of the Catholic Church by the exaggerated claims of theocracy which they put forward. Louis Veuillot of the paper *L'Univers* echoed all the most extreme arguments of Maistre. He was particularly important because he won the support of Pope Pius IX who, with considerable wishful thinking, persuaded himself that the authentic voice of French Catholicism was Veuillot rather than the powerful school of Liberal Catholics led by Dupanloup, Bishop of Orleans and Sibour, Archbishop of Paris. Because of this alliance between ultramontanes and Papacy, the Church remained closely associated with total opposition to the revolutionary tradition. The French prelates and clergy who held more moderate views strove, through papers like the *Correspondant*, to dissociate the French Church as a whole from these embarrassing ideas. But they were confounded by the Papal publication, in 1864, of the *Syllabus of Current Errors*. The *Syllabus* meant the official adoption of the ideas of Maistre and Veuillot, and securely tied Catholicism to the anti-revolutionary party. The subsequent declaration of Papal Infallibility in the Vatican Council of 1870 sealed this

M. Barbé: *Étude Historique des Idées sur la Souveraineté en France de 1815 à 1848* (1904); N. E. Hudson: *Ultra-Royalism and the French Restoration* (1936).

bond: and the Third Republic was bequeathed one of the thorniest of political and social problems which it had to tackle. It is, indeed, difficult to assess all the future ramifications of this association between the Catholic religion and Monarchist reaction, so far-reaching and complex were its consequences during the next seventy years. The cleavage in French life created by the separation of Church and State in 1905 is but the sequel and counterpart to the rift created by 1870, before the Republic was born.[1]

Side by side with this 'anti-revolutionary' current, the total negation of 1789, flowed what may be called the 'counter-revolutionary' current. It took various forms during the nineteenth century, but common to all forms was the blunting of some consequences of the Revolution by accepting and turning against them some of its other consequences or implications. In politics this current took two forms—Liberalism and Bonapartism: in religion it took the form of Liberal Catholicism.

French Liberalism, with all its strength and weaknesses, belonged almost entirely to what has been called above the political strand of the revolutionary tradition. The ideas common to nearly all its theorists and practitioners are insistence on the need for a strong centralized government, preference for a sovereign national assembly, and resistance to the social and economic implications of the revolutionary principles. Though constantly pre-occupied with questions of political organization, most Liberals were ready to compromise with Monarchy or Bonapartism so long as these regimes combined a strong executive with 'the indispensable liberties'. It is perhaps this pliability, combined with over-rigid refusal to compromise with Socialism, which explains the failures and relative ineffectiveness of French Liberals in the nineteenth century. They suffered the fate of many middle parties—being regarded as revolutionary by the Right and as reactionary by the Left: and

---

[1] On Louis Veuillot (1813-83) there is a biography by Eugène Veuillot; see Soltau: op. cit., p. 176 ff.; E. L. Woodward: *Three Studies in European Conservatism* (1929) and *War and Peace in Europe, 1815-70* (1931) for much valuable material on the period; and cf. Chapter IV, below, pp. 139–143.

by its fluctuations French Liberalism did little to refute either charge. It constantly fell between two stools. It concentrated on legalistic formulae without relating them adequately to existing social and economic conditions. It emphasized the need for parliamentary government without insisting that parliament should be sensitive and responsive to public opinion. It claimed for the middle classes and for property-owners freedoms which it was slow to extend to humbler wage-earners.

These generalizations can be plentifully borne out by the writings and actions of the leading French Liberals. In their faith in the efficacy of tinkering with political machinery, a writer like Madame de Staël and a politician like Guizot are the heirs of that early phase of the Revolution, prior to 1791. The best of them, such as Benjamin Constant, accept the revolutionary principle of the 'sovereignty of the people' whilst opposing the tyrannical perversions of it which had produced the Reign of Terror or the plebiscitary dictatorship of Napoleon. Civic rights and political liberties are seen as the safeguards of popular sovereignty. But the orthodox Liberal is opposed, somewhat inconsistently, to universal suffrage, as being likely to result in mob rule and the tyranny of the majority. Even in their opposition to extension of the vote, the Liberals attached exaggerated importance to a political device, and they failed to see that peasant proprietors and well-to-do artizans would be just as conservative in politics as many *bourgeois*. Their wooden, oligarchic outlook goes far to explain the fact, described above, that extensions of the vote were normally the result not, as in Britain, of Reform Bills, but of political revolutions. Likewise the persistent failure of France to appreciate and tackle the constitutional riddle of how to secure ministerial responsibility lies chiefly at the door of the Liberals: they could see little reason why ministers should be responsible, so long as they themselves were likely to be the ministers.[1]

The period which sent Liberalism sliding down the slope of association with the Right rather than the Left, which turned

[1] On French Liberalism in this period see Soltau: op. cit.; J. P. Mayer: *French Political Thought from Sieyès to Sorel* (1943); G. de Ruggiero: *European Liberalism* (1927).

them into Conservatives rather than Liberals in the English sense, was the reign of Louis Philippe, 1830-48. By the end of these years Liberalism had failed as decisively in France as in Germany or Italy to assert its leadership of the movements and forces of the future. Thiers alone, of the leading politicians of the reign, saw clearly the implications of ministerial responsibility to parliament, and tried to build up a constitutional monarchy reconciling tradition and democracy on the English model. But he was out of power for most of the period, and Guizot, like the King himself, followed in practice few political ideals other than total inertia and stubborn preservation of the *status quo*. As Professor E. L. Woodward puts it, he made 'the curious mistake of trying to establish the sovereignty of the people without the co-operation of the people'. This was the most common mistake of the early Liberals, and it taught Frenchmen to look for reform and alleviation of distress not to them, but almost entirely to the parties of the Left. To the Radicals, the more extreme Republicans and the Socialists was bequeathed the social strand of the revolutionary tradition. Guizot wrote his own epitaph in one of his letters: 'In seventeen years we used up all the capital of good sense and political courage which the country had accumulated since 1789. In 1848 no further drafts on this capital could be honoured. Hence the bankruptcy of France and of ourselves.'[1]

This divorce of the movement of Liberalism from a spirit of liberality weakened it in battle with its chief enemy, Bonapartism. The traditions and achievements of the First Empire, redecorated by the myth of St. Helena, had from the first stolen much of their thunder. It was Napoleon who had opened up *la carrière ouverte aux talents*, who had whetted and appeased the appetite of the peasants for land and hope and glory, and who had debased the spirit of freedom in the name of greater equality. The *mystique* of Bonaparte throve equally under restored Bourbons and Liberal Orleanists, amidst the hesitations of Louis Blanc and of Lamartine. The spell was re-

[1] On Guizot, see E. L. Woodward: *Three Studies in European Conservatism* (1929), Chapter II; of Guizot's own works, especially his *De la Démocratie en France* (1849).

THE REVOLUTIONARY TRADITION

cast by Louis Napoleon, assisted by the timely return of Bonapartist bones from St. Helena and Bonapartist nephew from England, so that for the second time in two generations the Republic merged into the Empire. The formula of the spell was the assertion that Napoleon had himself been a Liberal. The histories written by Liberals like Thiers had lent colour to the notion. The programme of promises drawn up by Louis Napoleon crystallized the legend so as to elicit the support of peasants who feared the 'Reds' of Paris, soldiers impatient with Republican theorists, and merchants who hoped for stability and order. Anti-revolutionary Monarchists and Liberal Orleanists equally tended to support him against Democratic Republicans like Lamartine. And it is significant that the forces of Socialism were routed by General Cavaignac under the direction of the Republican government in the 'June days' of 1848, six months before the election of the Bonapartist President. It was the cleavage between the political and social strands of the revolutionary tradition which opened the door to the counter-revolutionary forces of Bonapartism.[1]

The humiliation of Sedan did not, as is commonly supposed, kill Bonapartism as a political force. It had nearly thirty representatives in the National Assembly in 1871, and even in 1875 the party's candidates could poll as many as 42,000 votes in some constituencies. To the first Chamber of Deputies of 1876, some seventy-five Bonapartists were returned. Only slowly did the strange spell lose its fascination for Frenchmen, and at no stage did it lose its counter-revolutionary character. Its disciples stood, like the Liberals, for a strong centralized national government in opposition to the decentralizing tendencies of both extreme Right and extreme Left. Bonapartism represented the tradition of *étatisme* as strongly as the Liberals; the appeal to demagogy (in the form of plebiscite) as strongly as the Jacobins; and the sentiment of social equality only less strongly than the Socialists. That it was still associated with the mob tradition of violence came out clearly in 1874, when Gambetta

[1] Cf. Louis Napoléon: *Des Idées Napoléoniennes* (1840); Lord Rosebery: *Napoleon: The Last Phase* (reprint 1928); H. A. L. Fisher: *Bonapartism* (1908), Chapters IV-VI.

was personally attacked at the Gare Saint-Lazare by a gang of Bonapartists. In methods and appeal, the post-1870 Bonapartists were the ancestors of those later semi-fascist, authoritarian movements, such as the *Croix de Feu* of Colonel de la Rocque.[1]

The third element, which may rightly rank as a counter-revolutionary force, was the movement of Liberal Catholicism. In reaction against that cleavage between Republic and Church which dated from the Civil Constitution of the Clergy in 1790, there grew up in the latter half of the nineteenth century a body of opinion which sought to heal the wounds, and to reconcile the counter-revolutionary force of Liberalism with the anti-revolutionary force of Catholicism. It was associated in origin with the great names of Lamennais and Montalembert. It inevitably fought a losing battle on two fronts: against the Liberal conception of the omnicompetent State because its champions demanded freedom of education; against Papal orthodoxy because they sought freedom of conscience and the Press and the disestablishment of the Church. The effort to dissociate Catholicism from the Monarchist 'Ultras' was supported by the Gallican clergy as part of their resistance to Ultramontanism. Men like Dupanloup claimed for Catholicism all that was best in the Revolution, whilst condemning the more egalitarian, Socialistic tendencies of the revolutionary tradition. This meant, in effect, exalting the ideal of liberty above the ideal of equality. 'Freedom, and freedom only', wrote Montalambert, 'is what the Church needs.' This school of thought, eloquently and inspiringly expounded, attracted many of the finest characters amongst the French clergy. It failed chiefly because it was repudiated by the Papacy itself, in the way that has been already described. It bore temporary fruit in the eighteen-eighties, but reconciliation was short-lived.[2]

---

[1] See also Chapter III, for the activities of the Bonapartists after 1870, and Chapter V, p. 195f., for the Fascist leagues after 1919.

[2] On Lamennais, Montalambert and the movement of Liberal Catholicism, see the collected works in the *Collection Michel Lévy* (1872), with a study of Lamennais by Renan; H. J. Laski: *Authority in the Modern State* (1919); E. L. Woodward: op. cit., Part III; R. P. Le-

THE REVOLUTIONARY TRADITION

Its story is full of paradoxes. The two greatest triumphs of the movement were won under the Second Republic. These were the passing of the *Loi Falloux* and the overthrow of the Roman Republic of Mazzini by French Republican troops. The educational system established by the *Loi Falloux* is the best evidence of the 'counter-revolutionary' affinities between Liberals, Bonapartist President and Liberal Catholics. It set up freedom of secondary and university education under the supervision of State inspectors, and allowed the giving of State grants to free schools in certain circumstances. Since only the religious orders had funds enough to compete with the State *lycées* on anything like equal terms, the practical effect was to divide the younger generation of the upper and middle classes into two camps—those brought up in lay schools and those brought up in clerical schools. The greatest success of the Liberal-Catholic compromise resulted, in fact, in the permanent disruption of the Republic, which was only further aggravated when the compromise was rescinded in 1905. Then it was Combes, ex-pupil of the Jesuit schools, who repealed the *Loi Falloux*. Similarly, the Republican preservation of the temporal power of the Papacy in 1849 was to encourage, twenty years later, that assertion of Papal Infallibility which destroyed the movement of Liberal Catholicism. The paradox inherent in the movement was well illustrated by the career of its chief founder Lamennais. Starting as the echo of Maistre and Bonald in his extreme traditionalism, he moved through the phase of Liberal Catholicism to complete disillusion, excommunication by the Pope, and adoption of an extreme democratic and Socialistic faith.[1]

The Climax

We have followed the main currents of ideas and movements which emanated from the great upheaval of the French Revolu-

canuet: *Montalambert d'après son journal et sa correspondence* (3 Vols. 1895-1902).

[1] On the Falloux Law see Comte de Falloux: *Mémoires d'un Royaliste* (3 Vols. 1926), Vol. II; H. Michel: *La Loi Falloux*.

tion. They eddied and swirled throughout the nineteenth century, now converging powerfully in one direction, now colliding in a turbulent spurt of foam, tossing on their crests a rich profusion of men and parties. France was in a sea of troubles, but it was not without its moments of beauty and greatness. Spun at last into the whirlpool of overwhelming national defeat, diverse men and movements were drawn closer together for a moment—for long enough, perhaps—to join hands and gain more tranquil waters. From this moment of enforced collaboration was born that prolonged experiment in reconciliation which history knows as the Third Republic. But none could forget the past, and to memories of old disputes were added new discords. This chapter has been necessary because the Third Republic was haunted by history. Frenchmen thought incorrigibly in historical terms. Her great political leaders—Guizot and Jaurès, like Thiers and Lamartine before them—wrote big-scale historical studies of the French Revolution and its consequences.[1] Political oratory, no less than political writing, constantly appealed to the experience of recent history. Even the stoutest champions of the democratic republic were tied as securely to the past as had been the *ancien régime* of the eighteenth century. Frenchmen remained traditionalists even when they were being most progressive and revolutionary.

Perhaps the central weakness of the revolutionary tradition, in the last analysis, was the lack of a skilful political leader whose faith in the ideal of liberty was matched by his faith in the ideal of equality, and whose personality and statecraft were competent to bridge the apparent gap between democracy and government. This two-fold dichotomy, as we have seen, was the geological 'fault' running through all strata of the revolutionary tradition. Who, after all, were the outstanding French Radicals of the early nineteenth century? Victor Hugo and Lamartine? Both were greater as romantic poets than as practical statesmen: both started as Bourbon Royalists: both were democrats by emotion rather than by intellect. Their senti-

[1] Cf. A. Thiers: *Histoire de la Révolution Française* (1827); Jean Jaurès: *Histoire Socialiste* (1924); F. Guizot: *Histoire de France* (1879); A. de Lamartine: *Histoire des Girondins* (1847).

THE REVOLUTIONARY TRADITION 37

mental attachment to democratic ideals failed to withstand the Bonapartist appeal of benevolent despotism. Michelet and Quinet? Both were academicians, cultivators of the *mystique* of Republicanism rather than effective and realistic craftsmen in politics: both did much to infuse French Republicanism with a burning faith in the destiny of the French people. But they generated forces which others might harness and guide towards practical achievements without giving a lead themselves. De Tocqueville? He was a Liberal with a real spirit of liberality, who saw the meaning of democracy more clearly than his contemporaries, yet who shrank back from much that he saw, and whose active political life was extremely short. None of these great figures fills the bill. Men like Ledru-Rollin, Garnier-Pagès, Marrast and Arago might have had the faith that moves mountains, but they had not the political genius that moves masses of men into action. Radical democracy failed by political default.

As will be shown later (Chapter VII) the emergence of the Fourth Republic after 1944 has been marked by fresh attempts to reconcile the political and social strands of the revolutionary tradition, and to remedy this deep-rooted defect of inspiring democratic leadership. Will the men of 1944 succeed where the men of 1870 failed? The founder of the democratic Republic, as of the modern Radical Party, was Léon Gambetta. In 1870 it was he who when the gunfire had died away around Sedan, proclaimed (on 4 September) the end of the Second Empire, and the dawn of a new Republic. It was a revolutionary act, supported as usual by the people of Paris. He was the direct heir of the revolutionary tradition: and despite his erratic and disconcerting genius he probably did even more than Thiers to base the Third Republic on broad democratic foundations and to infuse it with democratic ideals. The social bases of the Republic require separate investigation.[1]

[1] The foregoing analysis may serve as an antidote to the tendency of many writers in France and about France to reduce the effects of the revolutionary tradition to the alleged existence of 'the two Frances'—the 'red' France of Jacobinism and the Revolution and the 'black' France of the Counter-Revolution. First elaborated by the

Swiss writer, Paul Seippel in his book *Les Deux Frances* (1905) under the spell of the Dreyfus Case, an enormous amount of theorizing and discussion has ensued as to the 'split personality' of the French nation, how far there is a 'third France' neglected by this division, and so on. This peculiarly barren controversy, revived from time to time (even for Vichy: e.g. Thomas Kernan: *Report on France* (1942) Chapter II), ignores the real complexity of French politics and French political life. The notion is even, apparently, accepted by so shrewd a student as Roger Soltau (op. cit., Chapter XV). Inevitably in an unstabilized society, a clear and wide social and intellectual cleavage is apt to appear in times of stress: but, as will be shown below, the connexions between the main cleavages which have arisen during the Third Republic are not those of identity or even of consistency, and the whole trend of French development between 1870 and 1940 is misunderstood if it is assumed that every crisis is ultimately the same crisis.

The truth is more accurately expressed by Miss Katharine Munro (*France Yesterday and To-day*, p. 63): 'The Right-wing parties never quite forgot the possibility of a counter-revolution, while the Left-wing parties revived the Revolution militant in their Marxism or Communism; each side suspected the other of using the Republic to achieve its own ends and of being loyal only so far as suited it. This suspicion threatened, time and time again, to make the Republic unworkable, since it led to obstruction in both the political and the economic sphere, and difficulties of government in turn undermined confidence in the regime and its rulers.' See below, Chapter III.

II

THE SOCIAL BASES

The Peasants

THE first general elections to the first Chamber of Deputies of the Third Republic were held in February 1876. Gambetta toured the provinces of France in a whirlwind campaign of speech-making, and everywhere he found large and enthusiastic audiences, Here is his own description of them, written at the time to Juliette Adam.

> Everybody comes as he likes, there are more than 3,000 people, and I am made to get up on an improvised platform. Here, indeed, is the audience I love—workmen, peasants, ordinary folk, whose natural generosity and common sense have not been changed by their contact with civilization. It is they I am fighting for. . . . But we had to leave Orange, and I thought for a moment that we wouldn't get out, so large, dense and enthusiastic was the crowd pressing round us. We had to shake hands all round, and only after a thousand speeches were we given a free passage, and not until we had been loaded with blessings and flowers. . . . We gallop on through the loveliest villages, and everywhere people run out, for the women and children know my name and connect it with the Republic. Peasants leave the fields and come to stop our carriage, seeking news of the rest of France. They go away with light step and moist eyes, when they learn that in three days France, the real France, will be free.[1]

That Gambetta did not exaggerate popular enthusiasm for either the Republic or his own leadership was proved by the election results. There was a Republican Left-wing majority of nearly two-thirds. Yet these same peasants, only five years before, had elected a National Assembly of which two-thirds were Monarchists. The most significant event of the years 1871-76 was not the definition and establishment of France's

---

[1] L. Gambetta: *Lettres, 1868-81* (edited Halévy et Pillias) (1938), Letter 269. Cf. Daniel Halévy: *La République des Ducs* (1937), pp. 214-20.

new political institutions. It was the conversion of the mass of French peasants to faith in a democratic Republic.[1] And that was the achievement partly of Thiers, who taught them by experience that *une république conservatrice* was possible; partly of Gambetta, who generated popular enthusiasm for democracy, and made it an operative ideal.

Perhaps these men built even better than they knew. Testimony comes, seventy years later, from the resistance of defeated France to the anti-Republican manœuvres of the Vichy Government. On 29 June 1940 only a week after the signing of the armistice with Germany, the French officer Barlone noted in his diary:

> Naturally, the idea of dictatorship in France, for the moment at least, is in the minds of both officers and men. Literally I have never met a single one of my poilus who has not expressed his disgust for the parliamentary regime and has not insisted on the Deputies and their policy being solely responsible for the disaster. These people express their thoughts inadequately. Being sincerely democratic, they feel that democracy has been distorted by the misuse of the last thirty to forty years of our parliamentary government: they are so profoundly attached to the Republic, so accustomed to make use of their deputy, that when they return home they will write him for a grant of money to rebuild their houses or in order to get a job on the railways. It is therefore the form of democracy which must be modified. We must give back to the people the habits of high thinking, we must make them understand again the necessity and the joys of sacrifice for the common good and the Fatherland.[2]

Even prolonged disillusionment with parliamentary machinery scarcely blurred the ordinary Frenchman's vision of the democratic ideal: it hardly even shook his faith in Republicanism.

After the loss of Alsace and Lorraine in 1871, there were over 36 million citizens of France. Only 10 million of these were given a vote by the new Constitution, and only 75 per cent of these actually voted in 1876. Over half the electorate—5,383,000—lived by agriculture, and 3,552,000 of them owned

[1] Cf. F. H. Brabant: *The Beginning of the Third Republic in France* (1940), p. 378.

[2] D. Barlone: *A French Officer's Diary* (1942), p. 97.

THE SOCIAL BASES

the land they tilled. Just over 3 million were engaged in industry and three-quarters of a million in business and trade—many of them, of course, village craftsmen and shopkeepers. Despite the great progress of the industrial revolution under the Second Empire, democracy in France meant still a rural democracy. Political life centred ultimately in the 36,000 *Communes* of the French countryside, and politics had still much of the atmosphere of the parish-pump. Just as Thomas Jefferson visualized American democracy as a democracy of frontiersmen, imbued with the spirit of freedom and equality of the frontier farming community, so Gambetta thought first of a democracy of peasant proprietors and little men. It was to the 'new social strata' of little men, enfranchised by the new grant of universal male suffrage, that he looked for the successful working of the Third Republic.

He made a famous speech at Grenoble in 1872 condemning the short-sightedness of the older ruling classes, and demanding:

Have they not seen the workers of town and country, the world of workers to which the future belongs, make formal entry into our political life? Does not their entry give notice that France, after due trial of other forms of government, is turning to a new class to make trial of republicanism? I foresee, I can see, I proclaim the coming of a new social stratum into our politics. I feel that the democracy of to-day has left behind the somewhat misty sentimentality of the last generation. We now have to deal with this new personnel—practical experienced people, used to business, prudent and politically wise. Every resolve they take, every decision they reach, will have a special quality, an individual accent, which will affect the conduct of the whole government of France.

He saw France being pulled in opposite directions by two forces which he described to Madame Adam as 'the old and the new social strata, the debris of oligarchy and democracy'. He believed that France could regain 'her former political and military lustre' only by the triumph of these new forces. He grasped the fact that the new regime must, if it was to survive, be based on the broadest national foundations of the common people: and that the common people must be infused with the operative ideals of liberty and equality if democracy was to be built in France.[1] In 1940 some 40 per cent of Frenchmen still worked on the land, and according to the last figures available, in 1931, 7,579,000 people were employed in agriculture, and 4,657,832 owned their own land. There were—even more significantly—some 1,343,000 peasant farms employing no paid labour. Even of the similar number of people in industry, 60 per cent worked for small firms employing less than twenty workers. France remained a half-way house between the top-heavy industrialization of Britain and the top-heavy agrarianism of most of the peasant countries of Europe. By their very means of livelihood, most Frenchmen are individualists, economically 'little men'. Their economic life has kept its continuity, with the village and the small market town as the basic units of social life. Freedom and equality were translated into terms of individualism, economic independence and social equality. This outlook and this particular conception of democracy found most self-conscious political expression in the Radical parties. And they laid claim to be, *par excellence*, the heirs of the revolutionary tradition and the defenders of the Republic.

This close linking of the direct revolutionary tradition with the powerful class of peasant proprietors and small property-owners had certain important consequences for the working of democracy in France. It perpetuated that divorce between the political and social strands of the tradition which has already been noted as a feature of nineteenth-century history. It has become a common-place that 'the French carry their hearts on the left and their wallets on the right', that they are politically Radical but socially Conservative. The prejudices and interests of the small property-owners are the reality behind these generalizations.

With our knowledge of subsequent developments, and our experience of how Conservative were these beneficiaries of 'universal suffrage', it is difficult for us to appreciate either the fanatical enthusiasm or the exaggerated hopes with which Left-wing democrats of the eighteen-seventies viewed the introduc-

[1] L. Gambetta: *Lettres*, Letter 206; H. Stannard: *Gambetta* (1921), pp. 143-7.

tion of the vote for all male Frenchmen over twenty-one. An occasional Conservative like Taine was able to welcome the change without violent misgivings. In his pamphlet, *Du Suffrage Universel* of 1872, Taine justified it on the grounds that 'it is in conformity with justice that, whether I wear a smock or a black coat, whether I be capitalist or navvy, no one should have a right to dispose without my consent of my money or my life. It is therefore reasonable that a peasant or a worker should have a vote, as much as a *bourgeois* or a nobleman; even if he be ignorant, dull, ill-informed, his savings and his life are his own.' A Liberal like Prévost-Paradol could write of it dispassionately as early as 1868, in his remarkable and prophetic book, *La France Nouvelle*. Whilst fully aware of the dangers of *un défaut de lumières*, he welcomed universal suffrage as at least having the advantage of stealing the thunder from all political agitators who could demand nothing further, so that universal suffrage is 'a reinforcement of material order and public peace'.[1]

But Conservatives and Liberals alike joined hands in devising constitutional checks such as second-chambers and indirect elections against the possible consequences of this logical application of the revolutionary doctrine of the 'sovereignty of the people'. And Radicals and Socialists equally united in demanding universal suffrage as a panacea for all the ills of France. The clash of opposing views came out forcibly in the debates of the National Assembly in 1874. The Left won the day because the Assembly itself was the product of universal suffrage, and the conviction grew that—as Louis Blanc himself put it—

[1] L. F. Prévost-Paradol: *La France Nouvelle* (1868), p. 52. This full-dress 'political testament' of a young man who had been a ringleader in the literary opposition to the Second Empire, may be recommended as a highly revealing exposition of what French Liberalism meant by 'democracy'. Paradol's thesis that since 1789 France has been 'a democratic society' in search of a 'democratic form of government' would meet with small agreement to-day. But his argument seems to have had extensive influence on the representatives who gathered at Bordeaux in 1871 to formulate, eventually, the constitutional laws of the Third Republic. A. Ésmein, *Éléments de Droit Constitutionnel* (1928), describes it as 'ce livre où se réflètent par avance les principaux traits de la Constitution de 1875'

'Universal suffrage is the instrument of order *par excellence*'. Since 1848, the movement of Republicanism itself was identified above all with the principle of universal suffrage: it had been the main plank of the Republican platform. Both Conservatives and Republicans upheld social order as the end: but whilst Conservatives opposed universal suffrage as likely to cause disruption and civil strife, Republicans regarded it as marking the end of the Revolution, and perhaps of all revolutions. The exaggerated fears and hopes of both sides arouse little sympathy to-day, until one remembers that Britain did not venture to extend the vote to agricultural workers until ten years later—nor to all women until fifty years later.[1]

It is significant that the chief argument for basing the central government on universal suffrage in 1875 was the fact that local government had already been based on it by the laws of 1871. The *conseils généraux* in the *Départements* were elected by universal suffrage, and renewed half at a time every three years. Municipal councils, though their powers of control might be small, were likewise popularly elected. It seemed illogical that a citizen of the Republic deemed capable of voting in local affairs should be denied the right to vote about the more important issues of national policy. The Republic was thus built up from the locality to the centre—and this remained the direction in which political influence was to flow. The combination of circumstances which in 1875 gave great weight to local and provincial outlook, to the peasantry above all other social classes, and to the countryside as against the towns, left permanent marks on the structure of the Third Republic. Constituencies were arranged to give weight to the countryside: the Senate, at first based on an arrangement which treated all Communes as equal, regardless of whether they were as

---

[1] For a full discussion of the 'supreme importance of universal suffrage' see G. Hanotaux: *Histoire de la France Contemporaine* (1871-1900), Vol. III, Chapters I and V. Gambetta's own view is summed up in a letter of 12 September 1874 (Letter 207): 'Le suffrage universel finit toujours par discerner et récompenser ses véritables amis. Il appartient par essence à la démocratie pure et loyale, mais il fait incessamment s'occuper de lui, lui prodiguer les soins et les lumières.'

THE SOCIAL BASES

large as Paris or as small as the smallest village-community, grossly over-represented rural France. In spite of frequent attempts to redress the balance, the constitution of the Republic never adequately adjusted itself to a more highly industrialized nation, dependent for prosperity and national security on her industry more than on her peasant agriculture. The industrialists and the industrial workers were at times forced to feel that it was less 'their Republic' than it was the peasants': and the peasants came to fear the political movements associated with industrialism as a potential menace to their own political power.

The Industrial Workers

When the Third Republic was founded, the industrial revolution was really only beginning to make itself widely felt in French life. The period of greatest industrial expansion was to come between 1870 and 1914, and continued between the two wars: though even then France developed more slowly and less uniformly than her powerful neighbours in Europe. If the output of her blast furnaces increased six-fold between 1870 and 1904, Germany's grew ten-fold in the same years. Being able to export agricultural produce and buy manufactured goods in return, she tended to leave many branches of manufacturing to others. There were two exceptions to this general policy. The needs of national defence dictated the fullest possible development of her coal resources and metallurgical works. And in the sphere of fine craftsmanship and precision-work, she became one of the great workshops of the world. But only the urgent demands of the war between 1914 and 1918 made France develop her industries on a massive scale, and produced a second industrial revolution, violently carried through in the worst conditions, so that scars and disequilibrium were left in her economic and social life. The silent French revolution of 1914-18 was the displacement of the pre-war industrial worker, technically skilled, alertly intelligent and politically individualist, by the operatives of mass-production, herded into the big towns, and including among their ranks many foreign immigrants.

This immigration began just before 1870, but had not assumed a scale big enough to influence the foundation of the Republic. Its immense increase after 1914 aggravated the changing social balance to which the constitution had to be adjusted. Between 1921 and 1931 the net influx of foreigners was over 1,340,000 people, many of whom came to be naturalized and so acquired citizen voting-rights. In the census of 1936, nearly 2,500,000 (nearly 7 per cent of the whole population) declared themselves to be aliens—and these figures are, of course, likely to be less than the actual number. There were probably something like 5,000,000 by 1939. And the majority of these immigrants normally went into the ranks of industrial workers, especially in the heavy industries, mining, building and road-making. Here, then, is one element in society which acted as a reinforcement of town as against countryside.

More important as a social division is the *communard* traditions of the larger towns. When the Paris Commune broke out in 1871, most other big towns followed suit. This was a straw in the wind. Heavy industry and mass-production industry, as distinct from the small concerns scattered throughout the provincial towns, tended to concentrate in the big towns. The new industrial classes, owing allegiance to their factory-community, their trade union or their town, had a different political outlook from the old craftsmen or the peasants: an outlook associated with neither the *étatiste* outlook of Republican Nationalists and Bonapartists, nor the Radicalism of the peasants, but rather with the old *communard* sentiments of civic action, resorting in times of stress to violent self-help and the barricades. The revolutionary creeds of Marxism, Sorelian syndicalism and even anarchism were most in tune with their political feelings. French trade unionism inherited and absorbed these sentiments. It is significant that the Third Republic did not legalize the existence of trade unions until 1884: and that when it did, it prohibited them from political activities.

How much French syndicalist organizations owed to the direct French Revolutionary tradition is shown by the fact that the syndical movement was founded by a Republican journalist, Barberet. He urged the formation of a movement which would not supersede or destroy capitalist production, but which would concern itself with technical education of the workers, settle problems and conditions of apprenticeship, promote arbitration in industrial disputes, and aim at forming producers' co-operatives. By 1875 there were 135 syndicates in Paris alone, and in the following year they arranged a Labour congress. It demanded working-class representation in the Chamber. But a later 'Socialist Labour Congress' in Marseilles, in 1879, which also tried to organize Labour as a political party, demanded full socialization of the means of production. The reason was that the Paris Socialists, led by Jules Guesde and now influenced by the First International, had joined the Congress. Endless internal schisms began to appear, first between the Marxist followers of Guesde (the Parti Ouvrier Français) and the more moderate Socialist reformers who followed Paul Brousse (the Parti Ouvrier Socialiste): then within each of these parties themselves. The Broussists—or 'possibilists'— urged the gradual seizure of power by slow infiltration into Parliament, municipal government and civil service. Between Guesdists and Broussists grew up a small but influential group of Independents, which was to produce some of the greatest of French parliamentary Socialists—Jaurès, Millerand and Viviani.

Thus when trade unions became legalized in 1884, they tended to develop along divergent lines. The position has been aptly summarized by Mr. John Hampden Jackson in his study of *Jaurès*:

The new unions developed on very varied lines, sometimes as large peaceable industrial syndicates, sometimes as small revolutionary craft unions, sometimes round employment exchanges (*Bourses du Travail*) organized by the workers but often subsidized by the town council and to that extent harmless. But in every case the spirit of trade unionism was anti-political. The organized workers distrusted all politicians, especially Socialists of bourgeois origin—and every Socialist leader of the Third Republic, except Allemane, was of bourgeois origin. They condemned parliamentary reforms as worthless palliatives; their slogan was 'direct action', by which they might mean anything from ca'canny, minor sabotage and isolated strikes to the syndicalists' dream of the general strike aimed at overthrowing the State and introducing a new society controlled by producer-groups. This attitude made them difficult grist to the political Socialists' mill—as difficult indeed as the co-operative societies which seemed unable to get further than the ideal of cheapening prices for the workers' food by cutting out middlemen.

The result of this anti-political character which organized labour had assumed by the eighteen-eighties was a gulf between the trade unions and the parliamentary Socialist parties which was never bridged. The trade union movement, after an abortive attempt to found a National Federation of Syndicates in 1886, and a more successful attempt to form a Federation of Labour Exchanges, managed to fuse the two ideas and the two organizations into the *Confédération Générale du Travail* (*C.G.T.*) at Limoges in 1895. The first article of its constitution was that 'the elements constituting the C.G.T. will remain independent of all political schools'. This deliberate divorce from party politics—and therefore from Parliamentary politics—meant belief in the efficacy of economic 'direct action' over political action, and reliance on the general strike as the chief weapon of gaining reforms and eventually of seizing power. It meant a permanent split and divergent development between organized Labour and the parliamentary Socialist parties. It meant, also, that the C.G.T. could become the militant agency of syndicalism, a power-weapon, freed from the 'friendly society' and other benevolent and charitable functions of English trade unions, because these functions were performed by the Federation of Labour Exchanges. The Labour Exchanges, originally an organ of workers' self-help in the finding of jobs, became working-men's clubs, with libraries, reading rooms and a friendly club atmosphere also divorced from party politics. Thus the three functions of friendly society, collective bargaining and political representation, which in England were fused together in the T.U.C. and the Labour Party, remained in French life three separate functions performed by three different kinds of democratic association.[1]

[1] For the full story of French Socialist and Labour movements, see P. Louis: *Histoire du Socialisme en France* (1925); Léon Blum: *Les Congrès ouvriers et socialistes français* (1901); Léon Jouhaux: *La C.G.T.*

Until the years of large-scale rearmament before 1914 there were in France very few completely industrialized districts, populated by masses of specialized workers such as Lancashire or the Ruhr. It was the concentration of industry, and especially mining and metallurgy, which first created such conditions, and precipitated Labour problems in the form of strikes and agitation for a general strike. By 1902, at its Montpelier Congress, the C.G.T. was able to formulate the main principles of syndicalism which distinguished it from parliamentary Socialism. These were to obtain concessions from employers not by arbitration but by strike, boycott and sabotage; and from the State by agitation and demonstration: to oppose militarism in all forms, because the worker has no country, wars only divide the working class, and military discipline destroys working-class initiative and independence: and finally to work for a successful general strike, which would abolish class-divisions and create new forms of society. This amalgam of Utopianism and physical violence was vigorously denounced and resisted by the parliamentary Socialists, and by none more effectively than by Millerand and Jean Jaurès, who after 1892 strove to produce working-class unity in France and canalize it into democratic, parliamentary channels. They regarded the Republic as the means towards the end of Socialism, and tried to lead organized labour with them. The arguments they used are significant.

'To accomplish social reforms', wrote Millerand, 'we must ask the help of all branches of Socialists, no matter how bold their theories, so long as they do not desire to triumph by methods other than pacific and constitutional.' 'The democratic Republic', wrote Jaurès, 'is not, as our self-styled doctrinaires of Marxism so often say, a purely *bourgeois* form . . . it heralds Socialism, prepares for it, contains it implicitly to some

(1937). There are good shorter accounts in English in J. Hampden Jackson: *Jean Jaurès* (1943) and Sally Graves: *A History of Socialism* (1939), Chapters II and VII. For the *Bourses du Travail*, see F. Pelloutier: *Histoire des Bourses du Travail* (1921). See Daniel Halévy's perceptive work *Essais sur le Mouvement Ouvrier en France* (1901) and the massive study by E. Dolléans: *Histoire du Mouvement Ouvrier, 1830 à nos jours* (3 vols., 1947-53).

extent, because only Republicanism can lead to Socialism by legal evolution without break of continuity.' He rebuked the trade unionists. 'Those who on the pretext of revolution and of doctrinal purity hide miserably behind abstention from party politics are deserting Socialist thought. They are also deserting the revolutionary tradition of the French working class.' He and Millerand opposed the idea of a general strike as a tactic likely neither to preserve working-class unity nor to win sufficient public approval to be effective. They both worked to put the parliamentary Socialist Party at the head of the industrial working-class, and to put Socialism in its true line of descent in the French Revolutionary tradition. How they temporarily succeeded in doing both, amid the storm of the Dreyfus case, will be told later (Chapter IV). But the death of Jaurès in 1914 and the effects of the Great War led to the re-splitting of C.G.T. from Socialist Party. When Léon Blum, the heir of Jaurès, took office as Prime Minister at the head of the 'Popular Front' government in 1936, the old split took the acute form of the 'stay-in' strikes and further disruption in the ranks of the industrial workers: this despite the share taken by the C.G.T. in the formation of the *Cartel des Gauches* in 1924 and in the early stages of the Popular Front itself.

By its stormy history and its chronic divisions, political organization of the French industrial workers thus failed to compensate for the bias of the Third Republican regime in favour of the peasantry and the countryside. If the regime only too often failed to reflect the true social balance of French life, if the governments and policies of the Republic tended too often to defer to the preferences of the peasants at the expense of the interests of the industrial workers, it was a fault not only of the Constitution itself, but also of the weakness of Labour organizations. This weakness became most apparent just when it mattered most—in the critical years between the two wars. Some real consolidation existed between the Amiens Congress of the C.G.T. in 1906 and the Saint-Étienne Congress in 1922. But in 1920 the Left Wing of the Socialist Party split off to become the French Communist Party, and a large section of the trade unions split off from the C.G.T. to form the *Confédération*

Générale du Travail Unitaire (*C.G.T.U.*), affiliated to the Moscow International. They reunited in 1936, when the reunited C.G.T. represented some five million out of the eight million industrial workers. (Others were organized into the *Confédération française des Travailleurs Chrétiens*, or Catholic unions.)

And the consequence of these unhappy divisions? It was not that the Radical Parties represented exclusively the peasants, or that the Socialists never got peasant support. The majority of Senators and Deputies represented rural or semi-rural constituencies, for the simple reason that most French constituencies were rural or semi-rural: but they bore every party-label, from Right to Left. In 1929 Léon Blum was returned by Narbonne, a constituency of wine-growers and well-to-do peasant proprietors. No single party specifically represented the peasants as distinct from the industrial workers, and any group which in substance stood for a special agrarian interest was usually careful to disguise the fact—like the *Parti Ouvrier et Paysan*. Every party tried to win the support of both peasantry and industry: and this had consequences which were more bad than good. The broad division of economic interests was between small land-owning agriculturists and wage-earning industrial workers: between those interested in high prices in the home market and tariff protection from foreign competition, and those interested in low prices and high exports. That this division did not coincide with any clear party division might have helped to soften the conflict. But the main result was that economically the conflict was never resolved or even seriously tackled: and politically there grew up habits of dishonest and inconsistent angling for votes on one hand, cynical or sceptical voting on the other. Because of the nature of their constituencies and the weakness of organized Labour, most politicians tended to be over-impressed by the voting power of the peasants.  Their policies thus still further accentuated the bias of the Republic away from industrial interests. In 1939, a French economist could still write, 'In the pursuit of any economic policy, the only guide for the central authorities has hitherto been the number of electors interested in agricultural production.' And men like Marshal Pétain and Laval, launching a 'back to the land' movement in tune with German policy, could make much of their own peasant origins in their propaganda and self-publicity, as evidence of virtue and a sign of grace.

This hiatus or lack of correspondence between social and political alignments was partly a result, partly a cause, of the power of the revolutionary tradition. France kept what M. Pierre Maillaud has called 'a party system based on historical memories rather than on hard economic facts', and party formations which were 'like the luminous rays of those stars whose light only reaches us some hundred years after the star itself is extinguished'.[1] The French habit of historical thinking (comparable only to the Irish or Polish cherishing and nursing of historical memories) became in this sense a burden on French political life and on the working of her democratic regime. Political controversy was too often carried on in unreal and out-of-date terms, battles long ago were refought while battles of to-day, which clamoured to be fought, were left in suspense or lost by default. The slowness and inadequacy with which social services were developed, the inefficiency of the French financial and fiscal system, the distrust of all government which characterized much Radical thought (as, for example, the writings of 'Alain' in recent years) all have some of their roots in the burdensome continuance of outworn ideas and irrelevant controversies.[2] The revolutionary tradition, in its diverse forms,

---

[1] Pierre Maillaud: *France* (1942)—a brilliant short introduction for English readers to the background and problems of modern France.

[2] Cf. Chapter V, for discussion of these shortcomings: for Radical individualism see especially 'Alain' (i.e. Professor Chartier): *Éléments d'une Doctrine Radicale* (1925). Typical of his constant thesis is the principle: 'Democracy resides in . . . what I call *le contrôleur*, which is nothing but the continually effective power of deposing kings and specialists the very moment they no longer manage affairs according to the interests of the greatest numbers. . . . To be a Radical is to accept without restriction the principles that universal suffrage must have all power and all ultimate control and checking authority.' The theories of 'Alain', as of all extreme Radicalism, mean constant incipient anarchy—the determination to preserve freedom by keeping the government weak, 'Everything which limits and controls powers is democratic—or if you like Radical.'

has often been a source of inspiration for France. In times of crisis—as in 1871, in the storm of the Dreyfus case, in 1914 and in 1944—it has helped France to renew her vitality with a resilience which has amazed the world. But in times of greater normality, it has been more of a drag on social progress and democratic evolution than a spur.

The Middle Classes

The social basis of the Third Republic had its centre of gravity in the middle classes. Whereas the peasantry, from the first, gained solid advantages from the Republic in the form of consolidation and protection for their property: and the industrial workers gained freedom to organize themselves for collective bargaining and direct action; the middle classes found, in the parliamentary Republic, an avenue for career, power and wealth which gained them ultimate political predominance. In so far as there was tension between agriculture and industry, peasant and industrial worker, the middle classes held, by reason of their entrenched position, a sort of casting vote between the two main blocs of economic interest.

To explain broad historical development by the 'rise of the middle classes' has become an overworked device of historians. This peculiarly self-raising class has been made unduly responsible for the growth of nationalism, imperialism, monarchy, democracy, dictatorship, and every other 'ism' and 'archy' invented by historians. But there is a real and concrete sense in which 1875 was a far more complete triumph for the French *bourgeoisie* than either 1789 or even 1830. With nobility rendered powerless, peasantry placated and industrial interests still kept subservient to *bourgeois* needs, the middle classes after 1875 gained solid control of all the apparatus of the State, and of most of the key positions in French society. The sequence of epithets applied to the Third Republic—*La République des Camarades, La République des Professeurs*, even *La République des Complices*, are but variants of this general truth.[1] M. Albert

---

[1] Cf. Daniel Halévy: *La République des Comités* (1934); Robert de Jouvenel: *La République des Camarades* (1934); A. Thibaudet: *La*

Guérard has spoken, with some force, of 'the dictatorship of the middle class', the rule of a '*Bourgeois* bureaucracy'.[1] And there is enough truth in the description to merit closer examination.

M. Guérard's thesis is that under the Third Republic the doctrine of a 'separation of powers' was still observed, but in a different sense from either the French Constitution of 1848 or the American Constitution of 1787. On the one hand there was the strictly *political* power, both executive and legislative, and in both cases elected. On the other hand, there was the *administrative* power—the judiciary, the permanent officials, the many branches of the civil service ranging from diplomats to railway officials, from colonial administrators to school teachers. The administrative power was little affected by political changes, and little even by revolutions, since substantially the same framework of officialdom lasted from Napoleon onwards, throughout the many political upheavals of the nineteenth century. Its professional traditions stretch back even behind the great Revolution to the days of Richelieu and Colbert. Its power was augmented by every successive increase in State activity, and its technical skill matured through many genera-

---

République des Professeurs (1927); A. Fabre-Luce: *Le Secret de la République* (1938), Chapter III, on 'La République des Complices'. Perhaps one should add also Robert Dreyfus: *La République de M. Thiers* (1930); and Daniel Halévy: *La République des Ducs* (1937) among the historians of the early years of the Republic; and Jacques Fourcade: *La République de la Province* (1936).

This tendency of French historians and political theorists to philosophize about the Third Republic in terms of one underlying principle became something of a cult: and such tendentious nicknames became part of the small change of political controversy.

[1] Albert Guérard: *The France of To-morrow* (Harvard, 1942). This interesting work by an American-born Frenchman is too little known in England. It has many penetrating remarks on the whole character of the Republic and of French national development in modern times. The central part of the book (Part II) is a study of 'Democracy in France'. Cf. also L. D. White, W. R. Sharp *et al.*: *The Civil Service Abroad* (1935) for a brief survey of the administrative organization; or W. R. Sharp: *The French Civil Service: Bureaucracy in Transition* (1931).

THE SOCIAL BASES

tions. Little is found in the constitutional laws of 1875 about the administration or the judiciary. The formal constitution of the Third Republic is even more significant for what it leaves unsaid, and takes for granted as being automatically carried forward, than for what it explicitly mentions.

This generalization was familiar among the many critics of the Republic. Thus Daniel Halévy wrote in 1931, 'Republican France has, in reality, two constitutions: one, that of 1875, is official, visible and fills the Press—it is parliamentary: the other is secret, silent, that of *l'An VIII*—the Napoleonic constitution which hands over the direction of the country to the administrative corps.'[1] He cites, as an example of the relative power of these two 'constitutions', the contrast between the Labour code drawn up in the eighteen-nineties by the *fonctionnaires* in the *Office du Travail*, attached to the Ministry of Commerce and Industry, and the social legislation drafted between 1899 and 1905 by the parliamentary Socialists. The one found concrete expression in the measures of the eighteen-nineties setting up workers' delegations, limiting the hours of work for women, fixing standards of hygiene, pensions and accident insurance, which were put through by the moderate Republicans. The other found little concrete expression, and became a dead letter while the work of the bureaucracy survived. Other considerations determined this contrast, and the Conservative bias of Halévy requires some allowance. But his general point

[1] Daniel Halévy: *Décadence de la Liberté* (1931)—a brilliant Conservative analysis of the political forces in the Third Republic. The general thesis here described was not, be it noted, peculiar to any political wing. It is shared by a Conservative like Halévy, a moderate Liberal like Guérard, a doctrinaire Radical like 'Alain', and a Left-winger like Blum. Cf. 'Alain': *Éléments d'une Doctrine Radicale*, p. 25: 'En France, il y a un très grand nombre d'électeurs radicaux, un certain nombre de députés radicaux, et un très petit nombre de ministres radicaux: quant aux chefs de service, ils sont tous réactionnaires. Celui qui a bien compris cela tient la clef de notre politique' (written 1906).

Carlton J. H. Hayes estimates the proportion of French citizens who were in some sense paid State functionaries at one-twentieth (*France, a Nation of Patriots*, 1930).

is true and significant enough: reforms passed by the middle class, as Conservative politicians and officials, went through quicker and worked more smoothly under the Third Republic than measures devised by more progressive and Radical political groups, and then imposed upon the *fonctionnaires*. The experience of the Popular Front Government under Blum still further illustrates and endorses the same general truth.

One important channel of middle-class influence on French life—even on French political life—was the Chambers of Commerce. There were over 140 Chambers of Commerce, each of twenty-one members, save the Paris Chamber which represented the Department of the Seine as well as the capital, and had forty members. Chosen by the wealthiest and most firmly established business men (who had to have been in business for at least five years and to have paid taxes upon a business enterprise for which they were responsible), they were semi-official bodies connected with the Ministry of Commerce, and had both privileges and responsibilities. In towns like Paris, Marseilles and Bordeaux, certain port taxes were allowed to them, and they served as advisory bodies in all problems affecting commerce and industry. Directly representing some 270,000 well-to-do business men, and including among their members the 'aristocrats' of each business locality, who served for six years at a time, the Chambers of Commerce were able to take a direct share in the formulation of government policy in business matters. The largest, such as Paris, made itself responsible for a dozen Business Schools, wherein primary school pupils learnt trades and a wide variety of business and commercial techniques: it built and equipped the schools itself. In both local and national business life, their influence and power were throughout considerable. And the part played in North Africa by the Algerian and other Chambers of Commerce after 1942 was important, when other more formal kinds of local administration were in a state of flux.

Of the lodges of freemasonry as a further channel of middle-class influence on politics, something will be said below (Chapter III) for their influence is inseparable from that of the Radical *cadres*.

At the time of the great Revolution, the Abbé Sieyès had asked, 'What is the Third Estate? Nothing. What ought it to be? Everything.' But the Third Estate meant the assembly of middle-class folk, provincial lawyers and intellectuals, who came to represent 'the people' as against the nobility and clergy. The assumption of the professional classes under the Third Republic, too, was that the 'Third Estate' should be everything—everything, that is, *in the State*. They provided the staff for all government offices, for the armed services, the universities and higher educational establishments, the colonial, diplomatic and foreign services, the judiciary: and people recruited for these services, if not *bourgeois* by birth, became *bourgeois* by training and outlook before they could enter the ranks of *fonctionnaires*. This position was not, of course, peculiar to France. It prevailed, with differences only of degree, in Germany and Great Britain. The sieve through which all had to pass was the network of the educational system.

Higher education was divided, on social lines, into two main branches.[1] On one hand, there was higher primary, commercial and technical education, provided free for all competent to pass the necessary examinations. On the other hand, there was secondary education proper, longer in duration and more costly in charge until as late as 1937. The one was democratic —the 'career open to talents'—but a career in the business and industrial worlds and not in the administrative professions. It was the educational ladder of the *lycées* and *collèges*, the universities and the professional institutes, which was the normal means of access to the levels of the *fonctionnaires*. The fees charged, the long delay before earning could begin, and the still further delay before earning could be large, all deterred any save the well-to-do from embarking on a professional

---

[1] Cf. C. Richard: *L'Enseignement en France* (1925), pp. 549-55, where the new scale of fees charged from 1926 onwards is given for the Lycées of Paris, Poitiers and Grenoble. See also the admirable summary of the French educational system in Carlton J. H. Hayes: *France, a Nation of Patriots*, Chapter III, and of the French civil service in L. D. White (ed.): *The Civil Service in the Modern State* (1930), p. 215 ff.

career. The number of scholarships available was not great enough to make the ladder more than a narrow one for the poor: and a suitable 'marriage of convenience', a further ladder to social position and power, was available only to those who were already moderately well-to-do.

Politics offered more openings than administration, and Daladier, son of a baker, Laval, son of a café-proprietor, could become Prime Minister. But a parliamentary career, too, was easier for those with a more classical and literary education or legal training, and those with private means enough to risk the chances of elections and cover the expenses of holding a seat. Deputies were not lavishly paid. Their salaries were raised from 9,000 to 15,000 francs (£600) in 1906: and were worth about the same at 82,500 francs in 1938. To this must be added privileges of free travel. Lawyers, teachers, doctors, journalists tended to go into politics more than any other classes of the community, and half the Chamber and Senate were normally lawyers and journalists. The competition for election was considerable. In 1919, 2,129 candidates stood for 615 seats: by 1936, there were 4,807 at the first ballot. In general, the middle classes tended to dominate parliamentary government almost as much as they dominated the administration: for the power of the central groups, the Republicans and Radicals which were normally indispensable ingredients of any government, reflected the political power of the middle and professional classes. The 'separation of powers' between the political and administrative branches of the constitution was real in a constitutional but not in a social sense. The Third Republic was throughout, in spirt and operation, middle class rather than either aristocratic or peasant or proletarian.

Yet, despite the similarity of social recruitment for both branches of the State, there developed a certain contrast and even conflict of outlook between the men employed in each of them. This sprang partly from the more rigid selection and training of the *fonctionnaires*, partly from the different functions which *fonctionnaires* and deputies performed in the constitution. The broad function of the deputy, apart from taking part in the establishment or overthrow of the Cabinet (which was in effect the executive committee of the two assemblies) was to serve as a watchdog and a check on the administration. He was, as M. Guérard suggests, 'the defender of the people, whose business it was to protect his constituents against the delays, the errors, the petty tyrannies of the Administration. Some obscure deputies, who never made a speech or wrote a report, were faithfully re-elected every four years, because they faithfully performed this their essential duty. They were not themselves the source or even the agents of power; they were the elected inspectors of the appointed bureaucracy.'[1]

The testimony of Lieutenant-Colonel Pierre Tissier, himself *Maître des Requêtes* (or Public Prosecutor) in the *Conseil d'État*, is of some interest. The *Conseil d'État*, the apex of the highly integrated and centralized administrative system bequeathed to modern France by Napoleon, had before that been an instrument of the monarchy of the *ancien régime*. It latterly contained many elements either Royalist or semi-Fascist, in direct opposition to the whole nature of the parliamentary Republic. 'The life of every high official in France', writes Tissier, 'begins on the benches of the Law School—the *Faculté de Droit*—and about the green-topped tables of the School of Political Science.' Some of the professors chosen by the latter were men whose political views were reactionary and definitely anti-Republican and it became the great rallying-point for the avowed enemies of the Republic. 'While it was just possible, if one wanted to study for the Foreign Office exams., to do so elsewhere (there was the School of Commercial Studies, also a private concern) it was in effect quite impossible for anyone who wanted to get into the Council of State or the Finance Inspectorate to do without the "Science po". Thus the Republic confided the training of its highest officials to its acknowledged enemies.'[2]

Indeed, the *Conseil d'État* and the Chamber of Deputies were the two poles around which the divergent tendencies of the

---

[1] Albert Guérard: op. cit., p. 168.
[2] Pierre Tissier: *I Worked with Laval* (1942), pp. 7-17. Cf. also P. Allard: *Le Quai d'Orsay* (1938), p. 38 ff. for a description of how the Quai d'Orsay staff was recruited.

Third Republican form of government may be said to have focused. The one—permanent, judicial, administrative, professional—the final bulwark of authority: the other—the arena wherein local and rival interests reached either working compromise and agreement or total deadlock, according to the issues involved, but always fluid, political, controversial, turbulent. The *Conseil d'État*, which survived through every political regime of the nineteenth century until it became the very centre of political power under Vichy, was normally not a political body. On one hand, it was the supreme administrative tribunal to judge disputes between the State, departments or Communes and the ordinary citizen, contriving to hold the scales fairly between the great powers of the public authorities and legitimate private interests or individual rights. In this role, its greatest virtue was its independence of politics: and its judges showed no marked partiality for the State against the private citizen. On the other hand, it served the Government in an advisory capacity, concerning new bills and decrees. In both capacities, it was normally very jealous of its independence: and its inborn hostility to the Republic made it a powerful check on hasty or arbitrary legislation, since it was extremely rare for any government to reject its counsels.

The outlook of the officials of the *Conseil d'État* is characteristic of the whole body of *fonctionnaires* as a class. It is the outlook of *étatisme*—of authoritarianism verging at its worst on totalitarianism, but at its best expressing concern for the cause of national unity and the stability of the national community as a whole. Perhaps the basic assumption, so manifest in a body ready to serve any form of regime, is the English Tory belief expressed pithily in the Duke of Wellington's maxim, 'The King's government must be carried on', or more classically by Alexander Pope:

> For forms of government let fools contest,
> Whate'er is best administered is best.

It means concern for law and order, stable government and good (in the sense of efficient) administration: an impatience with political controversy, conflicting ideologies and interests, and all party divisions: a longing to 'lift government out of politics' and provide regular administration by experts. It is an outlook instinctively anti-democratic in nature and tendency, yet with qualities which make it an indispensable ingredient in the effective running of a modern State, however democratic. Could any modern democratic State, assuming responsibility for the social welfare and public service of its citizens, work through a civil service which was not in some measure apart from politics, and impartially willing to serve any party in power? The United States, with its 'spoils system', tried to make its civil service political: it has increasingly abandoned the attempt.

The family from which sprang the greatest of all colonial servants—Marshal Lyautey—is characteristic of the environment in which so many *fonctionnaires* of ability and importance were brought up. The authorized biographer of Lyautey describes it in these words:[1]

> In his home two traditions and two conceptions of social life were harmoniously blended. From the father's side there came the tradition of service to the State—whether as soldiers or administrators, with the principle and practice of duty and work—while from the mother's side came the traditions of the landed gentry, with the art of living a cultured life of leisure. . . . When but twelve years of age (i.e. in 1871) he wrote down the reasons for his being a Royalist. Considering his home atmosphere, that he should hold such opinions was but natural; for while his father was a moderate Legitimist, his father's second sister had an ardent respect for the Comte de Chambord, the last scion of the oldest line of the House of Bourbon. His mother's people too, were Royalists, but with Orleans sympathies.

His grandmother of ninety, surrounded by her sixty de-

[1] Sonia E. Howe: *Lyautey of Morocco* (1931)—a highly illuminating study of how men of this social class and family tradition were virtually forced, by the anti-clerical and often anti-military spirit of the Republic into devoted service of the State. The Third Republic was happy in its inheritance of such public-spirited servants of the nation, whatever its régime and however repugnant the parliamentary regime might be to them: the spirit of *noblesse oblige* often served it well. See also André Maurois: *Lyautey* (1931).

scendants, summed up the family tradition and atmosphere in one sentence: 'I thank God that not one among you is a Republican.'

Educated in the School of St. Geneviève run by Jesuits, and in the Military Colleges of St. Cyr and *L'École d'État Major*, and profoundly influenced by the teachings of Comte Albert de Mun,[1] Lyautey grew to manhood in an environment which still further emphasized the ideal of service. Like the thousands of other able men who followed similar careers and also felt the teaching of de Mun, he learnt devotion to France as a nation and as a State, rather than to the Republic as such, or to democratic ideals.

This *étatiste* outlook was shared not only by *fonctionnaires* in the military and colonial services, but by the leaders of the home civil service, the judiciary, and even by some of the politicians. It has both its virtues and its vices. In so far as it rests on professional pride, on the ideal of State-service and national honour, it has immense social value. It makes for honest service, administrative integrity, even-handed justice. In so far as it is authoritarian, and attracts or breeds a narrow, rigid, over-traditionalist unimaginative type of personality, it lends itself to eager canvassing by totalitarian and undemocratic political movements which seek to overthrow the parliamentary system from within. By family traditions and technical training, by service-traditions and their working environment, the French *fonctionnaires* in the latter phases of the Third Re-

[1] Comte Albert de Mun: *Ma Vocation Sociale* (1926). Mun had a genius for winning disciples to his creed of social service and had more influence than any other single person in inspiring men such as Lyautey to a life of devoted service. He taught that 'it was the duty of the privileged classes to go to the humble folk, to learn to know them, to go with them in sympathy: to seek with them in perfect confidence and trust for a way of lessening this misunderstanding and of drawing hearts together'. Mun later described his disciples of St. Cyr as 'these young men, possessed by one idea only . . . to serve their country by love, by devoting themselves completely to it while remaining professed Christians' (quoted Sonia E. Howe: op. cit., pp. 26-9). Cf. Jacques Piou: *Le Comte Albert de Mun* (1925). Mun played a central part in the Boulangist plots.

THE SOCIAL BASES 63

public too often allowed these vices to overcome these virtues. Traditional Royalist movements such as the *Camelots du Roi* and the *Action française*, and semi-Fascist movements such as the *Cagoulards* and the *Croix de Feu*, won many adherents among the higher officials. The bureaucracy violated its own *raison d'être* and its inherent principles by coming down into the political arena: and the parliamentary Republic became not, like any other regime, the master to be served, but rather the enemy to be destroyed. The betrayal of the *fonctionnaires* was even more drastic and immediate in its effects than *la trahison des clercs* of which Julian Benda wrote so eloquently.[1]

This betrayal came to light, as will later be shown, in the willing response given to the experiment of Vichy in 1940.[2] That regime of dug-out army, naval and judicial officers to which so many North African colonial administrators paid ready homage, was not only 'the revenge of the anti-Dreyfusards'. It was also the revenge of the *fonctionnaires* for long years of parliamentary corruption and incompetence. But be it noted that the men of Vichy had to carry out many dismissals and replacements in the *Conseil d'État*, and in the ranks of the Prefects and the Army, before they could make these bodies pliable and servile tools of their dictatorship. The betrayal was never complete; and was no greater than the betrayal of the majority of the National Assembly—that other branch of middle-class predominance—which in July 1940 abdicated political responsibility by their grant of wide emergency powers to Marshal Pétain. The change of label, from 'the French Republic' to 'the French State', expresses exactly the transfer of allegiance which both bureaucracy and frightened parliamentarians made in the face of national disaster.

It will be shown below how far this attitude—this 'administrative outlook'—prevailed in such crises as the Macmahon crisis of 1877, the Boulanger and Dreyfus crises, and the supreme crisis of 1940. Suffice now to note its social roots in

[1] Julian Benda: *La Trahison des Clercs* (1927)—a study of the 'nationalization of intellect', which was widely discussed in both France and Britain in the late nineteen-twenties.

[2] See Chapter VI for a study of the Vichy regime.

the middle and professional classes, interested most in social order and the security of property. The peasantry, interested also in the security of property, could sometimes, and in some measure, be induced to support it. But while peasant interests dominated, on the whole, economic policy and industrial working-class interests were the driving-force behind social policy, it was the middle classes which dominated political and foreign policy. By this working compromise the Third Republic survived, in a sense unforeseen by Thiers, as 'the form of government which divides us least'. With the growing breakdown of this compromise, the Third Republic began to totter. And with its final breakdown, the Third Republic fell. It fell when the very issue of whether or not parliamentary institutions should survive became the one issue 'which divided us most'.

The Aristocracy and Gentry

The relics of the old nobility, the old Bonapartist officials, and the country gentry played a steadily diminishing part in the life of the Third Republic. When it was founded, they were still of considerable importance. During the eighteen-seventies, when the chances of a Monarchist revival were still not hopeless—and even the possibility of a Bonapartist resurgence could not be completely counted out—they were of immense importance. The period (1873-7) which Daniel Halévy has christened *La République des Ducs* was their time of greatest power. Only in 1879, with the clear failure of the Macmahon experiment in preliminary royalism and the complete capture by the Republicans of Presidency, Senate and Chamber, did the old nobility and gentry begin to sink into relative unimportance politically. By then, the constitution of the Republic had been cast in a mould not uncongenial to their interests and aspirations: and their lasting influence on the Republic through their decisive control of its formative stages will later be examined in some detail (Chapter IV). The gentry of the provincial châteaux lost their own grip even earlier—with the first dissolution of the National Assembly in 1876: a grip which had been loosening with each new batch of by-elections since

THE SOCIAL BASES

1871. *La Fin des Notables*—also Daniel Halévy's phrase—had come even before *La République des Ducs*. But like the greater nobility, they left their mark on the Constitution, since it was indeed their own child.

When the Republic fell into the hands of the Republicans, both greater and lesser nobility withdrew to their châteaux, from which only the crises of 1870-1 had first drawn them, and took a larger share in the social and economic life than in the political life of the Republic. With an attitude varying from monolithic aloofness to one of positive disdain and bitter contempt, they held apart from active public life, save in their own narrow locality. The *Annuaire de la Noblesse de France* went on appearing regularly, from its foundation in 1843 right through the Republic. Therein, at least, the supporters of the three rival houses of France at last merged—Bourbon, Orleanist and Bonapartist—in a concerted effort to keep alive their titles and pedigrees. Therein the lesser nobility created by all three dynasties recorded their births, marriages and deaths, and their centenary celebrations. In 1935 may be found recorded, significantly, the researches of the Duc de Gramont into methods of anti-aircraft defence; the appointment of General de Castelnau as Conservator of the Condé Museum in Chantilly; and the election of the Marquis de Bonneval in succession to the Baron de Bussière as President of the *Commission Française de Bridge*.[1]

A medium of continued aristocratic influence, of scarcely less importance than those already mentioned, was the Church. On the social borderline where old gentry and new *bourgeoisie* tended to merge, stood the folk who mostly filled the upper

---

[1] Whoever has not savoured the delicious snobbery of the *Annuaire de la Noblesse de France* has not fully understood the Third Republic. Produced mainly by the highly prolific writer, the Comte Georges de Morant, it reminds its readers: 'Une notice insérée dans l'Annuaire de la Noblesse de France, Nobiliaire précieux, est conservée dans les Familles, à la Bibliothèque Nationale à Paris et dans toutes les principales Bibliothèques du Monde.' It also points out (in 1935) that 'Quatre Ducs d'Angleterre, jeunes, beaux et riches, sont en quête de Duchesses', and provides details of their pedigrees, castles, wealth and expectations.

hierarchy of the Catholic Church and the Catholic Orders in France. According to the official figures of 1876, there were then 55,369 men employed in the organization of the Church in France. Nine-tenths of the priests, according to Lecanuet, were recruited from the sons of artisans or labourers: and the bishops were reproaching the upper classes for not giving their sons to the Church. But during the following generation the Catholic Orders—especially the Jesuits and missionizing societies—attracted many young men and women of the old gentry. Of the 2,464 Jesuits in France in 1878, over a quarter were also missionaries. The development of the French colonial empire in Africa and Indo-China opened up fresh opportunities for service of the Faith: and in the first decade of the Republic, some 40,000 Frenchmen served as Catholic missionaries.

In these ways the energies and ambitions of a section of the older aristocracy and gentry were diverted away from the democratic regime which they disliked: but were harnessed to the service of France as a nation, and of the Church as a social-service body. This social diversion was not without its influences, direct and indirect, on the functioning of the regime.[1]

The Oligarchy

An impressive feature of French life—as of British—was, throughout the Third Republic, the division between the old aristocracy of title and local prestige, and the new aristocracy of industrial wealth. In the latter decades of the nineteenth century, large industrial concerns, trusts and cartels, brought a new and startling element into French life, hitherto used to the small unit of production both in agriculture and industry. The later stages of the Industrial Revolution brought to power a new class of very wealthy—and very powerful—financiers and trust magnates, whose grip on French economy was sym-

---

[1] Cf. the valuable studies of E. Lecanuet: *L'Église de France sous la Troisième République, 1870-94* (2 Vols. 1910); C. S. Philips: *The Church in France, 1848-1907* (1936); A. Debidour: *L'Église Catholique et l'État sous la Troisième République* (2 Vols. 1906); and ibid., *Histoire des Rapports de l'Église et de l'État en France* (1898).

bolized in the notorious '200 Families'. Normally despised as upstart *nouveaux riches* by the older gentry, and feared alike by the peasants and industrial workers who depended on them for livelihood, the big industrialists between the two wars extended their grip to French political life through control of the Press, manipulation of the *Bourse*, and direct influence upon politicians in the Senate and the Chamber. This advent of a new social class between the two wars, and its manœuvres on the political stage (even when popularly exaggerated), was the main underlying cause of the new social conflicts which marked the working of the parliamentary regime in the nineteen-twenties and nineteen-thirties. The rise of what André Siegfried has christened 'industrial feudalism', and of violent opposition to the new oligarchy in the shape of a Communist movement, made the working of democracy in France since 1918 radically different from the working of democracy before the Great War. The Republican Federation became its chief parliamentary voice: though its power lay, like the organized Labour movements which opposed it, in 'direct action'.

The growth of big business in France was due to a wide variety of causes, some of them international and few of them peculiar to France. But four developments are worth specific mention for their bearing on the general change in social conditions of life and work.

One is the so-called 'concentration' of industry, which was taking place in the two decades before 1914, and which continued after 1918. The sugar industry, an important link between French agriculture and industry, shows the development well. In the season 1883-4, 483 sugar factories produced an average of 840 tons each. In 1900-1, 334 factories produced an average of 3,000 tons each. In 1912-12, 213 factories averaged 4,000 tons each. This process was due not to State policy but almost entirely to private enterprise. After 1918, the lead was taken by motor magnates, particularly Renault and Citroën, who tended to follow the American pattern. This attack on the small unit of production and the independent employer, and their replacement by bigger mass-production factories as the workers' natural communities, clashed with the familiar pattern of French economic life.[1] It made for greater efficiency of production, but had not gone far enough by 1939 to enable France to compete in output with Germany. Frenchmen had lost enough of their personal economic independence to put large numbers of workers at the mercy of cartels: but had not gained enough in national security to protect them from the enemy across the Rhine. As in so many other ways, France fell between two stools in 1940.

The second is the growth of joint-stock companies—*sociétés anonymes*. Though little used in industry until after 1865, joint stock had long been used for railways and public utility companies. But only when Napoleon III in 1868 did away with need for the separate official authorization of each company did they begin to be more extensively used. By 1870, 223 new companies were formed, and by 1878 it had become the normal type of organization for all large commercial and industrial undertakings. By 1911-12, the average annual crop of new joint-stock companies was 1,500. By the nineteen-thirties there were some 50,000 share companies in France. This immense expansion, which meant on one hand the rise of a vast class of small investors and even a new *rentier* class, meant also the exploitation of great blocs of associated and anonymous capital by wealthy directors and trust magnates. It meant putting new powers of direction and control of national wealth into the hands of big business, and professional finance. As Anatole France remarked in *l'Île des Pingouins*, 'After making its escape from the authority of kings and emperors, after three times proclaiming liberty, France has been brought into subjection by financial companies which command the country's wealth, and, by means of a bought Press, control public opinion.' Because these developments in France coincided in time with similar development in Britain and Germany, the companies

---

[1] Cf. J. H. Clapham: *The Economic Development of France and Germany, 1815-1914* (1921), pp. 258 ff. And cf. W. F. Ogburn and W. Jaffé: *The Economic Development of Post-War France: A Survey of Production* (1929); *L'oeuvre de la Troisième République* (1945), Part II, Chap. I on 'La chronologie économique de la IIIe République' by Jean Weiller.

formed international links, and as Sir John Clapham puts it, 'the nations had become each year part owners of one another's resources to an extraordinary degree'.[1]

Thirdly, there grew up a close connexion between the directors of industrial capital and the biggest financiers of the banks: and it was this link which cemented and entrenched the financial oligarchy. To the process of concentration of industry, and the accumulation of anonymous capital, was added the centralization of ultimate control in the hands of a few main companies; and the domination of most of these central controls by the magnates of finance. The oldest of the industrial associations—the *Comité des Forges*—dated from 1864. Though grouping together some 250 iron and steel companies, it was controlled by only thirty directors, with M. de Wendel at their head. He was also a Regent of the Bank of France. The *Comité Central des Houillères*, the *Union des Industries Métallurgiques et Minières*, and the *Comité Central des Armateurs de France* provided similar centralization for the mining, metal and shipping industries. These and other employers' associations in 1919 set up a still wider co-ordinating body, the *Confédération Générale de la Production Française*, comprising all the biggest concerns in all the main industries. At every stage there was the closest link, both financial and personal, between these associations and the main banks: the 'Big Four' which were national in scope, and the Bank of France itself. The *Banque de France* was ruled by fifteen Regents elected by the largest shareholders, and a Governor and two Deputy Governors appointed by the Government, who could be outvoted by the fifteen Regents since all had equal votes and the Governor had no more than a veto. The shareholders were represented by the General Council of two hundred: but this General Council, with the power to elect the Regents, was not elected by the shareholders. It was in both form and substance an oligarchy, since the Napoleonic Act of

[1] Cf. J. H. Clapham: op. cit., from which many of the figures quoted are derived. There is an interesting analysis, and much valuable material in the admittedly partisan work by the General Secretary of the Communist Party in France, Maurice Thorez: *France To-day and the People's Front* (1936).

1803 which created the Bank laid down: 'The two hundred shareholders who form the General Council shall be those whom the register shows to have been the largest holders of the Bank's shares at a date six months preceding the meeting.' These are the famous '200 Families'—the core of the industrial-financial oligarchy of the Third Republic. The Act of 1803 even stipulated that five of the fifteen Regents should be connected with commerce or industry. The position was changed only in 1936, when both the General Council and the Governor were brought under the effective control of the State, and banking was finally nationalized in 1945.[1]

Finally, as the culmination of this pyramid of power, all these big business organizations—trusts, employers' associations and financial oligarchy—devised various ways of directly influencing public opinion and controlling Government policy. As one member of the *Confédération Générale de la Production Française* put it in the nineteen-thirties, the Confederation 'is able to intervene, as often as may be required, by approaching individual Members of Parliament or Commissions of the Chamber of Deputies or of the Senate, in order to secure the introduction of amendments in the interests of general prosperity, to Bills or schemes which fail to take economic realities into account'. The attitude of the oligarchy to the Government was frankly expressed in a semi-official *communiqué* issued by the Bank of France in 1935:

M. Flandin's Government has some praiseworthy actions to its credit. The Budget was voted in good time. By opposing the abolition of the economy decrees, it has shown a sound instinct. Its economic measures—though a little less certain—still deserve a good mark, in view of the difficulties of the situation. This good mark has been given to M. Flandin in the form of credit facilities. These credit facilities

[1] Cf. Alexander Werth: *The Destiny of France* (1937), for a good journalistic account of the campaign against the '200 Families' and of the 'nationalization' of the Bank of France by the Blum Government: especially Chapter XX. The 'Big Four' were the Crédit Industriel et Commercial (1859), Société Générale (1864), Crédit Lyonnais (1865), and Comptoir d'Escompte (1889). All had many branches in Paris and the provinces.

may not prove sufficient. He will ask for more credit. Our reply will then depend on whether we are satisfied with the actions of the Government during the first respite we have given it as a reward for its present determination to defend the currency.

Few statements could better illustrate the stranglehold of the oligarchy on the duly elected government of the people: or the way in which government policy had normally to be a compromise between the desires of the Government and the dictates of the financiers. As the Finance Committee of the Chamber of Deputies declared in its report of 16 July 1936: 'the Bank is in the hands of an oligarchy which has succeeded in ruling the country over the heads of its chosen representatives'.

In addition to this direct stranglehold on the Government, the oligarchy had wide control of important sections of the Press. The extent of this control, and its influence on French opinion via the Press, has been brilliantly analysed by Charles A. Micaud. In addition to its official organ, the *Bulletin Quotidien*, the *Comité des Forges* had considerable control of *Le Temps* and *Le Journal des Débats*, and was partly responsible for setting up the famous *Comité France-Allemagne* under Fernand de Brinon to safeguard its close economic links with the German industrialists. But Mr. Micaud wisely gives a warning against explaining the attitude of the Right Wing by purely economic motives, and emphasizes that the Conservative and ideological motives common to the whole of the Right, from Monarchism, Fascism and Catholicism to simple anti-Communism and anti-Republicanism, probably did more to determine the anti-Soviet and pro-German stand of the French Right than either industrial profit-motives or foreign subsidies. The conclusion 'better Hitler than Blum' was an attitude indigenous to the ranks of the upper middle class, the old aristocracy and the financial oligarchy, and did not need to be created by Fascist propaganda. The effect of the large and often sinister Right-wing Press was rather to canalize and direct these indigenous feelings and beliefs, than to create them.[1]

[1] Cf. Charles A. Micaud: *The French Right and Nazi Germany, 1933-9* (1943); Carlton J. H. Hayes: *France: a Nation of Patriots* (1930), Chapter VI. *The Agence Havas* seems to have had direct connexions

Two Generations

From this brief outline of the social scene in France, and of the broad social divisions whose alignment and conflicts found reflection in the whole working of the democratic regime in France, a few general conclusions may be drawn. These will be further examined and illustrated in later chapters.

The story of the Third Republic falls into two equal parts—two generations each with different interests and a different social balance: and the watershed falls about the year 1905. The thirty-five years between 1870 and 1905 were spent, in a sense, in liquidating the past—in thrashing out the old conflicts between Church and State, clerical and anti-clerical, Monarchy and Republic, militarism and parliamentarism. And by 1905, the forces of anti-clerical, Republican parliamentarism had triumphed. The Dreyfus case, the *Bloc des Gauches* and the separation of Church and State cleared the old issues from the arena. The thirty-five years between 1905 and 1940 were spent, in a sense, in seeking working compromise within the now established parliamentary Republic between new social forces—the new industrial working class (the C.G.T. and the Socialist movements) and the new industrial and financial oligarchy. Dynastic, ecclesiastical and militarist issues were replaced by social and economic issues; after 1918 the German menace, though not killed, took a new and at first a less viru-

---

also with both the financial interests and the Quai d'Orsay (cf. P. Allard: *Le Quai d'Orsay* (1938), p. 179 f.) The big perfumier, François Coty, owned *L'Ami du Peuple*, which was pro-Fascist and even Bonapartist in outlook, but ceased publication in September 1938. He also owned *Figaro*, which had a circulation of some 50,000. These and the two influential weeklies owned by the publisher Fayard (*Candide* and *Je Suis Partout*) had their influence because they told their readers what they already believed and wanted to hear. Far wider in influence were the *Paris-Soir*, which was moderately Conservative and had a circulation of over 1,500,000: and *Le Petit Parisien* with nearly 1,000,000. The Communist paper, *l'Humanité*, sold between 300,000 and 450,000 copies daily in 1938. See R. Manevy: *Histoire de la Presse, 1914 à 1939* (1945) for full details.

lent form; in both home and foreign policy there was a new hesitancy, jerkiness and defensiveness, much aggravated by the losses and exhaustion caused by the Great War. With a few distinguished exceptions, such as Clemenceau, the first generation of political and national leaders had passed from the stage by 1905 and still more by 1914. Gambetta had died as early as 1882, Grévy in 1891, and Ferry in 1893; Renan had died in 1892 and Zola ten years later; Jaurès was killed in 1914. Meanwhile a new generation of leaders had come to the front. Briand and Blum had made themselves known during the Dreyfus affair: Poincaré, Barthou and Herriot were the new men in politics, as were Maurras, Anatole France, 'Alain', Duguit and Sorel, in political and social thinking. These very names reflect how much it was the Dreyfus crisis which threw up the 'new men' who were to dominate the next generation.[1]

And these new men represent a new social balance in French life: a balance in which the forces of conservatism were represented less by the classes of Church, Army and Aristocracy, and more by the commercial and financial oligarchy and semi-Fascist movements such as the *Action française*, the *Croix de Feu*, and *Jeunesses Patriotes*. The first, led by Charles Maurras, actually dates from Dreyfus days, the others from the nineteen-twenties. In this new social balance the forces of the Left were represented less by doctrinaire Republicans and more by Socialists, Communists, and the organized syndicalist movements: less by upper middle-class and peasantry, more by lower-middle class and industrial workers. The social content, no less than the ideological content, of the alignment of 'Right' and 'Left' Wings changed between 1905 and 1918. With this

---

[1] These names also reflect the new importance of the *École Normale*, or State teachers' training college—the fountain-head of so much anti-clerical Republican Radicalism: cf. A. Thibaudet: *La République des Professeurs* (1927), Chapter X, where it is pointed out that 'in the Liberal professions, teaching rigorously represents the class of "new men" . . .' and 'the Radical Republic, born in 1898, naturally found its *cadres* among these "new men".' Bursary-holders from the provinces—especially from Lyons—have often become the *normaliens* of politics.

fundamental distinction in mind, it is possible to proceed to an examination of the interaction between the actual democratic institutions as they evolved during these years, and the 'national vision' of democracy as an operative ideal.

III

THE DEMOCRATIC INSTRUMENT

The fundamental paradox of the Third Republican constitution was that it was a system of parliamentary sovereignty in a country where very few of the political parties or the broadly accepted schools of political thought really believed in parliamentary sovereignty. This paradox underlies its whole history, and is the clue to the political and social history of France in this period. In order to explain and expound this paradox, it is proposed to examine three questions:

1. How the Constitution of the Republic was born;
2. The principles and institutions of the Republic;
3. How the Constitution worked.

The Birth of the Republic

The Third Republic was a Republic before it was a parliamentary Republic. Events between 1870 and 1875 conspired to make the new regime a Republic: but only events between 1875 and 1879 determined that it should be a parliamentary Republic, with the centre of gravity of power lying inside the elected assemblies. It might at any time during these years have become either a system of cabinet government like the modern British Constitution or a system of presidential government like the American Constitution. After 1879, it could only have changed its character by either radical revision or revolution.

In another sense, the first turning-point in the formative stage of the Republic came not in 1875, when the main constitutional laws were passed, but two years earlier, when Thiers fell and the main attempt at 'fusion' of the Monarchist parties failed. The first phase—the struggle for a Monarchist regime—passed its climax in 1873: and the second phase—the struggle for a 'Conservative Republic'—began in the same year and continued until 1879. The fundamental difference between the two phases in their bearing on the working of democracy in France is that the first failed completely whilst the sécond substantially succeeded. The year 1873 saw the real rout of the Royalists: the year 1875 saw the real victory of the Conservatives—a constitutional and institutional victory, which the purely parliamentary triumph of the Republican forces four years later did not obliterate. Here is the first clue to the paradox.

The background to the years 1871-3 is the revolt of the Paris Commune, the urgent need to liberate French soil and plan French resurgence, and the clash of rival political parties. The forces in conflict were the moderate Liberal-Conservatives in power, led by Thiers; the Republican movement fostered and led by Gambetta; the Monarchist parties with a two-thirds majority in the National Assembly; and the small but active party of Bonapartists. The result was apparent governmental stability, in face of the national crisis, but a constant seething and manœuvring of parties, already lining up for the next stage of the battle. From this political fluidity was born the widespread desire for a Conservative regime, whatever its form, to preserve social order and security.

The regime under which France was governed between 1871 and 1873—usually called 'The Republic of M. Thiers'—was a rough-and-ready working compromise between the French tradition of investing 'national sovereignty' in a single, elected National Assembly, and the demands of urgent emergency. The National Assembly which met at Bordeaux in February 1871, had been elected under the shadow of military collapse and German occupation of the northern provinces. It was formally a carry-over from both the Second Republic of 1848, under whose laws of elections it had been created, and of the provisional Republican dictatorship dating from 4 September 1870, when Gambetta's Government of National Defence had proclaimed a Republic. On all grounds—of inheritance, form, spirit and leadership—the regime of the Bordeaux Assembly was a Republic. The Assembly recognized this when, on 17 February, it appointed M. Thiers 'Chief of the Executive

Power of the French Republic', and added that he would 'exercise his functions under the authority of the National Assembly, with the agreement of ministers whom he shall choose and over whom he shall preside'. On 1 March it affirmed the overthrow of Napoleon III and his dynasty—which had been proclaimed to the Paris mob by Gambetta on 4 September. The new 'Chief of the Executive Power' proceeded to strike a bargain with the Assembly, which became known as the 'Bordeaux Pact'.

Thiers declared in the Assembly, on 10 March: 'What we promise everybody, is not to deceive anybody; is not to behave in a way which would prepare, behind your backs, any exclusive solution which would distress the other parties. . . . We have accepted a heavy task. . . . We shall undertake nothing but the reorganization of the country. . . . I give you the word of an honest man that none of the questions which are reserved shall have been altered by any infidelity on our part.'[1]

The Republic of M. Thiers, which lasted until May 1873, and which accomplished successfully all its tasks of making peace, restoring order and liberating the country, was thus the most conditional, provisional and utilitarian of regimes. The precedent is of importance for the 'Provisional Government of the French Republic', headed by General de Gaulle, which governed France after her liberation in 1944.

But inevitably, in accomplishing such great tasks as suppressing the Paris Commune, raising the indemnity demanded by Bismarck in the Treaty of Frankfort, and reconstituting the French Army, even so provisional a government predetermined the conditions of the more permanent regime. To distinguish so clearly between military, social and economic reconstruction for which a strong government was urgently

---

[1] On the period 1870-3, see J. P. T. Bury, *Gambetta and the National Defence* (1936), especially Chapters IV-VI, XV-XVI; F. H. Brabant: *The Beginning of the Third Republic in France* (1940); Robert Dreyfus: *La République de M. Thiers* (1930); A. Bertrand: *Les Origines de la Troisième République, 1871-6* (1911); D. Halévy: *La Fin des Notables* (1930); Maurice Reclus: *L'Avènement de la Troisième République, 1871-5* (1900).

necessary, and political and constitutional reconstruction; and to postpone the second task believing that the process of accomplishing the first would induce no bias for or against the existing form of government, was itself an impossible bargain. That Thiers realized this is shown by his advice to the Republicans that they had a great vested interest in making his own regime a success.[1]

In the first place, greater definition was found necessary to enable the Government to carry on. At the end of August 1871, the so-called 'Rivet Law' was passed, conferring on Thiers the new title 'President of the French Republic', and defining both his powers and the method of exercising them. The long preamble suggests the qualms of conscience with which the Assembly assumed a more durable Republic, and it begins with assertion of 'constituent power' for the National Assembly. The step is presented as compatible with the 'Bordeaux Pact'. 'Considering that a new title, a more precise appellation, without changing anything fundamental, may have the effect of making clearer the intention of the Assembly to continue frankly *l'essai loyal* begun at Bordeaux. . . .' The second Article of the Rivet Law lays down that the President of the Republic shall promulgate laws as soon as they are passed on to him by the President of the Assembly; that he shall ensure and supervise their execution; that he shall stay near the Assembly and be heard by it whenever he wishes; that he appoints and dismisses ministers. It also stipulates an arrangement which remained operative into the Third Republic—that both Council

---

[1] For Thiers's attitude, see his *Notes et Souvenirs, 1870-3* (1903), pp. 131-410; and his letters, edited by G. Bouniols: *Thiers au Pouvoir, 1871-3* (1921), especially pp. 62-86. On 16 May 1871 he writes: 'Dans ma conviction, il n'y a de possible *actuellement* que la République. Hors de là on aura une affreuse guerre civile.' This seems to have been a constant factor in Thiers's belief in the Republic—its capacity as a salve of social friction and a safeguard against social disorder: hence his ferocious attack on the Commune. For the Treaty of Frankfort, see Sir A. Oakes and R. B. Mowat: *The Great European Treaties of the Nineteenth Century* (1918), pp. 274-88; and G. Hanotaux: *Histoire de la France Contemporaine*, Vol. I, Chapter V.

of Ministers and ministers themselves should be responsible to the Assembly, as was the President himself; and that every act of the President's should be counter-signed by a minister. The Rivet Law meant re-affirmation of the principles of parliamentary sovereignty and clarification of the shape of the executive organs of government, as well as consolidation of Republic rather than Monarchy or Empire. It could scarcely be, in substance, compatible with the Bordeaux Pact.[1]

In the second place, Thiers had to look increasingly to the parties of the Left for his support: and this, too, gave the regime a bias towards not only a Republic but a more Radical Republic. The Rivet Law had, paradoxically enough, been passed under pressure from Thiers's own supporters, the Left-Centre, by the Monarchists. They hoped that by concentrating authority in the hands of the President and the Assembly in which they held a good majority, they would retain the power of replacing Thiers by a king in due course. It was opposed by Gambetta and the Republicans (which was one reason why the Monarchists supported it) on the grounds that it broke the Bordeaux Pact. The party reactions, as described by Thiers himself, were that 'the Monarchists, furious at finding themselves in a Republic, and the Republicans, fretful at its not being Republican enough, are ready to fly at one another's throats, and I am obliged to throw myself between them to prevent them restarting the civil war, perhaps splitting the Army and destroying our growing credit, and so depriving me of the means for freeing our national soil from the presence of the foreigner'.[2] In the autumn of 1871, Gambetta launched a great campaign in the countryside for the dissolution of the National Assembly, and in the course of it made a series of speeches which became the basis of the new Republican creed. The campaign continued through 1872, and bore fruit in a long succession of Republican victories at by-elections, wherein

[1] For full text of the Rivet Law, see L. Duguit, H. Monnier and R. Bonnard: *Les Constitutions et Principales Lois Politiques de la France depuis 1789* (5th edn. 1932), pp. cxxi-cxxv and 315-16. Cf.: *Notes et Souvenirs*, p. 422 and Brabant, op. cit., p. 492.

[2] Bouniols: op. cit., p. 98; and see ibid., pp. 107, 130.

27 Monarchist seats were lost to 23 Republicans and 4 Bonapartists.[1] This pull towards the Left was offset by the various attempts at 'fusion' between the rival Monarchist parties.

The Monarchists' weakness was the split between Legitimists and Orleanists, each with their own candidate for the throne. The Comte de Chambord was the grandson of Charles X and the Comte de Paris was the grandson of Louis Philippe. The chance of a Monarchist restoration depended primarily on a fusion between the 'two branches of the lily', and such fusion was by no means inconceivable. The Comte de Chambord had no heirs, and was fifty-one in 1871, whereas the Comte de Paris was only thirty-three. The obvious tactic was agreement to get Chambord on the throne first, to be succeeded on his death by Paris. Despite repeated attempts of the more moderate Royalists to reach such an agreement during the years between 1871 and 1875, fusion was never achieved. The reasons were partly the memory, on both sides, of the year 1830, when Louis Philippe, entrusted with the baby Chambord by Charles X on his abdication, proceeded to make himself king: and partly the intransigence of Chambord himself.

The prospects seemed good in June 1871, when the National Assembly abrogated the laws imposing exile on the Duc d'Aumale and the Duc de Joinville, uncles of the Comte de Paris: and a committee of twelve Monarchist deputies, six from each party, was set up to serve as the 'Twelve Apostles' of Monarchist unity.[2] But each successive effort at fusion was frustrated by the stiff-necked Chambord, who insisted upon ill-

---

[1] On the propaganda campaign of Gambetta and the by-election, see H. Stannard: *Gambetta*, Chapters XIV-XV; Gambetta's letters for these years, in *Lettres de Gambetta*, ed. Halévy et Pillias; C. de Freycinet: *Souvenirs, 1848-93* (2 Vols. 1912-13).

[2] For the Monarchists' attempts at 'fusion' see F. H. Brabant: op. cit., pp. 217-348; D. Halévy: *La Fin des Notables* (1930), Chapter VII; Comte de Falloux: *Mémoires d'un Royaliste* (1926), Vol. III, pp. 224-338; Vicomte de Meaux: *Souvenirs Politiques, 1871-7* (1905), Chapters V-VII; C. Chesnelong: *La Campagne Monarchique d'Octobre, 1873* (1895); C. Lacombe: *Journal Politique* (2 Vols. 1907, edited by A. Hélot).

THE DEMOCRATIC INSTRUMENT

timed public pronouncements so uncompromising in tone as to amount to abdication. On 8 May 1871 he wrote to a Legitimist deputy a formal manifesto—the first of the series—which ended with the declaration that 'in my hands, and in my hands alone, mercy is also justice.... It is for France to speak and for God to act'. In July the long-proposed 'visit' of the Comte de Paris, aimed at reconciling the two rival claimants, was cancelled at the last moment by Chambord until he had 'explained his whole mind to France'. Four days later he issued his second manifesto addressed to 'the people of France', refusing to accept the tricolour flag instead of the white Bourbon flag, with the ominous if unhistorical vow that 'Henry V cannot abandon the White Flag of Henry IV'. It threw all Royalists into despair. 'Never', wrote one, 'have I seen such complete unanimity in despair.' 'It is no good hiding the fact', wrote another, 'that it is a farewell to France.' 'Henceforth', chuckled Thiers, 'people will denounce only one person as the founder of the Republic in France—M. le Comte de Chambord. Posterity will christen him the French Washington!'[1]

Yet a second movement for fusion took place between January and May 1872: this time concentrated in the ranks of the parliamentary Monarchists themselves. In January appeared Chambord's third manifesto, rejecting any idea of his 'abdication', but also refusing ever to become 'the legitimist king of the Revolution'. On 15 October the same year, he again forced an open breach with the Duc d'Aumale, now leading the Orleanist party, and proclaimed his belief that the Republic would bring certain disaster to France. Fusion became not only practically impossible but obviously impossible: and the third attempt at fusion, in 1873, was doomed from the start.

This third main attempt at fusion was led by the Catholic forces, instigated primarily by Dupanloup, Bishop of Orleans, and Pie, Bishop of Poitiers. In previous attempts the pretenders themselves and the parliamentary Monarchists had each failed in turn. Now the Church tried—with no more success. In

[1] For texts of Chambord's first two manifestos see (*a*) Brabant: op. cit., pp. 317-20; (*b*) ibid., pp. 339-40 (French text in Falloux: op. cit., Vol. III, pp. 235-8).

January Dupanloup wrote to Chambord and to the Pope, and tried to get the Pope to persuade Chambord that he could have an easy conscience about accepting the tricolour. He proposed a compromise, whereby Chambord might keep his white flag and France might also keep her tricolour: to which the retort of Chambord was, 'I have neither sacrifice to make nor conditions to accept'. By the summer, the two former tasks of the Monarchist supporters still remained to be achieved: reconciliation between the two pretenders and between the two flags. But now was added a third—the task which all were to pursue even when the other aims had been abandoned. This was to secure constitutional arrangements which would make restoration acceptable to the Orleanists and the Centre, and yet would be Conservative enough to satisfy the Legitimists and the extreme Right. The 'visit' of the Comte de Paris at last took place in August, and brought a new gleam of hope. But Chambord's famous Salzburg letter of October marked the breakdown of all hopes of reconciliation between the flags. His analysis of the problem of France was accurate enough: but now it could not be solved through a restored monarchy. As he truly declared:

> It is nothing less than a question of reconstructing a profoundly troubled society on its natural bases; of ensuring with energy the rule of law; of restoring prosperity at home and durable alliances abroad; and above all, of not hesitating to use force in the service of order and justice.[1]

The trouble was that this programme could no longer wait for the hesitations of the Royalists.

Each of the years 1871, 1872, 1873 had thus seen a fresh surge of Monarchist hopes, and a fresh disappointment and

---

[1] For the later manifestos of Chambord, see G. Hanotaux: op. cit., Vol. I, p. 392 f. and 489 and 538; for full text of the Salzburg Letter see Falloux: op. cit., Vol. III, pp. 324-7. The standard account of the fusionist negotiations from an Orleanist standpoint is C. N. Desjoyeaux: *La Fusion Monarchique 1848-73*. On all the events of these years see A. Daniel (really A. Lebon): *L'Année Politique (1874-83)*—a sort of 'Annual Register' of which ten volumes appeared between these dates.

THE DEMOCRATIC INSTRUMENT

anti-climax. This progressive deterioration in Royalist prospects consistently strengthened the hands of the Republicans, and drove Thiers to rely more and more on the Left for his parliamentary support. Each manifesto of Chambord was accompanied by another set of by-elections which brought Republican gains. Yet each new attempt at fusion had caused sufficient alarm on the Left and among the supporters of Thiers to rally their forces and strengthen their resolve. Each Monarchist anti-climax left the Republic more inevitable than before. It also left Thiers more firmly committed to *une République conservatrice*. He used each crisis as an occasion to reaffirm his fidelity to the Bordeaux Pact, and his own faith in a provisional Republic as the bulwark of social order and peace.

In 1871 he declared that 'every day of calm is a good thing for the Republic, and every day of disturbance is a bad thing'. In 1872, he opposed Republican celebrations of the anniversary of 4 September on grounds of France's need for 'calm and rest' in order 'to speed the liberation of her territory and to consolidate the Conservative Republic'. He declared, in his presidential message to the Assembly in November 1872, that 'The Republic exists—it is the legal government of the country. . . . The Republic will be Conservative or it will not exist at all'. In his last speech as President, on the day of his fall from power, 24 May 1873, he at last admitted, on the broad issue of Monarchy versus Republic, that he had come down on the side of Republic, because 'there is only one throne and three men can't sit on it'.[1]

This parting shot indicates one further disturbing force in the political life of France during these formative years—the Bonapartists. Bonapartists had throughout played a part, in both parliament and the country, out of all proportion to their

---

[1] Cf. Bouniols: op. cit., pp. 110, 207; Thiers: *Notes et Souvenirs*, p. 348 ff. Charles Chesnelong, a confirmed Royalist, regarded Thiers's speech of November 1872 as a complete betrayal of the Bordeaux Pact, and a further desertion of Thiers to the Republican Left (cf. *Le Gouvernement de M. Thiers* (1932), p. 122 f.). Thiers's speech of 24 May 1873 is conveniently summarized in Hanotaux, op. cit., Vol. I, pp. 604-10.

numbers. Napoleon III himself died only in January 1873, and there were always from twenty-five to thirty avowed Bonapartists in the Bordeaux Assembly. This group was led by a former Prime Minister of the Second Empire, M. Rouher, who was like his great successor in opportunism, Laval, a lawyer from Auvergne. The group of *l'Appel au Peuple* was powerful partly because of the survival of strong Napoleonic sentiments, traditions and even institutions—and partly too because of the divisions among the Monarchists. Through their paper *l'Ordre*, which they published in Paris, and their highly disciplined group in the Assembly, they strove to prevent the consolidation of more permanent institutions. They never failed to exploit the cleavage in the Monarchists, and as Republican gains at by-elections produced an even balance between Republicans and Monarchists inside the Assembly, the compact middle group of Bonapartists was able to control the balance of power between them. It played an important part in the fall both of Thiers in 1873 and of the Duc de Broglie a year later.

The year 1872 was the time of greatest alarm at the revival of Bonapartism. Bismarck used the threat of supporting Napoleon as a bargaining card with Thiers, and believed that 'the Bonapartist party is perhaps the party with which it would be most reasonable to hope for the establishment of a tolerable relationship between France and Germany'. In 1872 great plans were afoot for smuggling Napoleon III back into France and staging a restoration. A shadow-cabinet was already drawn up. In August, on the anniversary of Napoleon's birthday, there were shouts of *Vive l'Empereur* in the streets at Trouville where Thiers was staying, and rumours spread of a plot to kidnap Thiers. There were similar 'August scares' in 1873 and 1874, when the Prince Imperial made speeches at Napoleon's tomb at Chislehurst, and Bonapartist candidates won by-elections. The drive towards affirming and consolidating the Republic cannot be fully appreciated unless this standing threat be kept in mind. Bonapartism remained an active political force until 1875: and found fresh opportunities for action later, during the Boulanger affair in 1887 and even in the Dreyfus affair. The Bonapartists must share, with Chambord, part of the responsibility for the foundation of the Third Republic.[1]

This conflict of forces during the years 1871-3 left an important legacy to the Third Republic. It determined the basic question of the form of regime, and decided for a Republic as against a Monarchy. It gave the executive arm of this regime definition—in the Rivet Law, in the arrogation of supervisory power by the Assembly, to which President and ministers alike were to be responsible, and finally in the law of March 1873, regulating the conditions of ministerial responsibility, sometimes called the *loi des Trente*. This modified the Rivet Law by enforcing clearer separation between the President and the Assembly. It set the office of President on the course of becoming more and more of a figurehead, joined to the legislative body only through his ministers. In future the President could communicate with the Assembly either by messages which would normally be read by a minister, or by special previous permission to appear in person and address the Assembly. Debate could no longer take place in his presence, nor could he freely participate. Interpellation could be addressed only to ministers and not to the President. The Assembly undertook not to dissolve until it had decided the organization of legislative and executive powers, the structure and powers of a second chamber, and the electoral laws. Passed primarily to gag Thiers, the law in effect separated the two offices of President of the Republic and Chief of the Executive Power which Thiers had hitherto combined.

But though it separated the two offices it did not separate

[1] On Bonapartism in this period see Maurice Richard: *Le Bonapartisme sous la République* (1883); Robert Dreyfus: *La République de M. Thiers*, pp. 182 f. and 234 f.; Hanotaux, op. cit., Vol. III, Chapter I. Rouher was elected deputy for Corsica in February 1872. On the Bonapartist scares of 1872 and 1873, see Bouniols, op. cit., p. 205; Gambetta: *Lettres*, Nos. 174, 193, 200, 203 ff. Gambetta always used the threat of Bonapartism as an additional reason for intensifying Republican propaganda, just as Thiers used it as further proof of the need to maintain social order and achieve greater definition of the Republic.

executive and legislative powers. It had the opposite effect, for it squeezed the President out of the Assembly, but ensured that he should leave the bulk of his executive powers behind him, to be wielded by his chief minister in the Assembly. It meant a reversal of the traditional doctrine of the 'separation of powers', and was a step towards the English system of concentration of responsibility. It was a specialization of functions, and the 'Vice-President of the Council of Ministers' would henceforth be the operative head of the government, nominally acting in the Assembly on behalf of the President, but inevitably holding the real power of decision and leadership in the same way as the British Prime Minister. The office of 'Vice-President of the Council of Ministers' had been created in September 1871 as simple deputy for the President. It was now an office of key importance.[1]

The constitutional importance of the fall of Thiers, when he was out-voted in May 1873, hinged upon this law. The political change fulfilled and confirmed the intentions of the law. Marshal Macmahon was elected to succeed Thiers by 391 votes out of 392, because the Left abstained from voting. With the transfer of the Presidency from the veteran civilian politician to the veteran professional soldier it inevitably became more of a purely dignified and less effective office. Because Macmahon remained President for the next six years—throughout the whole formative phase of the Republic—this change became permanent. He did not feel that politics were his business: and his few intrusions into politics were so unhappy that no successor dared to repeat them.[2]

Personality mattered, too, in that the Duc de Broglie became Vice-President of the Council, and so inherited the

[1] For the text of the law of 13 March 1873, see Duguit, Monnier and Bonnard: op. cit., pp. cxxvi-cxxx, and 317-18, and Appendix I of this book.

[2] For the text of the nomination of Macmahon as President see Duguit, Monnier and Bonnard: op. cit., p. 318, and on Macmahon see G. Hanotaux: op. cit., Vol. II, *passim*; D. Halévy: *La République des Ducs* (1937), *passim*. The election of Carnot as President in 1889 clinched the inefficacy of the President in the constitution.

special position implied in the law of March. The ascendancy of this astute Conservative politician, who had been largely responsible for engineering the fall of Thiers, marks the main transition from the first to the second of the formative phases of the Republic. Substantially accepting a Monarchist restoration as out of the question, but resolved to make the Republic a bulwark of Conservatism in an even stricter sense than Thiers, he wove his schemes with subtlety and skill, in or out of office, during the next few years. With a cabinet which Edmund Burke would have called 'curiously inlaid', a medley of Legitimists, Catholics and Right-Centre politicians, Broglie had to cope with the last and most desperate attempt at Monarchist 'fusion', already described. In every way the first ministry of Broglie (May-November 1873) saw the confirmation of all the political and constitutional tendencies indicated above. Only in his second ministry (November 1873-May 1874) did the new and significant stage in the evolution of the Republic begin.

On the day after Chambord's Salzburg letter appeared, Broglie, according to the Vicomte de Meaux, expounded his plan to a few close friends. It was to keep Marshal Macmahon in power as 'the clay rampart' of the Monarchist majority in the Assembly, and 'to constitute authority by personifying it in a man in default of a dynasty'. Basing his power on the Right and Right-Centre, in contrast to Thiers's basis on the Left and Left-Centre, Broglie planned to shift the emphasis and put Conservatism first and Monarchy second in priority of purpose.[1]

The Broglie brand of Conservatism relied ultimately on gaining control of the cadres of administration and the *fonctionnaires*. A score of Republican Prefects were dismissed almost at once, and replaced by Monarchists or Bonapartists. The Press was controlled and Republican papers hampered. A law giving the Government power to nominate the mayor in each

[1] Cf. de Meaux: *Souvenirs Politiques* (1905), p. 184 f. ; *Mémoires du Duc de Broglie* in *Revue des Deux Mondes*, second and third series, published during 1929. The story is well told in D. Halévy: *La République des Ducs*.

Commune was eventually forced through in the face of great opposition: and many of the new mayors were old Bonapartist officials with administrative experience. The police was reorganized and placed under the mayors. The new police-State was rapidly taking shape by the spring of 1874.

But it aroused violent opposition locally, and in April Gambetta could write to his friend, Ranc, that he had 'not known any moment since 2 July 1871 more favourable to Republican interests. . . . The Law of the Mayors has put the seal on the popularity of the men and ideas of our party'. In other more formal ways too the Republic had been made more permanent. By the so-called 'Law of the Septennate', of November 1873, the Presidency of Macmahon had been assured for seven years, with the old title 'President of the Republic', and a commission of thirty had been set up to prepare the Constitutional Laws. Everything proceeded on the assumption that the Republic had come to stay, but that its institutions could be so moulded as to blunt the edge of the revolutionary tradition.[1]

It is significant that Broglie fell from power, like Thiers, when he was on the point of introducing an important new constitutional measure. Each was overthrown by the Assembly as soon as he was about to take a decisive step away from the purely provisional. Significantly, too, his successor was a soldier—General Cissey. Government was falling into the hands of the service-chiefs and the *fonctionnaires*, with a Marshal as President, a General as Premier, and Bonapartists like Magne and Fourtou in the key ministries of Finance and the Interior. This position lasted, with some reshuffle, until the end of February 1875, by which time the main Constitutional Laws had been passed. The Third Republican Constitution was born, as it died, in the hands of an authoritarian government of service-chiefs and *fonctionnaires*. History was to repeat itself oddly in 1940 with Marshal Pétain as President, General

---

[1] On this period, May 1873-May 1874, see G. Hanotaux: op. cit., Vol. II, Chapters VI-VII and X; Gambetta: *Lettres*, Nos. 159-193; C. Chesnelong: *L'Avènement de la République* (1934), Chapter I. Text of the Law of the Septennate in Duguit, Monnier and Bonnard: op. cit., p. 319.

THE DEMOCRATIC INSTRUMENT 89

Weygand and Admiral Darlan as his lieutenants, and a politician like Laval as its operational leader.

The prelude to the first of the Constitutional Laws was the defeat of the Cissey cabinet in January 1875, and its enforced carrying on because the President could find no alternative government. The Republic of the Dukes put through the Third Republic in its own death-throes, and the only real sense of urgency came from fear of deadlock and dissolution. In July 1874 the principle of male suffrage for all at twenty-one rather than twenty-five in municipal elections had been recognized, so that central government, too, had now logically to be based on the same electorate. This preliminary triumph was largely due to the parliamentary skill of Gambetta.[1] In January the Assembly began to debate the first two bills proposed by its commission—the Bills regulating the public powers and the second chamber. The first definitive resolution came at the end of the month in the form of the famous Wallon Amendment, resolving that 'The President of the Republic is elected by absolute majority vote of the Senate and the Chamber of Deputies, meeting as the National Assembly. He is appointed for seven years and is re-eligible'. It was passed by a majority of one vote. But it contained in germ the whole later framework: the reaffirmed Republic, the division into two chambers, and the definition of the Presidency. As in its earlier stages, the Third Republic was growing like a stalactite, from the top downwards.[2]

[1] Cf. D. Halévy: op. cit., p. 149 ff.; G. Hanotaux: op. cit., Vol. III, pp. 19-22; H. Stannard: *Gambetta*, p. 159.

[2] There had already, before 1875, been diverse draft proposals: e.g. Thiers's proposal of May 1873, printed in Annexe 26 of his *Notes et Souvenirs*; Broglie's proposal for a 'Grand Council' of May 1874, which was much more elaborately Conservative than the scheme of Thiers—given in full in A. Daniel: *L'Année Politique* (1874), p. 165 f., and summarized in Duguit, Monnier and Bonnard: op, cit., p. cxxxvi, or D. Halévy: op. cit., p. 133 f.

On the Wallon amendment see G. Hanotaux: op. cit., Vol. III, p. 166 ff.; C. Chesnelong: op. cit., Chapter III; A. Bertrand: *Les Origines de la Troisième République*, Chapter VIII, who calls it 'la consécration légale et définitive de la République'.

If the Wallon amendment be regarded, as it unanimously has been regarded, as the real basis of the Third Republic, then the paradox of its foundation is complete. The Republic was founded by a Monarchist assembly with a Right-wing President and Government in power, on the motion of a Catholic lawyer who insisted that he was not asking for the Republic—and it was passed by a majority of one vote, a deadlock being avoided only by the late arrival of one deputy who would have voted against the amendment.[1] Yet these remarkable circumstances do less than justice to the popular acceptance of the Republic in 1875. Between February 1871 and September 1874 126 of the 158 contested by-elections had been won by Republican candidates: the Monarchist forces had been frustrated in all their manœuvres: and the Conservative Government was in power only on sufferance and *faute de mieux*. The circumstances, and the background described above, are important only because they reveal how it came to be the Conservative forces which moulded the new institutions—not, indeed, without having to make some compromises with the Left, but yet with sufficient freedom of action to leave their permanent impression on the whole democratic instrument of modern France.

The constitutional laws determining the Organization of the Public Powers and the composition of the Senate were passed in February. The laws determining the relationship between the Public Powers and the methods of electing Senators followed in July and August. The law governing the election of Deputies was passed at the end of November. The ministry of M. Buffet, a Right-Centre man, had replaced General Cissey's 'cabinet of caretakers' in March, so the last three laws were passed under his government. It was merely a reshuffled coalition of the Centre parties, and in administrative policy it was every bit as Conservative as Broglie's or Cissey's. But dissolution was now in the air. It haunted the final labours of the Na-

---

[1] Cf. A. Zévaès: *Histoire de la Troisième République* (1938), p. 81 f.; D. Halévy: op. cit., p. 158 ff. M. Senart was the late arrival concerned.

THE DEMOCRATIC INSTRUMENT 91

tional Assembly. The spur to action came from anxiety to complete its labours before it broke up.[1]

The framework of government thus curiously created will next be described. But not least of the legacies of the Bordeaux Assembly to modern France was the experience of five years of real parliamentary government. One sovereign Assembly of elected representatives of the nation had ruled the country and had achieved the tasks it was set up to achieve. It had been a truly national body in the sense that noble and commoner, 'notable' and Radical, had met and debated it in, and had thrashed out in debate usually hectic and often brilliant, the most fundamental problems of modern France. Princes, Dukes and provincial *bourgeoisie* had played their part. In spite of its constant party feuds it had—almost without knowing it—done a great work of reconciliation, both social and political. The Royalist, Chesnelong, pays tribute to the many deputies whose names do not figure large in histories of the Assembly, yet who worked modestly and solidly behind the scenes, on committees and bureaux. The Republican Freycinet points out that the Assembly achieved precisely the opposite of what it had dreamed, and that had the Third Republic been born in a Republican Assembly it would doubtless have been more elaborate, with declarations of general principle and arrangements so absolute that they would have needed revision in a few years. The Republic was destined by conditions to sobriety and moderation, in its machinery and institutions. Yet like all compromises it satisfied few of its creators. It remained for many years longer a *modus vivendi*, a stop-gap accepted because of necessity. There was for a whole generation every intention of revising it soon.[2]

The Principles and Institutions

The collective form which emerged from the fierce interplay of sectional interests and opinions during 1875 may be briefly

---

[1] For the texts of all five Laws, see Duguit, Monnier and Bonnard: op. cit., pp. cxliii- clx, 319-35 and Appendix I of this book. The Assembly finally dissolved at the end of December.

[2] Cf. C. Chesnelong: op. cit., p. 210 f., and C. de Freycinet:

described as a system of parliamentary sovereignty checked by popular election. The Chamber of Deputies was from the first destined to be only the popular branch of Parliament, checked and counter-balanced by the two Conservative institutions of the Presidency and the Senate. That it should become the centre of gravity of political power, as it became after 1877, was neither the intention nor the arrangement of its creators. The basic principle on which all parties were ready to agree was that there should be a strong executive power. Monarchists and Bonapartists and even Conservative Republicans all alike wanted a powerful Presidency for their diverse designs. Republicans of the Left were willing to accept a strong executive, in the hope of one day capturing it and using it to hold their rivals at bay. None intended that either Presidency or cabinet should become as ineffective as they later became.

The powers of the President, laid down in 1875, were that he should have charge of the armed forces, make all civil and military appointments, receive foreign envoys and ambassadors, negotiate and ratify most treaties, and preside over all national solemnities. He was given power to adjourn and even to dissolve the Chamber of Deputies, in agreement with the Senate, and was responsible before the Chambers only in cases of high treason. He could initiate laws, and had to supervise the execution of all legislation.

But every one of his acts had to be counter-signed by a minister, and ministers were 'collectively responsible to the Chambers for the general policy of the Government, and individually responsible for their personal actions'. The existing arrangements for a council of ministers with an active president of its own were reaffirmed and carried forward into the new regime. The President, himself chosen by a simple majority of both Chambers sitting together as 'the National Assem-

---

Souvenirs, p. 319. Gambetta's view (Letter 261) was 'All goes well. The Republic is founded. It remains to make it great and strong, and lead it on to its "natural frontiers".' The plaintive summary of a Monarchist (de Meaux: *Souvenirs Politiques*, p. 279 ff.) was 'Under a Monarchist assembly which the King deserted, France recovered and the Republic was set up'.

bly', and holding office for seven years, was meant to represent continuity and stability of the executive power as compared with the four-year tenure of the Chamber which was liable to be broken by dissolution. Thiers had warned the Centre parties that if they would not cross the Channel with him, they would have to cross the Atlantic: and the Presidency was meant to be more akin to the American model than to the British monarchy of Queen Victoria.

So, too, the Senate was intended to represent both continuity of tenure and constitutional security for the Conservative forces. It was to represent the 'notables' of the provinces at least as much as had the Bordeaux Assembly, and therefore not only were 75 of its 300 members to be in the first instance nominated by the old National Assembly, but the rest were to be elected indirectly, through electoral colleges, on which each Commune was equally represented regardless of its population. This device placed, as it was meant to place, preponderant power in the hands of the small villages, and over-represented rural France as against the big towns. The countryside, it was hoped, would prove—as in 1871—Monarchist or at least socially Conservative. Each Senator was to sit for nine years, and only one third of the Senate was to be renewed every three years. All Senators had to be at least forty years old, to mobilize the alleged Conservatism of middle-age. Besides sharing full legislative power with the Chamber, the Senate could act as a court of law for judging the President or ministers, if they were charged with misdemeanours by the Chamber. So constituted, and having a virtual veto on all legislation, it was meant to be the bulwark of social order against over-enthusiastic Republicans, Radicals or Socialists.

The Chamber alone represented direct male suffrage, for it was to be elected every four years by secret vote in each *arrondissement*. Two special electoral arrangements require mention: the method of second ballot (or *deuxième tour*) because it lasted throughout the Republic, and the method of single-member constituencies (*scrutin uninominal*) because it had been before 1875, and was to remain afterwards, a contentious issue. By the system of second ballot (laid down in Article 18 of the

Law of 30 November 1875), no Deputy could be elected on the first ballot unless he had gained a clear majority of the votes registered, and also at least one quarter of the voters registered. If the candidate at the head of the poll failed to qualify on either of these grounds, a second ballot was held over a week later, when a simple majority sufficed. This device made possible in the interval a process of compromise and party bargaining, which in England normally precedes the poll. But it opened the door to considerable possibilities of bribery.

The issue of *scrutin uninominal* versus *scrutin de liste*, so much debated during the formulation of the Constitution, was in 1875 decided in favour of the former. But the Liberal Republicans, the Bonapartists and some Radicals argued for the alternative arrangement of making the *département* the unit of voting rather than the single-member constituency, on the grounds that *scrutin de liste*—collective voting of all *arrondissements* in one *département* for a party-list of candidates—would give the Deputy greater independence, and help to eliminate the pressure of the *sous-préfet* in the small unit of the *arrondissement*. Opinions were very divided on the issue, because the lessons which could be drawn from previous experience were conflicting, and the balance of considerations of expediency was subtle. The method of *scrutin de liste* was tried between 1885 and 1889, and again between 1919 and 1927: no clearer decision was reached even after both experiments. It freed the Deputy from constituency control but put him more at the mercy of the party organization which drew up the list: and the risks of administrative pressure on elections diminished anyhow, for different reasons.

Apart from these minor adjustments in details, the whole working of this democratic machinery was radically changed by the course of events. President, Senate and Chamber evolved differently from the intentions of the men of 1875. In 1877 President Macmahon used his constitutional power to dissolve the Chamber, and went to the country using every sort of influence and pressure to produce a congenial Conservative majority in the Chamber. The elections produced a large Republican and Radical majority, and dramatic demonstration of the kind of deadlock to which the Laws of 1875 could easily lead. A President Conservative in bias, with a firm sense of the 'balance of the Constitution' and of his own national responsibility, found that he could not pursue a policy which was unacceptable to the country and the majority of the Chamber. He was faced with either governmental deadlock or personal resignation. After some experience of the former, in 1879 he chose the latter. Never again did a President venture to use his power of dissolution: and the Chamber secured, contrary to the law, a guaranteed tenure of four years without general elections.[1]

In 1884, under the ministry of the Republican, Jules Ferry, the electoral basis of the Senate was overhauled. The balance between rural and urban power was changed by giving the larger Communes much greater weight in the electoral colleges than the small Communes. Representation was graded according to the size of the municipal council, which itself was determined by size of population. At the same time, the system of a quarter of the Senate being self-perpetuating was abolished. Thus its Conservative character was modified, and it was made more democratic and more broadly representative. But the countryside still held a preponderance, through the system of indirect election, and the Senate remained an obstacle to many measures passed by the more radical Chamber. Extension of the vote to women suffered such obstruction quite regularly. Remaining of equal legislative capacity to the Chamber, the Senate was always a more important body than

---

[1] On the system of second ballot, and the experiments with single-member and multi-member constituencies see G. Hanotaux: op. cit., Vol. III, pp. 433-49; A. Ésmein: *Éléments de Droit Constitutionnel Français et Comparé* (2 Vols. 1928), Vol. II, Chapter V; Joseph Barthélemy: *Le Gouvernement de la France* (last edition 1939), Chapters III and IV. There is an excellent short account of the whole working Constitution of the Third Republic by L. Trotabas: *Constitution et Gouvernement de la France* (second edition, 1933).

On the important events of 1877 concerning Macmahon—known as the crisis of *Seize Mai*, see especially D. Halévy: *La République des Ducs*, Chapter VII.

the British House of Lords, and more akin to the Senate of the United States.[1]

The Chamber of Deputies, though unchanged in structural basis, underwent a two-fold change. With the decline in importance of the President, the executive power concentrated completely in the hands of the cabinet, under the *Président du Cabinet*, which in turn depended for its existence and survival entirely on the support of a majority of the Chamber. Secondly, with the crystallizing of party groups, in great multiplicity, every cabinet had to be a coalition of several such groups to get its majority support. Great power therefore fell into the hands of the centre groups, virtually indispensable to all ministries, and the marginal groups, whose adherence or desertion made and unmade governments. The Chamber became the great arena wherein the groups shuffled, bargained and manœuvred: and the lobbies of the Chamber became the *Bourse* of politics. The whole centre of gravity of power shifted downwards, until the fate of French governments depended normally on the result of manipulations in the Chamber and its lobbies, and only in an ultimate way, at four-yearly intervals, on the expression of public opinion given in general elections. Governments became unstable and short-lived, being at the mercy of group bargains. Groups in the Chamber became semi-detached from the group-formations which appealed to the voters during elections. And the Chamber as a body of some 618 men of diverse calibre and outlook became, in effect, the real government of France. The Bordeaux National Assembly, one single body, gave birth, in the end, to an offspring remarkably like itself.

[1] For the texts of the laws revising the Senate, see Duguit, Monnier and Bonnard: op. cit., pp. 338-42. The obstructiveness of the Senate is discussed in W. L. Middleton: *The French Political System* (1932)—an excellent analysis in English of the French Republic: see especially Chapter VIII.

In the department Seine-et-Oise in 1938 the rural population, about two-sevenths of the whole, had the same number of representatives as the urban population, which was five-sevenths of the whole, in the electoral colleges which appointed Senators. Cf. D. M. Pickles: *The French Political Scene* (1938), p. 41 f.

The structure of local government, as defined in the Duc de Broglie's 'Law of the Mayors' of 1874, remained in force for only nine years. The mayors of the chief towns were appointed directly by the Government: the mayors of the smaller Communes by the prefect. After 1883, all mayors except the Mayor of Paris were to be chosen by the municipal council, which was itself already elective. A law of 1884 regulated elections to municipal councils on a very wide male franchise. The democratic nature of communal elections assumed new importance now that the Commune was the real basis of the Senate: and here, too, something was done to democratize the Senate, as well as to decentralize the highly integrated Napoleonic machinery of administration. Through his control of municipal police, as well as of the manifold activities of local government in social and economic life, the French mayor became the unique figure of active local democracy, symbol of the intense parochial and provincial life of France.[1]

But other units of local administration were less democratic and more authoritarian. The *départements* remained under the government of the Prefect, an agent and official of the central government: under him, the *Sous-Préfet* administered the *arrondissements* on the same terms of centralization. Each unit had its elected council—the *conseil-général* in the *département* and the corresponding but much less important *conseil d'arrondissement*. In August 1871 the Monarchist majority had met with bitter opposition from Thiers, over a measure which was intended to weaken the power of the central government and the prefects in local affairs. It was proposed by the Committee of Decentralization to set up an elective Departmental Com-

---

[1] On Broglie's Law of the Mayors see G. Hanotaux: op. cit., Vol. II, p. 437 f. The centralizing tendency of this law of 1874 was in complete contradiction to the law of April 1871 which Broglie himself had sponsored, and which gave municipal councils power to elect their own mayors in all communes with less than 20,000 inhabitants. Only the bitter opposition of Thiers had then kept for the central government the right to appoint the mayors of the larger communes, cf. Brabant: op. cit., p. 462. For the text of the law of 1884 see Duguit, Monnier and Bonnard, op. cit., p. 337.

mission drawn from each General Council, to supervise the carrying out of the Council's decisions by the prefect. The General Council consisted of one delegate from each *canton*—an artificial unit of purely administrative convenience between the *Commune* and the *arrondissement*—and men of local prestige and importance were normally returned. Its functions were—and substantially remained—advisory. The scheme of 1871 would have erected the small inner body, of four to six men, as a standing executive arm of the General Council, forcing the prefect to observe local wishes. But here the discipline and central loyalties of the prefect proved too strong to allow effective decentralization of authority: and in the *départements* there remained much more local administration than local self-government. The *Loi Tréveneuc* of February 1872 conferred great executive authority on the General Councils in an emergency: but the law was not evoked until General Giraud's memorandum of April 1943, and was later dropped by the French Committee of National Liberation in Algiers, and the Provisional Government of General de Gaulle in Paris. It thus remained also a dead letter. Although the office of *sous-préfet* at the head of each *arrondissement* became often superfluous, and M. Poincairé in 1926 eliminated 106 such offices, the unit remained important for administrative, judicial and electoral purposes. Its Council played little active part in local government. The key offices in local government and administration remained the prefect and the mayor, the one representing the centripetal, integrating forces of French democracy, the other the centrifugal, local forces. In this working balance and compromise, the conflicts of principle of the eighteen-seventies found remarkably permanent solution[1]

The judicial system was taken over even more intact and un-

[1] On the drive for decentralization in 1871, see Brabant: op. cit., pp. 463-4 and Appendix, p. 515 ff. where the statements of Thiers before the Committee of Decentralization are reported; and D. Halévy: *La Fin des Notables*, p. 49 ff. For the Loi Tréveneuc see Duguit, Monnier and Bonnard: op. cit., p. 316.

On the units of local administration, see J. Barthélemy: op. cit., Chapter IX; W. Anderson (ed.): *Local Government in Europe* (1939).

mentioned by the makers of the Third Republic. The only part of it specifically changed by the constitutional laws was the *Conseil d'État*. Article 4 of the law concerning the organization of the Public Powers (25 February 1875) laid down that as vacancies arose in future, the President of the Republic should nominate, in the Council of Ministers, councillors of State *en service ordinaire*, who would be revocable only by decree of the Council of Ministers. It also provided that those appointed by the law of May 1872 could be dismissed in the same way: but after the dissolution of the National Assembly, revocation could take place only by a resolution of the Senate. The explanation of this isolated attention to the very key-stone of the administrative hierarchy of institutions is that from September 1870 until June 1872 the *Conseil d'État* had been abolished. When Thiers asked for its reinstatement in 1872 the Assembly kept for itself nomination of councillors *en service ordinaire*—that is, to the purely judicial as distinct from the administrative personnel of the Council. Its administrative experts (*en service extraordinaire*) were anyhow appointed by the Government, usually from the ranks of prefects and higher civil servants. The Law of 1875 not only reaffirmed the existence of the *Conseil d'État*, but gave its members considerable security of tenure immediately, and even greater safeguards of independence in the future. The actual method of recruitment developed was a combination of very stiff competitive *concours*, followed by rigorous internal selection for promotion: and from the ranks of the *Maîtres des requêtes* so sifted, two-thirds of the vacant councillorships had to be filled. With this degree of independence and security of tenure, the Council acquired great professional pride and integrity, as well as dignity and prestige. Far from being an agency through which the State could act as judge in its own cause, the Council became the defender of individual rights, liberty and property against the administration.[1]

[1] There has been a controversy between French historians over the reasons for Article 4: cf. D. Halévy: *La République des Ducs*, p. 176 ff., and note on Robert Dreyfus's theory, p. 181. Cf. above, Chapter II, p. 59 f., and on the *Conseil d'État* see Ésmein: *Éléments de Droit Constitutionnel*, Vol. II, Chapter 3; and L. Trotabas: op. cit., p. 83 ff.

This spirit at the top governed the behaviour of all subordinate administrative courts—especially the *conseils de préfecture de département*, which after the administrative overhaul of 1926 gave place to the *conseils de préfecture interdépartementaux*. They were further reformed in 1934. These tribunals dealt with disputes in public works, local elections, and practically all disputes in which local authorities were involved. Here, and in the *Conseil d'État* to which appeals could go, lay the real machinery for harmonizing the autonomy allowed to Communes. All judges and magistrates were appointed nominally by the President of the Republic—actually by the Minister of Justice—and once appointed they had security of tenure.[1]

The general theories and principles underlying these constitutional arrangements are conspicuous by their absence. By nature and origin pragmatic, and confessedly a synthesis of conflicting party demands like the English settlement of 1688, the Third Republic was not built on finely drawn theories or absolute and consistent principles. This has not prevented jurists like Trotabas and enthusiastic Republicans like Gabriel Hanotaux from abstracting certain principles from the arrangements after the event. But their value and aptness are questionable. Universal suffrage—which Hanotaux thought fundamental? But no women had the vote. Sovereignty of the people? But the people had only the right to be represented in the Chamber and less directly in the Senate, which together

The Minister of Justice was himself, though a political appointment like the English Lord Chancellor, President of the *Conseil d'État* and also of the *Tribunal des conflits* which determined whether or not a dispute falls within civil or administrative jurisdiction.

[1] Cf. L. Trotabas: op. cit., pp. 78-91. Trotabas draws a parallel (p. 73) between the pattern of central and the pattern of local government. There is an executive power representing centralization, a deliberative power representing the idea of decentralization, and a consultative or juridical power, which 'controls' or checks. This 'regime-type' can be seen in the President and Council of Ministers—the Chamber and Senate—and the *Conseil d'État* nationally: in the Prefect, *Conseil général* and *Conseil de préfecture* locally. But at the really local level the parallel does not hold, and 'c'est le Conseil d'État . . . qui est le conseil et le contrôleur de toutes les communes de France'.

wielded complete legislative sovereignty and even appointed the President. Ratification and revision of the laws were not entrusted to the people, but were reserved for the chambers themselves: there was no system of plebiscite, referendum or popular initiative. The separation of powers? But the Senate had judicial powers, executive power lay theoretically with the President who was elected by the National Assembly, and in practice with the Council of Ministers who belonged to the Assembly and were controlled by the Chamber and Senate sitting separately. The *Conseil d'État*, under the presidency of a party man such as the Minister of Justice, formed a close link between judiciary and administration.[1] The only general principles on which the Constitution worked derive less from the constitutional laws than from the conventions and practical devices adopted to make it work.

It has been shown how a balanced constitution, with elements of democracy, oligarchy and even monarchy inherent in its structure, came to be set up in particular historical circumstances. How this system worked to produce a regime of parliamentary sovereignty must next be examined.

How the Constitution Worked

If the Royalist forces were frustrated by 1879, and the Conservative forces triumphed constitutionally in 1875, the Republican and Radical forces won a political and parliamentary triumph in 1877 and again in 1879. In 1877, the Republican parties, with the backing of Republican opinion in the general elections, robbed President Macmahon of his power to establish a Conservative regime with strong, authoritarian executive power. Two years later, when Macmahon recognized defeat by resignation, he was replaced by the Republican, Jules Grévy. At the same time, with the Republican leader, Gambetta, as President of the Chamber and a Republican party majority

---

[1] Cf. G. Hanotaux: op. cit., Vol. III, Chapter V, for a full-dress analysis of the 'theory of the Constitution'. Also L. Trotabas: op. cit., Chapter I, for a much more discriminating analysis of its principles.

in both Senate and Chamber, the 'Republic of the Republicans' really began. These events shaped the whole future working of the Constitution.[1]

The first result was to give France a period of almost unbroken Radical government for ten years, before the next serious threat to the Constitution arose in the form of Boulangism. Grévy himself, re-elected in 1885, remained President throughout this period. Both Senate and Chamber kept Republican party majorities, and although the ministries changed rapidly, reflecting the growing disunity in the ranks of that party, none attempted to challenge, pervert or overthrow the existing Constitution. These ten years consolidated the Third Republic. They also, unhappily, confirmed the failure of France to produce either strong political party-formations or stable ministries.

Before examining the reasons and consequences of these facts, it is well to summarize the social significance of the triumph of the Republicans after 1877. Alexandre Zévaès has put it thus:

As the conservative M. Jacques Piou observes, 'Is it not a struggle between the old governing classes and the new social stata? The Duc de Broglie led one, Gambetta headed the other.' . . . Each of the different political formations corresponds to a particular stratum either of the governing and possessing class, or of the middle and working classes: the Legitimists representing more particularly the big landowners, the Orleanists the wealthy industrial, financial and business bourgeoisie born and grown since 1830, and the Bonapartists a small section of the bourgeoisie trusting to the virtues of the sword and also that crowd of adventurers who seek in a new 'December the Second' the chance and possibility of fresh spoils. To these three forms of political and economic reaction are opposed the middle and lower bourgeoisie, who understand that they have become, and tend

[1] On the events of 1879 and their permanent importance see E. Lavisse: *Histoire de France Contemporaine* (1921), Vol. VIII (by Charles Seignobos), Chapter III; Alexandre Zévaès: *Histoire de la Troisième République* (1938), pp. 105-44. There are valuable accounts of the Third Republic, its origins and working in R. W. Hale: *Democratic France* (1941); W. Sharp: *The Government of the French Republic* (1938); K. Munro: *France Yesterday and Today* (1945).

to become more and more, the solid core of modern society. . . . Their elements are these: the doctors of small towns and villages, whom Balzac described, the skilled artisans, the small peasant-proprietors . . . the schoolteachers closely bound up with the life of the people and in bitter conflict with the priest in their Commune.

The industrial workers had been busy organizing themselves during the eighteen-seventies, and exerted some direct political influence by 1879. 'In 1879', writes Zévaès, 'the Labour Party properly so-called enters on the scene.' The social strand of the revolutionary tradition began now to intertwine inextricably with the political: and the demand for economic liberty and equality mingled with the demand for political liberty and equality.[1]

The political and parliamentary groupings and alignments therefore took shape against this confused background of conflicting social forces and movements. It has often been suggested that the party system of modern France is the result of two revolutions going on simultaneously: the political fermentation of the French revolutionary tradition and ideals, and the economic revolution of industrialization. Until the great climax of the Dreyfus affair, as already suggested, the issues which divided Frenchmen most were the residue of old political issues: authoritarianism, militarism, clericalism. But the social issues of labour conditions and industrial organization were already raising their head. After 1905 they came increasingly to dominate the political scene, until during the inter-war years they virtually precluded all others. By then a multiplicity of party groups had become inevitable and normal, and the working constitution had adjusted itself to these formations. And the main parties of modern France could trace their direct lineage back to the early nineteen-hundreds.[2]

The parties of the extremes will be considered later (Chapter V), for they did not form the ingredients of ministries. The

[1] Cf. A. Zévaès: op. cit., pp. 105-6; cf. above, Chapters I and II for discussion of the different 'strands' in the revolutionary tradition, and the social bases of the Republic.

[2] Cf. p. 72 f. above and W. L. Middleton: *The French Political System*, p. 16.

nuclei of parties which, in coalition, provided the governments of the Republic, were the old centre parties of the Bordeaux Assembly, Gambetta's Republican Union, and the Socialist parties temporarily united by Jaurès before 1914. Without exploring the innumerable subtleties of the tiny splinters of groups which ricochetted throughout the electoral and parliamentary history of the Republic, it is possible to trace the reasons and occasions which kept the Conservative, Republican and Socialist groups from becoming solid parties on the English or American pattern.[1]

The main parliamentary Conservative Party of modern France was the *Union Républicaine Démocratique*—or Republican Federation, formed in 1903 and led by M. Louis Marin. It represented Catholic opinion, industrialist and land-owning interests, and big business in general. It was the spokesman of the higher *bourgeoisie* and the new oligarchy in parliament: and of a spirit of Conservative nationalism in foreign policy. Historically it originated as an attempt to introduce stiffer party discipline and organization among the parties of the Right, and to serve as the Conservative counterpart to the Radical, Socialist and Communist parties. It was the heir of the Conservative groups which emerged in the eighteen-eighties, accepting the Republic as the form of regime, but opposed to anti-clerical policies and determined to use parliamentary institutions as the bulwark against Radical change. Though powerful in the Chamber during the nineteen-twenties, it lost power during the nineteen-thirties.

The moderate Conservative, or Right-Centre, Party was the Democratic Alliance, the party of Poincaré, Tardieu, Flandin and Reynaud, formed by Adolphe Carnot in 1901. Liberal in

---

[1] There are many excellent accounts of the political party-formations, their ideas and social bases; see especially: André Siegfried, *Tableau des Partis en France* (1930); Emmanuel Berl, *La Politique et les Partis* (1932); Roger Soltau, *French Parties and Politics* (1930); Albert Thibaudet, *Les Idées Politiques de la France* (1932); Fernand Corcos, *Catéchisme des Partis Politiques* (1932); Léon Ernest Jacques, *Les Partis Politiques sous la Troisième République* (1913); Georges Bourgin et al.: *Manuel des Partis Politiques en France* (1928).

outlook, representing orthodox finance and capitalist business interests yet seeking international co-operation through the League of Nations, it was the heir of the Liberal groups of Thiers and Favre, the old Left-Centre. Never attaining the party discipline of even the Republican Federation, it was a loose bundle of fluctuating groups co-operating for electoral purposes outside the Chamber. It was in general both anti-Catholic and anti-Socialist. In the Chamber it consisted mainly of groups calling themselves variously Left Republicans, Centre Republicans, Democratic Left and Left Independents, and tending to vote divergently on each issue.

There was normally much less cohesion among these groups of the Right than among the parties of the Left. They had a majority in the Chamber of 1919 partly because of the curious working of the 1919 experiment in proportional representation which hit the Left very hard, and partly because they were united on the purely nationalist issues of national security and 'making Germany pay'. Conservatism in France tended to depend more on the defences provided for it outside parliament, in the ranks of the *fonctionnaires*, the Bank, and industrial power, than on electoral or parliamentary party organization.[1]

The Left-Centre forces of politics found more organized expression in the so-called 'Radical and Radical-Socialist Party'—though here, too, fluctuating groups mattered almost as much as the general party structure. They were the direct heirs of the great party built up by Gambetta—the party which founded the 'Republic of the Republicans'. They liked to think of themselves as the descendants of the Jacobins. Champions of anti-clericalism, anti-militarism, anti-caesarism: of Dreyfus and individual rights; of peasant proprietorship and the 'little man'; of the *École unique*; of Republican defence and national security: the Radicals made themselves the voice of both the revolutionary tradition in politics and of the middle classes and the peasants in parliament. They represent the

[1] Cf. E. Berl: op. cit., pp. 27-38 on the U.R.D. Its leader, M. Louis Marin, escaped to England and joined General de Gaulle in 1943. For its period of greatest power, 1919-24, see Paul Vaucher: *Post-War France* (1934), and see below, Chapter V, p. 184 f.

defensive, distrustful individualism of French democracy, the suspicion of all authority and the hatred of all privilege. Their strongholds were therefore the villages and smaller provincial towns: and the basis of their party organization was the *cadres* or local committees, and the lodges of Freemasonry. These committees consisted of college professors and school teachers, petty officials and shopkeepers, doctors and journalists, artizans and well-to-do peasants. The *comitards*—the structural basis of Halévy's *République des Comités*—chose parliamentary candidates, and served as active agencies at elections. But they themselves were self-appointed and not elected. Here, again, was a powerful force of political decentralization in French democracy, making the Deputy, once selected and elected on this intensely local foundation, an agent of local, provincial interests and outlook.

Similar both in origin and spirit to the local Radical committees were the Freemasons' Lodges, whose anti-Catholic creed was inspired by the revolutionary tradition inherited from the eighteenth-century Deists, the *philosophes*, and the Jacobins themselves. The *Grand Orient* and the smaller *Grande Loge* organizations have shared between them since 1772 the membership of some 50,000 to 60,000 French Freemasons, and have played an active but little recorded part in the fight of the Radicals against Church, Army, Monarchy and big finance. Their social basis was middle class and not proletarian.[1]

As the most powerful Centre party, and the organization most deeply rooted in French national life, the Radical and Radical-Socialist parties made themselves a normally indispensable part of every governmental coalition. Their leaders provided the greatest names in the list of Prime Ministers of the Third Republic—Ferry, Combes, Clemenceau,

---

[1] On the Radical and Radical-Socialist local committees, see especially A. Thibaudet: op. cit., pp. 135-52. On Freemasonry in France, see Pierre Frédérix: *État des Forces en France* (1935), pp. 115-35, 152-6; Carlton J. H. Hayes: op. cit., pp. 118-23; Albert Lantoine: *Histoire de la Franc-Maçonnerie Française* (1925). For a virulent attack on it, see A. G. Michel: *La Dictature de la Franc-Maçonnerie sur la France* (1924).

Herriot, Daladier. The fact that the party of individualism *par excellence* played so consistently prominent a part in French governments made the Third Republic what it was: socially Conservative, politically progressive, and diplomatically nationalistic. Its chief internal division concerned its attitude towards Socialism, and the most important split came in 1910, when those Radicals who favoured Socialism formed the small but influential 'Republican Socialist Party'. But for most purposes 'Radicals' and 'Radical-Socialists' held together: though within the organizational framework of the *cadres* survived a rich diversity of shades of opinion.

The parliamentary representatives were organized by the Radical Executive Committee, which arranged several meetings a year. These meetings were normally attended by some 300 or 400 of the most active Radical leaders. The annual Congress of the Party, capable of making momentous party decisions, was loosely organized, and federations of local committees were but haphazardly represented as compared with hundreds of influential individuals in Paris who could wire-pull on the spot. The Party was not itself systematically or democratically run: and again ultimate powers of control relapsed to the local *cadres*.[1]

The Socialist Parties, though perpetually tending to split, from the first reached a higher degree of organization in the country and in parliament, and a closer connexion between the two. Indeed, the further Left the more thorough was party organization. The United Socialist Party dated from 1905, when it was defined as 'a class party, aiming at the socialization of the means of production and distribution: not a party of reform, but a party of class and revolution, united against all

---

[1] The 'Radical and Radical-Socialist Party' had, for example, 86 seats in the Chamber of 1919; 139 in 1924; 125 in 1928; 160 in 1932; 113 in 1937. The U.R.D. meanwhile dropped from 183 in 1919 to 103 in 1924, and 1928, and only 41 in 1932, and 54 in 1937; meanwhile the Socialist Party (S.F.I.O.) rose fairly steadily, too, from 68 in 1919 to 104 in 1924, 100 in 1928, 131 in 1932, and 151 in 1937, when it was the largest single party in the Chamber and Blum became Prime Minister.

bourgeois groups'. From time to time groups like the neo-Socialist group of Marcel Déat, or individuals like Briand and Boncour, inevitably split away from this rigid basis: and from the first various dissidents formed the 'Republican Socialist Party'. The Great War brought further splits, and in 1920 both the modern Socialist and the modern Communist Party were born by the division between the adherents of the Second and Third Internationals within the 'United' Socialist Party. The French section of the Workers' International (S.F.I.O.) became the modern Socialist Party headed by Léon Blum; the French section of the Communist International (S.F.I.C.) became the modern Communist Party, of which Maurice Thorez became the General Secretary. The old Socialist newspaper, *L'Humanité*, which Jaurès had founded in 1904, became the organ of the Communists, and in 1918 Blum founded the new Socialist paper, *Le Populaire*. This split, deliberately promoted by Lenin, was engineered at the Socialist Party Conference at Tours in 1920. By 1922 the trade unions split in a similar way, at the conference at Lille, into the old C.G.T. which remained Syndicalist-Socialist, and the new Communist *Confédération Générale du Travail Unitaire* (C.G.T.U.). They did not re-unite until 1936, during the Popular Front experiment. The Left-wing working class movement was split from top to bottom, and French democracy was so much the weaker for the collapse of that democratic Socialist movement which Jaurès had so laboriously and so successfully united.

And on the Left such party splits affected party organization at every level. Rival local committees and candidates appeared at elections, just as rival trade unions appeared in each industry. The Socialist Republican Union (U.S.R.) derived from a split of the late nineteen-twenties, when the mildest, non-Marxist Socialists led by Renaudel combined with various other individual dissidents, such as Briand, Boncour and Painlevé, to form a parliamentary group of ministers and former ministers more willing than the S.F.I.O. to collaborate with Radical governments. Socialist local committees, more systematically created than the Radical, found concerted expression in the annual party conference, and the party structure was more akin to British party organization, national and centralized.[1]

So, too, with the Communist Party. As a more absolutely revolutionary body, its organization was tight and its discipline strict. But despite its orthodox Marxist creed and its appeal to the more extreme among industrial workers, French Communism is not purely the product of industrialism. Communism was strong not only in the 'red belt' of the Paris working-class suburbs and the industrial departments of the north-east, but also in the centre (Cher and Allier) and in the south (Southern Provence) which are agricultural, and strongest of all in the completely rural area of Lot-et-Garonne in the south-west. André Siegfried has suggested that it there signifies 'red Republicanism' rather than strict Marxism, and that discontented peasant proprietors who voted Communist should be regarded as a sort of 'Irish Group', voting extremist on principle regardless of the ideology involved. It seems probable that the experience of active resistance between 1940 and 1944, sometimes led locally by the Communist Party, may have still further extended this peculiar appeal of the most extreme of all Left-wing parties in France. No Communist Deputy held office during the Third Republic: and only in 1944 did two Communist representatives take ministerial office in the Provisional Government.[2]

The excessive individualism and 'non-conformity' of French politics found expression not only in this complex spectrum of organized parties, but in the immense number of splinters which existed between these broad blocs of opinion. Small bands of independents or free-lance Deputies abounded in every Chamber. Lacking any wider party discipline, they reshuffled, bargained and voted as they pleased, and owed allegiance only to the constituents who had returned them to parliament. Once again, local and particularist interests found

[1] On the S.F.I.O. and the C.G.T., see above, Chapter II, pp. 47-51, and J. H. Jackson: *Jean Jaurès, passim*. On the modern policy of the C.G.T. see Léon Jouhaux: *La C.G.T.* (1937); Robert Bothereau: *Histoire du Syndicalisme Français* (1945).

[2] Cf. A. Siegfried: op. cit., pp. 169-70; E. Berl: op. cit., pp. 87-100; and the naturally favourable description in Maurice Thorez: *France To-day and the People's Front* (1936).

full expression, at the expense of parliamentary organization and governmental stability. In a regime where the Deputy was intended to be the *contrôleur* of Ministers, scores of Deputies were abundantly free to exercise their powers arbitrarily. It was often boasted that every nuance of public opinion, however subtle, could find expression in parliament. What mattered more was that every special interest, however local and exclusive, could encumber national politics with its demands.[1]

The regular means of exerting such power was through the device of *Interpellation*, or challenge. Any Deputy or Senator could call upon a Minister to explain his policy as regards any particular issue. A general debate followed, and this debate had to end with a resolution or general vote, before proceeding with the *ordre du jour*, or business of the day. Should the resolution go against the government, the ministry was expected to resign: and during the first fifty years of the Republic, three out of every five ministries resigned over an adverse *ordre du jour*. The device served excellently to sacrifice ministerial stability to parliamentary control over policy, and was one main plank in the structure of parliamentary, rather than cabinet, sovereignty during the Third Republic.[2]

[1] The suggested distinction between what Thibaudet calls 'parties of interests' on the Right and 'parties of ideas' on the Left has little real substance in fact. The *Action française* ideology is as absolute as the Communist, and the sectional interests appealed to by Socialists and Communists are no less real than the interests appealed to by the U.R.D. or the Democratic Alliance. All parties appealed equally to the combination of interests and ideas best calculated to win them active support among electors and readers.

[2] On the methods of parliamentary control over the executive see J. Barthélemy: *Le Gouvernement de la France* (1939), Chapter VII. The other two methods in addition to interpellation (inquest and question) were less important: inquest because, though elaborate and formidable in procedure, it was seldom used; question because, though abundantly used, it was usually concerned with details of administration rather than general policy. Formal printed questions and answers in the *Journal Officiel* might number as many as 5,000 in a year. Interpellation, in either Chamber or Senate, was the regular method of control over ministers and the Government's general policy.

THE DEMOCRATIC INSTRUMENT

More formidable in appearance, though sometimes less effective in practice as a means of parliamentary control over ministers, was the elaborate system of Senate and Chamber standing committees. By 1920, twenty permanent committees of the Chamber had been set up, covering between them most subjects of legislation and administration. Each had forty-four members, representing all parliamentary groups in proportion to their strength in the Chamber. Originally simply organs of criticism and advice in the formulation of Bills, they soon came to be used as weapons for directing government policy and controlling the action of the government. They meant that each important Minister had to face not only the Chamber or Senate as a whole, but a miniature Chamber or Senate of men who specialized in criticism of his own department and its activities. He was seldom likely to behave irresponsibly—however much the committees might behave irresponsibly. The committee's attitude would range from one of helpful co-operation to one of hostility and obstruction: depending usually on the personality, tact and skill of the minister himself. The Committees on Foreign Affairs were particularly imposing bodies, usually headed by a former Prime Minister. They had the right to keep in constant touch with the *Quai d'Orsay* through their *rapporteurs d'information*, as well as the power to invite the Foreign Minister or his subordinates to come before them for interrogation. But ministers could refuse to appear—and did refuse when they felt strong enough. They could be evasive when they did appear. And the Committees became channels of information about foreign policy, rather than agencies in making it. Parliamentary control over foreign policy was mainly indirect: through financial control over money spent on the diplomatic and armed services, and through political disapproval after the event. A dozen ministries were overthrown during the Republic on issues of foreign policy. Such control—or rather reprisals—after the event were in France, as elsewhere, the most effective method yet found in a democracy for control over foreign policy. Though clearly unsatisfactory, it must probably always remain the ultimate sanction. It cannot be said that French parliaments abused this power as regards foreign policy: largely because, until the inter-war years, there was broad and substantial agreement in French opinion about foreign policy.[1]

The results of these constitutional arrangements and customs and this party system of fluctuating groups are familiar enough: some 88 distinct ministries during the seventy years of the Third Republic (over 100 if abortive ministries be counted): some 50 different Prime Ministers and nearly 50 different Foreign Ministers: between 400 and 500 different Cabinet Ministers. Yet these absurd results should not be exaggerated. Where desired, both continuity and consistency could be achieved. M. Delcassé held the record for continuity with seven years' unbroken tenure of the Foreign Office: M. Briand the record for persistency with his total of ten years altogether at the same office, and his eleven different ministries. The democratic instrument in France was no better than the revolutionary tradition, the balance of social forces and the conflicts of public opinion would allow it to be.

From the 'revolutionary tradition' modern France inherited a double 'geological fault' which ran right through her social life and her political structure: the conflict between liberty and equality as ideals, and the gap between democracy and government. By permeation through the social bases of her national life, this inheritance produced a multitude of small groups and parties, many of which were opposed to a democratic form of government and democratic ways of life. The consequent clash of social and political forces led, in turn, to a compromise regime which was designed by Monarchists, adapted by Liberals, and made to work by Radicals. It was a system of parliamentary sovereignty in which very few of the political parties really believed. The first generation of this regime, between 1870 and 1905, was spent in liquidating the past, and the

[1] On the parliamentary committee system see W. L. Middleton: op. cit., Chapter VII, and the specialized studies by R. K. Gooch: *The French Parliamentary Committee System* (1935); and Lindsay Rogers: *The French Parliamentary System* (1929). On the Foreign Affairs Committees in particular, see F. L. Schuman: *War and Diplomacy in the French Republic* (1931).

chief unifying force amongst the parties seeking to make it more democratic was common hostility to the 'enemies of the Republic'. The series of flukes and hazards by which the Third Republic was established left a large minority opposed to its very existence and survival. The energy spent in resisting this minority in Church, Army and administration meant postponement of more vital questions about what the Republic should do and what sort of society it should seek to create. This cramped the early development of the Republic, for the only programme on which parties could unite was the minimum programme of opposition to the minority which opposed the whole regime: a policy of 'anti-monarchism', 'anti-clericalism', 'anti-militarism'. The Great War produced a temporary unity and reconciliation, but still further postponed the settlement of modern issues.[1]

The second generation of the Republic, between 1905 and 1940, was therefore haunted by a great time-lag and by powerful forces acting as a drag on smooth and timely adjustment of the Constitution, law, government and administration to meet modern and ever-changing conditions. Habits acquired during the previous generation died hard, old divisions formed on out-of-date issues survived. Now it was the parties of the Right which were united only in common opposition to the forces of

---

[1] The position can perhaps be understood by imagining a United Kingdom in which a Mosleyite Fascist movement attacking parliament were so great a danger that elections had to be fought by all the other parties as 'democratic' parties united only on the issue of anti-Fascism. In spite of having run the elections as a bloc they would, in power, have the most diverse views on what to do with their electoral victory and would shade off from Right to Left somewhat like the French. Whenever a domestic issue arose on which they were divided, they would be strongly tempted to shuffle and re-group within parliament rather than risk their wider (though negative) unity being impaired, or the parliamentary system running into a deadlock which would be grist to the Mosley mills. Such a situation has not arisen in Great Britain mainly because the vast majority accept the parliamentary system: and the whole nature of a democratic regime is conditioned by whether or not there is such general agreement about the fundamentals of the regime itself.

DEMOCRACY IN FRANCE

Republicanism, Democracy, Socialism and Communism; and they shaded off from Right to Left according to which of these forces aroused their greatest animosity. The Left parties might have developed greater solidarity and more stable party organization, but for the new disruptive force of Communism which split them as well. Opponents of the existing regime were now reinforced, for they existed both on extreme Right and extreme Left, and the Centre parties—the Republicans, Radicals, Radical-Socialists and moderate Socialists—although disagreeing among themselves about domestic issues, were forced to shuffle and reshuffle in a series of uneasy coalitions in order to carry on the government. Constant compromise was unavoidable if they were not to risk the whole regime being defeated and overthrown, and positive legislation could be no more than the highest common denominator of their agreement. The system survived and worked only so far as these Centre groups could agree to make it work: and perpetual half-measures were the price paid for making it work. Every government and every measure which got through both houses of parliament had to be a half-way house.

Thus arose the paradox that in a nation famed for its logicality and clarity of mind and vision, and amid a party system where every party took its stand on a clear-cut ideology and a fairly distinct social or sectional basis, the general atmosphere of politics and the tone of nearly all legislation was one of half-hearted, timid compromise of which the fruits were usually 'too little and too late'. The habit of *débrouillage* became chronic. A spirit of compromise may be essential in democratic government, but this was compromise without tolerance, and a series of half-way houses which were destinations rather than temporary halts on a journey. Democracy needs a constitution with balance but without deadlock; a party-system which produces compromise without stalemate; leaders who can bargain without sacrifice of principles; a social order which provides orderly progress but not stagnation or violent change. The Third Republic was not happy in finding or creating these prerequisites of a successful democracy. The tendency to deadlock between President and parliament was solved only by the

THE DEMOCRATIC INSTRUMENT

complete ascendancy of parliament over all governments. The tendency of parties to stalemate was avoided only by half-hearted compromise. The power of provincialism and the group-system were not such as to produce many leaders who were more than shrewd manipulators and skilful politicians. The changing balance of social classes was not one with which such a regime could easily keep pace, for the drag on legislative reforms was heavy and the dynamics of the parliamentary system were geared very low. If the democratic instrument in France was no better than the revolutionary tradition, the balance of social forces and the conflicts of public opinion would allow it to be, it was perhaps no worse than the extreme individualistic and separatist spirit of the French people wanted it to be. Indeed the very multiplicity of parliamentary groups helped to soften divisions which a more rigid two-party or three-party system would have intensified.

It can be judged by two standards: relatively, by its own standards and values, and not by those of other democratic nations such as the United Kingdom or the United States; and more absolutely by the standard of its response to the challenge of modern problems which are common to all twentieth-century nation-States, whatever the form of their regime. One criterion is that of the French national vision: the other is that of the adequacy of the Third Republic to meet the requirements of men in modern European civilization. Each must be applied in turn, before a just estimate of the achievement of the Third Republic can be attained.[1]

[1] The first of these criteria is applied in Chapter IV below, the second in Chapter V below. A final résumé of the whole argument will be found at the end of Chapter VII.

IV

THE NATIONAL VISION

The Democratic Ideal

'I HAVE always believed', said Thiers in 1871, 'that there is only one kind of good government and one kind of real liberty. Good government means unity of action; real liberty is the opportunity of dismissing the authority to whom the action has been entrusted. But once you have set up an authority you must let it act and not weaken it.' Herein lies the clue to the basic conflict of conceptions within the French democratic ideal.[1]

It has already been suggested that part of the peculiar 'revolutionary tradition' of modern France was the difficulty of reconciling democracy and government—freedom and administration—the sovereignty of the people with the rule of law. The explanation of the strong appeal of traditionalist and conservative ideas in France is the belief, shared alike by extreme democrats and extreme anti-democrats, that liberty and authority are ultimately irreconcilable. The failures of the nineteenth-century experiments in monarchy and Liberal Catholicism seemed to endorse this belief. Furthermore there has always been a gulf between nationalist Liberals like Thiers and Radical democrats like Gambetta: the same sort of gulf as between Bonapartists and traditionalist Monarchists. It is the contrast between men who believe in the need for a strong centralized authority in the modern State, and men who see in decentralization and local autonomies the essence of good government.[2]

These contrary conceptions of government remained an issue throughout the Republic, though the controversy took varying forms. At first it crystallized into the conflict between centralization and decentralization, with Monarchists and Radicals and

[1] Cf. F. H. Brabant: op. cit., p. 516; and cf. above, p. 16.
[2] Cf. pp. 98 and 112.

THE NATIONAL VISION

even some Socialists on one side, Liberals and Bonapartists, odd allies, on the other. Later it became involved with the question of how far the Deputy should be the agent of the national 'general will', and how far he should be the agent of local, particularist interests. The fluctuation in electoral methods between *scrutin de liste* and *scrutin uninominal*, already described, implied similar questions. Some of the many issues involved in the Dreyfus affair were the issues between the claims of individualism and personal rights and the claims of authoritarianism and 'national security'. Largely as a result of the affair, Radicalism came to be stated in the extreme and anarchistic form of the philosophy of 'Alain', whilst authoritarianism was stated in an equally extreme form: the traditionalist *étatisme* of the *Action française* and the post-war semi-Fascist movements. Underlying these varied contests of principles, which in one form or other dominated the whole political life of the Republic, lies a permanent, many-sided issue. It merits further enquiry, since it involves the whole national vision of what constitutes the 'good life', and of what is regarded as the most desirable kind of national society. It is an issue which was constantly influenced during the Republic by the standing menace of the Third Reich—the perennial threat to French national security, which threw France periodically into a state of siege and emergency conducive to authoritarian control.[1]

The notion that democratic government should be weak government, that more government meant less democracy, was always a heresy to the French Liberal. The very concern of French Liberals with the doctrine of the 'separation of powers'—a doctrine derived from Montesquieu's writings but seldom interpreted as Montesquieu had defined it—implied the grant of wide powers to the central authority as a whole. It was, historically, the first answer of French democrats to the charge that centralized power would inevitably be undemocratic and even uncontrollable. It was an answer concerned with what Montesquieu had more accurately called 'the *distribution* of powers'—the allocation of authority between complementary organs of the central government. As such, it found full ex-

[1] Cf. Chapter III, pp. 76-78, and Chapter V, pp. 179-184.

pression in the first two French Republics: indeed, such perfect expression in the Second Republic of 1848, that deadlock between executive and legislature, each resting on direct popular mandate, was wellnigh inevitable. The absence of any real attempt to embody the principle in the constitution of the Third Republic was partly the consequence of this previous experience, and partly a sign of how little the Liberals shared in the moulding of the constitutional laws. French democrats like Gambetta pinned their faith more in the efficacy of universal suffrage to control the Chamber and Senate, than in any attempt to achieve some automatic check on executive power within the mechanism of the central government itself. 'If the Chamber should show itself decidedly powerless', he wrote in 1875, 'it would not only be it but the whole Republic which would be blamed.'[1]

Paradoxically enough, it was the extreme Legitimists who were the chief advocates of extensive measures of decentralization in the eighteen-seventies: they and the *communards*. The Monarchist Committee of Decentralization which was created within the Bordeaux Assembly pressed Thiers very hard for greater local autonomy in the *départements* and in the municipalities, and for *scrutin uninominal* (single-member constituencies) in national elections. The local gentry, as Daniel Halévy describes them, 'elected in the disaster of the Second Empire, pursued a Liberal dream whose traditions went back to the aristocratic risings of very ancient France': in short, to the traditions of the *Frondes*, to defence of local privileges and immunities against royal bureaucratic centralization. Parlements, provincial Estates, Chambers of Agriculture and Assemblies of

---

[1] Cf. Gambetta: *Lettres*, No. 256 (14 November 1875). An influential Liberal propagandist such as Prévost-Paradol specifically rejected the principle of 'separation of powers' in 1868. 'Un ministère présent aux Chambres, homogène, responsable, amovible surtout, voilà donc l'instrument le plus indispensable du gouvernement parlementaire et la plus forte garantie de la liberté publique' (*La France Nouvelle*, p. 101). Cf. L. Trotabas: op. cit., pp. 27-32, for an attempt to maintain that the Third Republic was based on a 'separation of powers'.

THE NATIONAL VISION 119

'notables' haunted this dream, and led to the anti-Rousseauist doctrine of the need for 'intermediary bodies' between the individual citizen and the State. Louis XVI in particular had experimented with them and after 1870, as earlier in the nineteenth century, reaction against Napoleonic integration expressed itself among the gentry in revival of this dream. The Liberal Prévost-Paradol made it popular and topical in *La France Nouvelle* of 1868; but it had already been promoted by ultramontanes like Veuillot, who had argued that a centralized State is a weak State, since it can be knocked out by one blow at its nerve-centre, whereas dispersed power and local liberties made for a tough and durable State. Sedan revived this belief with dramatic effect.[1]

Indeed, the views of all parties were clearly reflected in their characteristic reactions to the Second Empire and its defeat. In 1864 Thiers had made his famous demand for the 'indispensable liberties' which became the programme of the Liberal Party. He had defined them as 'security of the citizen against personal violence and arbitrary power; liberty but not impunity of the Press, that is to say liberty to exchange those ideas from which public opinion is born; freedom of elections; freedom of national representation; public opinion, stated by the majority, directing the conduct of Government'. This remained the essence of Left-Centre ideals in the eighteen-seventies. In Gambetta's Belleville Manifesto of 1869, this moderate programme was restated in more Radical terms. 'For those who believe that the People is the one lawful sovereign, and must really exercise power, mere responsibility of ministers to parliament is not enough: all those who hold any kind of office must be effectively checked, especially the head of the executive power.' To underline his divergence from Thiers, he added, 'Those who *can* reconcile universal suffrage with the "indispensable liberties" granted by limited Monarchy can join Thiers.' His demands were for universal male suffrage in both local and

[1] On the movements for decentralization see Brabant: op. cit., p. 420 ff. and Appendix; D. Halévy: *La Fin des Notables*, pp. 49-54; Prévost-Paradol: *La France Nouvelle*, p. 77 ff.; Falloux: op. cit., Vol. II.

national elections; complete freedom of the Press and public meeting; freedom of association; the abandonment of standing armies; the complete disestablishment of the Church; the abolition of all privileges; a secular, free, compulsory system of elementary education; and economic and social reforms. Napoleon's plebiscite of April 1870, on the belated 'Liberal Constitution' which granted Thiers's 'indispensable liberties', won the bulk of the Liberal votes but none of the Republican votes. Yet even Gambetta's readiness for direct democracy was limited: and in November 1870 he is found resisting the theory of *mandat impératif*, or instructions imposed on representatives by their constituents, as vigorously as Edmund Burke resisted it in his speech to the electors at Bristol nearly a century before.

Both Liberals and Radicals, then, had much in common, and much to distinguish their programmes both from the decentralizing tendencies of the extreme Right and extreme Left, and from the 'direct democracy' favoured by the Bonapartists with their slogan of *appel au peuple* and their plebiscitary caesarism. Liberals and Radicals alike believed that the form of the regime, political reforms and civic liberties, were essential prerequisites of social and economic reforms. They had the same priority of purpose, which Gambetta stated categorically in the Belleville Manifesto.[1] 'I believe that the progress of these social reforms depends absolutely on the political regime and on political reforms: and for me it is axiomatic in these matters that the form involves and determines the substance.' This attitude set both of them apart from the Socialists, who gave primacy to social and economic reforms. Political liberties and rights once ensured, both became readily satisfied: and to the Socialists, Syndicalists and Communists was left the task of pressing for more social and economic reform. As late as 1921, M. Painlevé's *Ligue de la République* in its manifesto defined as Republicans 'those who accept without qualifications the Republic

[1] Cf. Henri Malo: *Thiers* (1932), p. 449; J. P. T. Bury: *Gambetta and the National Defence* (1936); Appendix II of this book for the text of the Belleville Manifesto; and cf. Bury, p. 16 ff. On the distinction between Liberals and Radicals, see above, p. 36f.

as defined by Gambetta in his Belleville programme of 1869'.

In this sense, the domestic history of the Third Republic might be written in terms of the progressive satisfaction of the 'moderate' parties of each generation, and the consequent relegation of each 'moderate' party in turn to the ranks of Conservatism. The Republicans of the eighteen-seventies, satisfied by the new parliamentary regime, became the Conservatives of the eighteen-eighties. The Radicals of the eighteen-eighties, satisfied by the triumph of anti-clericalism and anti-militarism, became the Conservatives of the early nineteen-hundreds. The Radical-Socialists, satisfied by the mild social reforms of the nineteen-hundreds, joined the ranks of the Conservatives in the post-war period. The Socialists of the inter-war years, satisfied by the social-reform and nationalization programme of the Provisional Government, already rank among the moderate parliamentarians of the nineteen-forties. The so-called *sinistrisme* of French politics has often been commented upon, in the sense that Conservative parties adopt or cling to Left-wing labels. It would be equally true to speak of the *dextrisme* of French politics—the accumulative recruitment of the moderates to the forces opposing still further social change: or—while phrases are being coined—of the essential *modérisme* of French politics—the invariable triumph and satisfaction of the forces of moderation. It all depends on the standpoint of the commentator: and all three generalizations are equally true and equally false, being but different aspects of the same central historical fact. The essential fact is that the national vision has shifted its range with each generation, and has led to a fresh alignment of political forces amid changing circumstances.[1]

---

[1] Cf. Albert Thibaudet: *Les Idées Politiques de la France* (1932). M. Thibaudet analyses the six main schools of political thought—Traditionalism, Liberalism, Industrialism, Social Catholicism, Jacobinism and Socialism—and concludes that they form a complementary whole, *une République platonicienne d'Idées*, held together by the comprehensive ideology of Liberalism. André Siegfried (*Tableaux des Partis en France*, p. 89) speaks of the *toujours à gauche* of French political life—though with some scepticism.

Throughout these many changes of emphasis and objective, French political thought has seldom ceased to regard the individual and human personality as the very basis of politics. The basis of all is humanism, ranging from an extreme individualism which is tantamount to anarchism, to a respect for small and intense human communities which are but the individual writ large. France herself, as a nation and even as a state, is thought of in terms of individual personality. It is no accident that the Third Republic was nicknamed Marianne. The powerful traditions of classical humanism, of Roman law, of revolutionary sentiment and emancipation, have all conspired, with the institutions of peasant proprietorship and the small business, to exalt the individual in French thought, habits and social organization. This is the constant reality underlying the desire for decentralization, local autonomies, a weak government, strong communal life in small farms and villages, and above all in independent family life. It breeds the spirit of resistance to all dictatorship: and even the most complete of dictatorships have had to make much of their respect for peasant proprietorship and the family, for the ideal of the 'career open to talents' and the rights of Labour. Even the unsought system of parliamentary sovereignty which was the Third Republic had to come to terms with this reality by making the Deputy the most effective personal agent of local desires and interests, and of individual requests. Every French regime except Vichy, and nearly every French school of political thought except traditionalism, has been able to claim some lineage from Rousseau: at one moment an *étatiste*, at another a *communard*, at another a Socialist, yet always, at bottom, an incorrigible individualist.[1]

---

[1] The French cult of individuality and of individualism is apparent in innumerable aspects of French life and culture, some of which are described elsewhere in this book. It has been frequently acknowledged and elaborated by prominent French writers—e.g. André Siegfried: op. cit., Chapter I on *Le Caractère français*; Pierre Maillaud: *France* (1942), p. 41 ff. to quote only two very modern examples.

On the many-sidedness of Rousseau, see Alfred Cobban: *Rousseau and the Modern State* (1934); and the brilliant Catholic analysis of

THE NATIONAL VISION

The French national vision has remained, indeed, deeply coloured in politics by the legacy of eighteenth-century thought, whether classical or romantic, rationalist or emotional. After the great age of French literature in the seventeenth century, France had a national heritage of culture which remained great beyond challenge. That culture linked classical traditions and national literature with political institutions such as the monarchy of Louis XIV, and with political theories such as the rationalism of Descartes or Voltaire, or the classicism of Racine or Montesquieu. Culture, nationalism and political thought became interconnected and associated ideas. As one writer has remarked, 'the eighteenth-century ideal of civilization, based on rational and human values, has remained a dominant characteristic of the French mentality'. Some consequences of the close connexion between literary men and politics in the nineteenth century have been already indicated. In the twentieth century, too, the classical scholarship of M. Herriot and the French literary learning of Léon Blum, the literary leadership of Royalist forces by Barrès, Maurras and Léon Daudet, have continued this connexion. Journalism and literary polemics are the life-blood of French politics, and the influence of *normaliens* in the *République des Professeurs* tends in the same direction. M. André Philip and M. Georges Bidault, prominent in post-Vichy France, were both academic scholars at French universities before the crisis of 1940 brought them into active politics as champions of democratic liberties and national recovery.[1]

In 1936 Jean Guéhenno could write, 'In a world where property and interests know no frontiers, nations can henceforth represent only those ideas which our will and our courage have kept alive, a way of thinking, a way of living, which men who speak the same language, who live under the same sky and have lived through the same history, have discovered through the

---

Jacques Maritain: *Trois Réformateurs* (1925). Cf. A. D. Lindsay: *The Modern Democratic State* (1943), Vol. I, pp. 129-34; 235-40.

[1] Cf. D. M. Pickles: *The French Political Scene* (1938), Chapter I; and D. Mornet: *Les Origines Intellectuelles de la Révolution Française* (1933).

centuries.... The only legitimate imperialism is that of reason.'
To identify nationalism with rationalism is characteristically French. Few distinctions are more significant in modern French political thought than the famous distinction drawn by Charles Péguy between *mystique* and *politique*. When traditionalists like Barrès had spoken of nationalism in superstitious terms, of the feelings inspired by the bones of ancestors in the soil, Péguy raised the conception of national feeling once again to a moral, Christian level, to a conception which satisfied both French rationalism and French nationalism. His famous epigram—*tout commence en mystique et tout finit en politique*—might seem to express a sort of *fin de siècle* disillusionment, though Péguy himself defined his terms carefully enough. But the actual effect of his personal influence on French thought—the greater because of his death in action on the Marne in 1914—was to revive and purify, in modern terms, the spirit and tradition of the Revolution. His passionate belief in personal integrity, obedience to conscience against all authority at whatever the cost, the quality of his revulsion against the forces which tried to crush Dreyfus, made him the hero of modern Republican individualism, and the dramatic antithesis to Charles Maurras and all that French traditionalist Conservatism represents.

In reply to requests to define his meaning, Péguy declared that '*la mystique républicaine, c'était quand on mourait pour la République; la politique républicaine, c'est à présent qu'on en vit*'. He saw Caesarism not only in the Second Empire, in Boulangism, in the anti-Dreyfusards, but also in the electoral committees and the parliamentary party machinery of the Radicals and Radical-Socialists. Indeed, he saw a tendency to Caesarism in all political organization, for he saw politics as the degeneration of pure spirit. Only in the untrammelled realm of pure human spirit could there be freedom and truth. Morals and politics are for him interdependent. 'We can in no wise distinguish the social from the moral revolution, in that we do not believe the moral revolution of mankind can be sincerely, deeply, seriously effected without a complete revolution of his social environment; and we equally believe that no formal revolution would avail in any way unless it be accompanied by the ploughing up and turning over of consciences.' Combes and his attacks on the Church after the Dreyfus affair incurred as much abuse from him as had the anti-Dreyfusards themselves: the spiritual must not be devoured by the political to which it has given birth. The real enemy—because it is the source of degeneration—is personal ambition and acquisitiveness: and the real social remedy is individual moral integrity. This attack on ambition and the power of money made him an enemy of the new oligarchy and a certain kind of Socialist. But he regarded the wage-earning class—the proletariat—as infected with the same vices as the *bourgeoisie*; and he attacked the political leaders of the Left as much as those of the Right.

It has been necessary to say this much of Charles Péguy's ideas and influence, for as it has been suggested 'his intellectual and religious evolution is a mirror of twenty years of French thought', and 'few men have been more truly representative of their generation'. He presented, in vivid personal shape, the eternal protest of the prophet against the lawgiver, the spiritual against the material. He did much to ennoble the ideas and sentiments of the young men of his generation. The incorrigible non-conformist, in a perpetual minority of one; the rebel and heretic, cherishing integrity above power, exerted a strong fascination over many Frenchmen. Few writers are more expressive of the finest elements in the national vision of France during the first half of the Third Republic, with its blend of patriotism and individualism, its passions and rebelliousness. Few are more revealing of that instinctive distrust of all authority *qua* authority, that mutinous spirit of anarchism which inflamed the democratic ideal in these years. There is little doubt that had Péguy lived he would have been a perpetual critic of the Republic during the inter-war years: yet equally certain would he, in 1940, have rallied to the Cross of Lorraine, and fought all collaborationism; and equally certainly would he have leapt into violent criticism of the Provisional Government as soon as it tackled the tasks of concrete reconstruction and political reorganization. Here, too, the poet in politics bears the hall-mark of much that is familiar and characteristic in modern French political life.[1]

Fortunately, perhaps, there is also a very different element in the national vision of France, to which we must now turn.

French homage to the classical ideals of ordered unity and rational harmony takes many forms: the power of the *Académie française* over the French language; the belief, which persisted through every regime since 1789, in a positive set of ideas to be inculcated by the national system of education; the national prestige accorded to distinguished scientists and artists; the instinctive rejection of racial prejudices and theories; the colonial policy of assimilation and the generous extension of citizenship. It was simply assumed that the cultural unity of French civilization is such that it must be formally expressed in national institutions and policies. Only belatedly and reluctantly was it admitted that this unity could admit of other loyalties and individual rights within the nation: and the rights of a free Press, free Labour organization and free public meeting date from the very end of the nineteenth century. In this curious way—again so reminiscent of Rousseau—French individualism has been tempered and restricted by a totalitarian nationalism and *étatisme*, and the Renaissance antithesis of sovereign individual and sovereign State has persisted in sharper terms than in England. Even when France has been most anxious to make men free, she has been tempted, the next moment, to believe that they can be forced to be free. This rapid transition, so foreign to British habits of thought, remains an important factor in the schemes for a more 'social democracy' in France since her liberation in 1944. The ill-fated Algiers scheme for a unified national news-agency—*une agence unique*—is but one instance.[2]

Religion and ecclesiastical traditions have reinforced these

---

[1] Cf. Jean Guéhenno: *Jeunesse de la France* (1936); Charles Péguy. *Notre Jeunesse* (1916) and other works; D. Halévy: *Péguy et les Cahiers de la Quinzaine* (1941).

[2] Freedom of the Press in France really came only in 1881; free association in trade unions in 1884; free public meeting in 1907. For the draft schemes of Algiers for the *agence unique* see *France*, published in London, 3 August 1944, and other issues of that period.

THE NATIONAL VISION

tendencies to conscious unification of the whole nation. Again, there is a sharp contrast with Britain. It has been suggested that 'The articles of faith of the Church of England were like the constitution of the Third Republic, that which divided Englishmen least'.[1] In a country where Protestantism had first been tolerated by granting it exclusive territorial and political privileges, and later repudiated by withdrawing these privileges and driving out the Huguenots, men were driven to be pro-Catholic or anti-Catholic: and where Protestantism took but little root, to be anti-Catholic meant to be primarily anti-clerical, and often, in the end, to be anti-Christian. The Third Republic inherited the struggle between Church and State from the whole of modern French history: from the seventeenth century alliance of altar and throne under Louis XIV; the eighteenth-century antithesis between Christianity and agnosticism, priestcraft and reason; the French revolutionary battle between Church and Republic; the nineteenth-century divorce between Catholicism and Liberalism. The events of 1870, which brought sharp conflict between Papacy and State in Italy, raised new complexities for the Third Republic. It now had to choose between a nationalist foreign policy which dictated friendship with the Italian kingdom, and Catholic pressure for a pro-Papal foreign policy of hostility to the new kingdom. Bismarck's *Kulturkampf* of the eighteen-seventies in Germany still further complicated the choice of France.[2]

The well-established connexion between altar and throne,

[1] R. B. McCallum: *England and France, 1939-43* (1944), p. 9.

[2] Protestantism in France, though not attracting numerous adherents during the Third Republic, was chiefly influential by reason of the brilliant and distinguished theologians it produced. The names of Sabatier and Couchoud are international in importance, and the French characteristics of rationalism, logic and individualism are apparent in their writing, cf. Canon W. J. Sparrow Simpson: *Religious Thought in France in the Nineteenth Century* (1935), Chapters IV-VIII. The men who effected the separation of Church and State in 1905 thought in the historical terms here used. M. Briand, who first made his name as *Rapporteur* of the Chamber Commission on Church and State, traced the history of the Church in France from the baptism of Clovis! Cf. J. E. C. Bodley: *The Church in France* (1906), p. 20.

and the naturally anti-clerical bias of French Republicanism, edged France steadily towards a positive anti-clerical policy, both at home and abroad. Gambetta was ever ready to raise the cry of 'Clericalism the enemy', and he was echoed in later decades by Ferry and Combes and Clemenceau, loudest among a host of others. These echoes died away only during the Great War, though they left a legacy of divided public opinion to modern France. A doctrinaire rationalism and laicism, forced into becoming a creed as absolute and as intransigent as its opponent, has therefore remained throughout the Third Republic a persistent feature of the French 'national vision'. And politically it chimed in with the Rousseauist refusal to tolerate competing loyalties which might mar the direct relationship between State and individual. To be a democrat without becoming an anti-clerical, an agnostic or an atheist, required both intellectual valour and moral conviction. The *école unique*, infused with the spirit of the *école normale*, became the moral foundation of the Republic. Even after liberation, in 1945, this issue revived enough to cause real friction between the Catholic party (the *Mouvement Républicain Populaire*) and the Socialists and Communists in the Fourth Republic.

The establishment of the Republic and, after 1879, the triumph of the Republicans, created a new alliance between the Church and the Army. Here again was an authority, a power bloc claiming absolute allegiance from French citizens, which the Republic was bound to regard with jealousy and suspicion as a competing and rival authority to the State.

But here was a complete dilemma for the Republicans. As regards the Church, the solidarity of the Republic and the security of the nation could both be pursued by hostility to clerical policies, at home and abroad. As regards the Army, the solidarity of the Republic demanded a policy contrary to the security of the nation. France needed a large and powerful Army: great military establishments; national conscription; and measures which placed a large portion of national wealth and national energies at the disposal of the High Command. But to do this was to strengthen the very authority which the Republicans feared as a power bloc liable to be hostile to parliamentarism, and liable to grow beyond the control of parliament. The social connexion between Church, Monarchists and Army leaders has been already described. Every *sou* spent on increasing France's military power seemed to strengthen the social classes most dangerous to the survival of the Republic: yet their power was necessary to the survival of France. Nor was it for the Republicans, traditional champions of the *guerre à outrance* against the enemy beyond the Rhine, and of national defence by *levée en masse*, to withhold any power from the nation in arms.[1]

This vital difference between the clerical problem and the military problem goes far to explain that watershed in the history of the Republic which falls between 1905 and 1914, and which has been already described. The clerical problem could be solved by simple organization—by separation of Church and State (achieved in 1905) and by promotion of the *école unique*. The military problem could not be so easily solved; for even the cultivation of good Republican generals did not prevent the growth of an authoritarian professional caste, hostile to parliamentary control by the very nature of its technical training and discipline, yet ever more exacting in its demands in face of the growing international tension between 1905 and 1914. It was inevitable, especially after the Dreyfus affair, that men of the Left should tend towards anti-militarism and pacifism. The support of the great financial and industrial oligarchy for the authority to which it owed so many orders and so much prosperity, linked Army and oligarchy more closely even than altar and throne had been joined in the earlier nineteenth century. The terms 'Right' and 'Left' came to mean an antithesis quite different from their alignment in the first half of the Republic's history. They meant the antithesis between

---

[1] Cf. A. Siegfried: op. cit., p. 107. 'Hoche, Marceau, Bonaparte lui-même avaient été révolutionnaires et républicains, mais les grands chefs militaires de la troisième République étaient royalistes et catholiques. Il y avait désormais divorce idéologique—mais en France quoi de plus grave?—entre l'armée et la République, entre la patrie elle-même et la démocratie.' For elaboration of this problem and its consequences for democracy in France, see below, pp. 152-163.

militarism and capitalism on one hand, parliamentarism and Socialism on the other. This new alignment was to last until the nineteen-thirties, when—as will be shown later—yet another reshuffle of parties took place, splitting both Right and Left into the alignment which culminated in Vichy versus Resistance.[1]

André Siegfried dates the spread of Marxism and of antinationalist feeling from the eighteen-nineties: starting with the young intellectuals, but spreading to all who were dissatisfied with the existing social order. A generation of peace and the diversion of colonial expansion had damped down the passion for *revanche*, and military service had become, for the ordinary citizen, a burdensome duty which he wanted to see curtailed. The last big war-scare had been nearly a decade before, at the height of the Boulangist crisis. The Left produced no fiery nationalist leader to cry that the nation was in danger and the frontiers should be manned—that had been Boulanger's cry, and he had been utterly discredited. Gambetta was dead and had become *vieux jeu* for the rising generation. The hey-day of Clemenceau in foreign policy was not yet come. The hour belonged to the internationalist and pacifist Left, though the less optimistic Delcassé, ever alert against the German threat, was at the *Quai d'Orsay* from 1898 until 1905. Perhaps his very success in frustrating German designs in these years helped to breed a false sense of security in France, as the new century dawned. It is characteristic of French politics in this new century that Clemenceau himself, in his first Ministry of 1906, should—despite his fears of Germany—accept reductions in the Army's budget which were imposed on him by party competition between Radicals and Socialists.[2]

The nationalist function of democracy, in the eyes of a Radical like Clemenceau, was the systematic reconciliation of individual and group interests so as to produce 'solidarity'—solidar-

---

[1] Cf. Chapter II, pp. 66-71 for the new oligarchy of the Republic and Chapter VI on the alignment of forces under Vichy.

[2] Cf. A. Siegfried: op. cit., p. 106 ff., and D. Halévy: op. cit., pp. 33-4. Péguy wrote of 1894—'un socialisme jeune homme venait de naître'.

ity in the sense in which Ernest Renan used the word when he declared that 'every nation is a great solidarity'. In his essays, *Sur la Démocratie*, Clemenceau wrote: 'Democracy alone is capable of making the citizen complete. To it alone belongs the magnificent role of reconciling all citizens in a common effort of solidarity.' Years later, in *Au Soir de la Pensée*, he wrote: 'All social activity is a resolving of forces, an association of interests, in which the individual and the group cannot serve one another to advantage, cannot prop one another up, except by mutual thrust and counter-thrust.' The philosophy of the *Ligue des Droits de l'Homme*, which he and others founded in 1888 to combat Caesarism, could be reconciled with the military demands of national security only by such a conception of democracy. But the interplay of group and party interests did not, as this theory assumed, automatically produce that harmony of interests in which he believed. The *mystique* and the *politique* of Republicanism were not so easily reconciled.[1]

One result—or at least one accompaniment—of this tension between individualism and *étatisme*, pacifism and nationalism, has been the prominence of force and violence in the repertoire of democratic movements in France. The philosophy of violence expounded by Georges Sorel (1847-1922) may have its immediate basis in the Marxist analysis of *bourgeois* society. Its popularity among Left-wing syndicalist movements in France is better explained by its appeal to the peculiar French experience of revolutions. Just as, in 1793, the breakdown of attempts to reconcile monarchy and democracy in the form of constitutionalism ended in the raising of the barricades and disorder: or as, in 1848, the failure of the Orleanist Monarchy led to the experiment of the National Workshops and the June Riots; or as, in 1871, the collapse of the Liberal Empire produced the Paris Commune: so the social and political tension of the early nineteen-thirties led to the Paris Riots and demonstrations of

---

[1] Georges Clemenceau: *Sur la Démocratie* (1930), p. 98; *Au Soir de la Pensée* (2 Vols. 1930), Vol. II, p. 375. On Clemenceau see the balanced study by Geoffrey Bruun in the 'Makers of Modern Europe' Series (Cambridge, Mass. 1943); Jean Martet: *Clemenceau* (1930); Léon Daudet: *Clemenceau* (1940, English translation).

February 1934, and the stay-in strikes during the Popular Front Government of 1936. In France democracy, and later Socialism, have always been something to fight for, something for which recourse to the barricades has become a time-honoured vindication. This peculiar tradition is alien to British ways of thought, for which 'the rule of law' is so essential a basis of democratic methods and aims that violence is instinctively distrusted. The experience of organized resistance between 1940 and 1944 has deepened this old conviction in France. In 1943 a genial Socialist such as Louis Lévy could write that 'the regime of the Commune was wholly democratic', and proceed to take his reader on a descriptive tour of the French provinces, showing how 'democratic' and 'Republican' each has been by recounting its record of active resistance and rebellion to successive authorities in French history. He assumes throughout that democracy is a faith which may demand civil war as much as a war of national defence. It involves a temper sharper and more drastic than that fostered by the parliamentary habits of Britain. To raise the barricades to defend the Republic in 1848 or the Commune in 1871 are for him as much proofs of democratic spirit as to have voted against Marshal Pétain in 1940.

This permanent factor in French life is closely linked with that 'social strand' of the revolutionary tradition already described. It is as if, at moments of crisis, this force asserted itself in two ways. On one hand, the demand for a more 'social democracy' comes to the front—whether with Babeuf in 1796, Louis Blanc in 1848, Blanqui and the Communards in 1871, Marxism in 1934-6, or Resistance in 1945. On the other hand, faith in the 'sovereignty of the people', in the form of direct popular action, became the habitual last sanction against those who would cheat the rebels of the fruits of their efforts, or who would check the revolution half-way. In practically every French revolution the chief gains have gone less to the men who made the revolution than to the more moderate elements which contrived to check the drift to anarchy and divert the benefits of change in their own direction. Perhaps the main reason is that recourse to the barricades is apt to strengthen, not prevent, the

THE NATIONAL VISION

drift to Caesarism which all French democrats so greatly fear. The power of reaction, of the backwash from the revolutionary tide, is usually under-estimated. The dramatic interest of France to-day is how far the Fourth Republic can ride both the demand for further social reconstruction and the Conservative fears aroused by this demand, and so guide France towards that more 'social democracy' which once again has become the favourite slogan of Left-wing parties and organized resistance movements.[1]

To sum up. The operative ideals of democracy which have sustained democratic government throughout the Third Republic may be said to have both a negative and a positive aspect. The negative side—according to which democracy means suspicion, distrust, watchfulness, resistance, hostility to all government however democratic in origin—is closely connected with the intense individualism of the French people. It produced the hierarchy of checks which was favoured by the Republic—the Deputy checking the Minister, the constituent checking the Deputy, elected councils checking the Prefect and the Mayor, and so on. It meant the disparagement of all politics, such as is found intellectually in a Péguy or an 'Alain', and practically in the cynicism shown towards all politicians and political parties by the average French elector.

The positive side—according to which democracy means independence and self-help, the readiness of the citizen armed to defend the nation, the Republic and himself by recourse to violence when necessary—springs from very similar national characteristics. Intellectually it takes the form of restless, incessant demand that the 'revolutionary tradition' be carried out to its logically complete conclusion, with the effective establishment of liberty, equality, fraternity, sovereignty of the people, and the addition of social and economic democracy to political democracy. Practically it merges into the demand for real national security and abolition of class privileges or oligarchic power.

[1] Cf. Louis Lévy: *France is a Democracy* (1943). For present-day demands for a more 'social democracy' see below, Chapter VI and Appendix II.

Both sides are essential in the 'national vision' of France. From their interpenetration derive the French distrust of racialism, Caesarism, Fascism: the French devotion to the values of human freedom, dignity, reason: the French conception of nationalism, imperialism, internationalism, and of civilization itself. The working of democracy in France can best be illuminated by a more close-up view of the impact between these operative ideas and ideals and actual conditions during the Third Republic. The four crucial issues were the problem of the Church, the problem of national security, the problem of overseas expansion and the problem of industrialism. The fourth of these will be reserved for special consideration (Chapter V). The other three will be considered forthwith. But first it is important to indicate the quite new circumstances which confronted the Third Republic from the day of its birth. All four issues were prominent in French politics because of conditions which were not peculiar to France. They were issues raised by a revolution in the whole balance of power, wealth and population in Europe, a revolution which was in its critical and decisive stage in 1870, when the Republic began to raise its head.

The New Europe of 1870

The dramatic events of 1870-1 heralded a new Papal policy: a united Germany and a united Italy: a new era of overseas expansion: and a new era of industrialization in Europe. They meant that France was confronted with four sets of conditions which she had never had to face before. They raised problems peculiar to the Third Republic, and little known to previous regimes. In emphasizing the historical continuity of political, national and social forces in France, it is also necessary to emphasize the sudden jerk which such forces were given by these events. Democracy in France may not, in future, be confronted with similar conditions. All may well be, both in origin and duration, in prominence and intensity, peculiar to democracy as it worked under the Third Republic. Yet they are vital to understanding of how that democracy worked and evolved. They demanded nothing less than a fundamental re-thinking and restatement of France's ecclesiastical, foreign, colonial and domestic policy. If any system of government is to be judged by its powers of adjustment and adaptability, and any ideal by its power to be perpetually restated in terms of the practical problems which confront it, then here are the four criteria of both the democratic instrument and the democratic ideal in France.

All four, it should be noted, involve a conflict between a democratic order in politics and a hierarchical organization. As Lord Lindsay has said: 'The organs of power in a democratic State are not and cannot well be themselves democratically organized.' The hierarchical, authoritarian organizations of Catholic Church, foreign policy and armed services, colonial administration, and large-scale industry, almost simultaneously raised this one great fundamental conflict. French democrats had to make such strenuous exertions to resolve the first three of these conflicts during the first half of the Republic's history that the further labours of adjustment and adaptation which confronted them after 1918 proved insuperable. The old half-won battles left Frenchmen so deeply divided that the springs of fresh energy, needed to undertake still more profound political and social overhaul, ran dry.

The revival of ultramontanism which grew out of the great Vatican Council of 1870 raised the first of these problems. The Pope, Pius IX, summoned the Council because he wanted a formal declaration of papal infallibility. Representatives were chosen for their support of ultramontanism, and the procedure of the Council was controlled to give the desired result. Because the dominant school of Catholic thought in France and Germany was not ultramontane, the most eminent representatives of these countries were ignored. The declaration of papal infallibility, which duly issued from the Council two months before Italian troops entered Rome and ended the temporal power of the papacy, tightened and centralized the structure of the Catholic Church. It hardened the conflict between papal absolutism in doctrine and all Gallican, Liberal or Republican opinion. The inevitable result was the conflict between Church and State which straightway developed in Italy, Germany and

France: and was only very partially healed by the great social Encyclicals of Pope Leo XIII in the eighteen-eighties.[1]

Because of the peculiar condition already described, the Catholics had a majority in the National Assembly of 1871. Their best policy was obviously to be moderate and to avoid internal divisions and any irritation of moderate opinion. But the new spirit of the Church militant made this impossible. It was even urged that, with German troops still on French soil, French soldiers be sent to help the papacy against the new Liberal kingdom of Italy. The Monarchist intransigence of Chambord had its counterpart in the ecclesiastical intransigence of the most ardent Ultramontanists.[2]

Secondly, the years 1870-1 saw the unification of France's eastern neighbours into the two great nation States of Germany and Italy. Until then these lands were split into some fifty—latterly a dozen—small states, each tending to raise its own tariff barriers, cherish its own 'State sovereignty', and keep up its own separate army. The population, economic resources, industrial potential and administration of this whole area of central Europe had until 1870 been splintered up; and to manipulate the balance of power between them had been easy for a strong, centralized and organic state such as France. But now there appeared on her flank two vigorous new kingdoms, still flushed with victory and success, each under a single popular national government eager to harness its wealth, manpower and unified administration in the cause of national independence and expansion. The centre of gravity of power shifted eastwards—away from France and Britain; and old generalizations about the position of France in Europe, her security and defence, were no longer true. Principles of French foreign policy which had been valid guides before 1870 were out of date, now that she had been defeated decisively at the very moment when these new Powers arose. Diplomacy in western and central Europe had hinged upon a London-Paris

[1] Cf. E. L. Woodward: *Three Studies in European Conservatism*, III; M. Oakeshott: *Social and Political Doctrines of Contemporary Europe* (1939), Section II; E. Lecanuet: op. cit., *passim*.

[2] Cf. above, Chapter II. Lecanuet: op. cit., Chapters IV and V.

axis—even when London and Paris had been at war. Now there emerged the shadow of a Rome-Berlin axis—which took concrete form when Italy joined the German-Austrian alliance in 1882, and still more concrete form in 1936, when Nazi Germany and Fascist Italy joined hands. Here was a profound revolution in the problem of security, which haunted the whole history of the Third Republic.[1]

Thirdly, there appeared more slowly, but equally relentlessly, a new problem for France which was closely connected with her international position: the problem of overseas colonies. By the second decade of the Republic's history this issue had been pushed to the forefront of politics. Italy, as a new naval power in the Mediterranean, was seeking colonial possessions on its southern shores. France had already acquired control of the stretch of North African coast-line nearest to herself—Algeria. The problem which faced her was whether she should enter freely into the growing race for overseas possessions, upon which future international prestige and even national prosperity seemed likely to depend: or whether she should concentrate on preserving her military strength as a continental power and avoid overseas exploits which might embroil her with maritime powers already better placed, and add them to the list of possible German allies. Her own previous colonial experience, and the anti-colonial policy of Bismarck, equally urged caution: but the menace of an expanding Italy and the problems of French national security in the Mediterranean were powerful arguments in favour of staking out colonial claims in North Africa, at least. Here was a disturbing, perplexing issue, which still further divided French opinion, and often cut across other existing divisions of opinion. The answer of France was always ambiguous, and was provided in the end less by popular decision than by the private enterprise of a few enthusiasts who presented French democracy with a series of *faits accomplis*.[2]

[1] Cf. David Thomson: *French Foreign Policy* (1944), and below, Chapter V, pp. 200-10.
[2] Cf. D. W. Brogan: *The Development of Modern France* (1940) Book V.

Finally, as has already been suggested, Republican France was embarked upon a decisive stage of industrialization—an economic revolution, which proceeded slower in France, and went less far, than in Germany or Great Britain.[1] The full internal social effects of this revolution were not to be felt in France until the twentieth century. But, from the first, industrialism was affecting the balance of population both inside France herself, and between France and her great neighbours: the war potential of France in relation to her possible allies and enemies: her whole capacity for national independence and self-defence. War was becoming dependent on large resources of man-power and on heavy industry. In neither was France favourably placed. In 1815 she had still been the largest of all the great European Powers in population, with some 30 million as compared with 13 million in Great Britain, 11 million in Prussia, and 26 million in the Habsburg Empire. By 1870, this superiority had gone. Great Britain had doubled her population: united Germany numbered 41 million: but there were still only 36 million Frenchmen in the world. Industrially, France had lost her rich provinces of Alsace and Lorraine, and they had been added to German industrial power. Her defeat in the Franco-Prussian War, partly due to superior German military technique and equipment, such as the new needle-gun, left her painfully conscious of her shortcomings. She was compelled to perform prodigies of reconstruction and rearmament during the eighteen-seventies before she could even hope to hold her own.

In these various ways the new France found herself in a new Europe. The course of her development was the result of interaction between new France and new Europe. Foreign affairs had constant repercussions on domestic affairs. Democracy had to be restated and remodelled in a quite rigid framework of given circumstances over which France had little control. The ideas of the revolutionary tradition were fermenting in new and unpredictable conditions, and it was more than usually difficult to avoid conducting political debate and national policy in unreal and out-of-date terms. It is of great importance that

[1] Cf. Chapter II, p. 45.

THE NATIONAL VISION 139

the four new conditions described could not, in the nature of things, present themselves to France as distinct and separate problems. The 'Roman Question', the colonial question, the problems of industrialization were all issues of foreign policy: the problem of population affected colonialism and industry and military strength: Church and Army were bodies vitally connected with both foreign and colonial policy. The complexity and perplexity of democratic ideas and institutions in modern France are not entirely due to revolutionary traditions and idiosyncrasies of national outlook: they are inherent in the whole intricate network of modern international affairs in western Europe.

The Church

The renunciation and condemnation by the papacy of all forces of Liberalism, Republicanism and tolerance in the modern world, and the alliance of so many French Catholics with monarchy, predetermined a clash between clericals and anti-clericals during the Third Republic. But the twist which that clash gave to democratic ideas and government is the only aspect which concerns the present argument. Had the breach of 1790 been healed by 1890, democracy in France would have been very different. The passions of anti-clericalism which so dominated French politics during the first generation of the Republic left an acerbity, a cleavage and an intolerance which distinguish French democracy from British, American, Swiss or Scandinavian. It was also the operative force in the first real triumph of the Republican parties in 1877-9.

In March 1877 the French bishops, profoundly influenced by the new ultramontanism, petitioned the Government of France under the Presidency of Marshal Macmahon 'to do all they could to secure respect for the independence of the Holy Father and his government'. This petition was interpreted as agitation for French policy to undertake restoration of the temporal power of the Pope, and meant, if so, war with Italy. French foreign policy, beset by Bismarck's schemes to isolate the Republic and keep France without allies in Europe, was anxious for friendship with Italy, and was then in process of negotiating a commercial treaty with her. The attempt to forbid the circulation of the bishops' appeal provoked violent debates in country and parliament, and from Gambetta the famous cry: 'Clericalism —there is the enemy!' The Chamber moved that the Government should 'use its legal powers for the suppression of the antipatriotic agitation of the ultramontane parties, whose increasing activities might become a danger to the internal and external security of the State'. What were these legal powers?[1]

They were the laws of the Civil Code governing all associations. Napoleon's Concordat of 1802 had legalized the rights and powers of only the secular clergy. Monastic orders, convents, and religious congregations were on a par with any other association within the State, and therefore could not exist legally without formal and official authorization. Napoleon had authorized only a few missionary and philanthropic orders, but many others had been tacitly allowed to exist during the monarchies and the Second Empire. Many were engaged in teaching, and Church schools had been recognized by the Falloux Law of 1850. But the orders themselves existed illegally and only on sufferance.

In 1880 all unauthorized congregations were instructed to apply for formal authorization within three months. During the next two years some 300 congregations were thus forced to dissolve, although Carthusians and Trappists were allowed to remain. The Church schools also remained, and the programme for replacing them by free primary schools in each Commune was an eventual, long-range project launched in 1882. In this position of stalemate, with the Republic secured against the spread of clerical power, many moderates would have been content to remain. But the doctrinaire and extremist temper of French Radicalism gained the day, in the sense of perpetuating the clerical controversy and splitting Moderates from Radicals. It continued, despite the conciliatory gesture of Pope Leo XIII in 1892, who declared that the Church was 'not opposed to any particular form of government', and so gave rise to a group of

[1] Cf. G. Hanotaux: op. cit., Vol. III, Chapter IX.

Catholic Republicans, accepting reconciliation with parliamentary democracy.¹

One aspect of the Dreyfus affair was the culmination of this conflict in its most bitter form. The fact that Dreyfus was a Jew, and that his condemnation led to a wider drive by the authoritarian militarists and clericals to exclude not merely Jews but Protestants and Republicans from positions of military and administrative power, raised the issue in dramatic form. It was a clash of rival absolutisms—a challenge of intolerance which bred an equally severe intolerance amongst the Radicals and Freemasons, the anti-Clericals and Socialists. Democracy had clearly to be a social and political order based on common citizenship and civilian rights within the Republic: or else it would be replaced by an authoritarian, hierarchic order, dominated by Church and privileged ruling classes in the Army and civil service. French logic interpreted the conflict in these clear terms, and the battle began.

That the political issue should become a pitched battle between Church and State was not inevitable, but was the consequence of extremists like Maurras on one side and Combes on the other. Movements of reconciliation existed on both sides. The Pope himself was not anxious for an open breach, and distrusted the mixture of ultra-Catholicism with paganism in the *Action française*. The movements originated by Albert de Mun and Marc Sangnier stood for reconciliation, and even in 1902 Sangnier held that 'Catholicism contains the moral and religious forces which democracy needs'. As one French writer has aptly suggested, 'The social shock of the affair determined two movements: one to win over modern democracy, the other to dominate it. The former leads to Marc Sangnier, the latter to Maurras.' By social activity, charitable works and mutual aid the former hoped to find reconciliation between Church and democracy. They might well have succeeded, and they were in tune with the Papal Encyclical *Rerum Novarum* of

¹ On the whole development, see J. E. C. Bodley: *The Church in France* (1906), where the texts are conveniently printed of the Concordat of 1802, the Associations Law of 1901, and the Separation Law of 1905.

1891. But they were frustrated by the absolutist doctrines of political reaction and political extremism. In July 1904 France broke off diplomatic relations with the Vatican. In December 1905 the law separating Church and State was passed by the *Bloc des Gauches*, led by Émile Combes, and disestablishment and expropriation were pushed through with a brusque thoroughness producing lasting bitterness.[1]

Between 1905 and 1925, 'the majority of the men who became French bishops came from schools, circles and social spheres where the political outlook of the *Action française* prevailed'. When, in 1926, the papacy finally broke with its costly and burdensome supporter, placed its paper on the Index and publicly condemned the movement itself, its former sympathizers tended to turn to the still more scurrilous journals, such as *Gringoire* and *Candide*, and violent movements such as the *Croix de Feu* and the *Camelots du Roi*. There is, in short, a direct link between the bitterness of the Dreyfus affair and the feuds of the inter-war years which helped to kill the Republic in 1940, although anti-clericalism sank into the background of political issues after 1918.[2]

One reason for this persistence of violent pro-Catholic political movements long after the clericalist issue itself was substantially settled lies in the effects of separation on the Church in France. As Mr. J. E. C. Bodley pointed out in 1906, the separation meant two things. The abrogation of the Concordat of 1802 was 'the first serious breach made in the administrative fabric constructed by Napoleon'. And separation, though done by anti-clericals, was 'an Ultramontane Act. For the first time since the French people became a nation, the Pope is the absolute master of the Bishops and Clergy of France. Gallicanism, long declining, has received its death-blow'. Earlier in the nineteenth century ultramontane writers such as Lamennais had urged disestablishment to free the Church from State control. It now had that effect, and the Pope could appoint bishops, and bishops parish clergy, without the need

[1] Cf. Pierre Frédérix: op. cit., p. 136 ff.
[2] Cf. Yves Simon: *La Grande Crise de la République Française* (1941), Chapters III and IV.

for governmental confirmation previously required by Articles 5 and 10 of the Concordat. Carried through in different circumstances, the separation would have had a healing effect—like a skilful amputation. But the amputation was not skilful. Combes and his disciples carried out the Associations Law of 1901 with more rigour than had been intended, refusing nearly all applications for authorization. And after the diplomatic breach with the Vatican in 1904, separation included ruthless measures of expropriation of Church buildings and property by lay bodies. Church and State were torn apart, not neatly separated: and political bitterness was fed with new fuel.[1]

Another reason for the perpetuation of anti-clericalism throughout the history of the Republic was the controversy over control of education: a controversy which did much to mould the spirit and substance of education in France. The long struggle between Church and State hardened the outlook and creed of both, and reinforced the natural tendency of both to regard a national system of education as a means of spreading and inculcating certain positive beliefs. Condorcet, during the French Revolution, and Napoleon after him, elaborated schemes for a national system of schools in every Commune which should form the basis of a pyramid of instruction with the universities and the Ministry of Public Instruction at its apex. Neither completed the pyramid. Condorcet swept away more than he replaced, and Napoleon concentrated on the levels of higher education. In 1808, Napoleon founded the 'University of France', on the principle that 'as long as children are not taught whether they ought to be Republican or Monarchist, Catholic or irreligious, the State will not form a Nation'. He based education on principles which one historian has called the 'principles of political hygiene'. France was divided into seventeen *Académies*, or academic regions, each with a university at its head whose rector would be responsible for all public instruction within the region. In his wide field of jurisdiction and his direct responsibility to the central government he was the academic counterpart to the Prefect. The framework has lasted until to-day. But it was the task of the

[1] Cf. Bodley: op. cit., p. 3 ff.

Third Republic to complete the base of the pyramid which all previous regimes had left incomplete.

The Republic inherited a dual system of Church schools and State schools which had been permitted by Napoleon and the restored Bourbons, confirmed by the Second Republic in the *Loi Falloux* of 1850, and perpetuated by the Second Empire. A series of laws in the eighteen-eighties were passed largely under the inspiration of the anti-clericalists led by Jules Ferry, who was Minister of Public Instruction several times between 1879 and 1885. The result was, for the first time in French history, a real national network of free, compulsory, primary, secular schools. Many 'free schools' run by the Churches survived, though under State inspection and limited supervision, and the number of children attending them steadily declined between 1885 and 1940. In 1886 there were 1,919,134 children in Church primary schools as against 3,598,007 in the State primary schools. By 1925 there were only 767,000 as against 3,061,000, so that the ratio dropped from about a third to about a fifth of the total.[1]

The laws of the Republic were also responsible for making primary education in France remarkably uniform in purport, syllabus, and even time-table. The 'higher primaries', for children between the ages of thirteen and sixteen, continued this uniformity. The State *lycées* and *collèges*, providing education which ran parallel to and beyond the 'higher primaries', charged fees but were subsidized and supervised by the State. At every level immense emphasis was put on French language and culture, French history and geography, French national traditions and citizenship. The guiding principle was that a positive set of beliefs and moral values had to be impressed upon each new generation. The State teachers' training colleges—the *écoles normales*—provided the necessary staff of highly indoctrinated teachers, drilled in anti-clerical sentiments and barred by the syllabus from providing any religious instruction. The result was an army of Radical and Socialist sympa-

---

[1] Cf. C. Richard: *L'Enseignement en France* (1925); Carlton J. H. Hayes: *France a Nation of Patriots* (1930), Chapter III, where many interesting statistics are given.

thizers—lay missionaries—dispersed in strong strategic positions in every Commune, whether village or township, throughout France.[1]

The national vision of democracy might be abundantly illustrated, in this particular facet, from the speeches, writings and official instructions of the leading organizers of French education. A few must suffice. Jules Ferry, in a circular letter to the primary teachers explaining the meaning of the law of 1882 which required moral and civic teaching, emphasized the role of the teacher as 'a natural aid to moral and social progress'. His task was 'to prepare a generation of good citizens for our country'. He must teach 'those simple rules of moral conduct which are not less universally accepted than the rules of language or of arithmetic'. Ferry's official programme of moral education for children between eleven and thirteen includes the following significant section on society.

1. The family: duties of parents and children; reciprocal duties of masters and servants; the family spirit.
2. Society: necessity and benefits of society. Justice, the condition of all society. Solidarity and human brotherhood. Alcoholism destroys these sentiments little by little by destroying the mainspring of will and of personal responsibility.

Application and development of the idea of justice: respect for human life and liberty; respect for property: respect for the pledged word; respect for the honour and reputation of others. Probity, equity, loyalty, delicacy. Respect for the opinions and beliefs held by others.

Applications and development of the idea of love or brotherhood. Its varying degrees; duties of benevolence, gratitude, tolerance, mercy, etc. Self-sacrifice, the highest form of love; show that it can find a place in everyday life.

[1] Cf. the valuable anthology of French theories of education in F. Buisson and E. E. Farrington: *French Educational Ideals of To-day* (1920), from which the quotations which follow are taken. The purport of French education is admirably illustrated by the 'Digest of typical textbooks in French schools for instruction in History, Morals and Civics, Geography and Reading' in Carlton J. H. Hayes: op. cit., Appendix A. Also *L'Oeuvre de la Troisième République* (1945), Part III.

3. The fatherland: what a man owes to his country: **obedience to** law, military service, discipline, devotion, fidelity to the flag. Taxes (condemnation of fraud towards the State). The ballot: a moral obligation, which should be free, conscientious, disinterested, enlightened. Rights which correspond to these duties: personal freedom, liberty of conscience, freedom of contract and the right to work, right to organize. Guarantee of the security of life and property to all. National sovereignty. Explanation of the motto of the Republic: Liberty, Equality, Fraternity.

This blend of Christian ethics without Christian religion or faith, nationalist principles and middle-class virtues, was the creed inculcated by one of the most highly centralized educational machines in the modern world. They were the ideals which infused French thought, if not always French practice, in the twentieth century.

Octave Gréard, Ferry's right-hand man whom he called 'the first schoolmaster of France', instructed teachers that 'in history we must emphasize only the essential features of the development of French nationality, seeking this less in a succession of deeds of war than in the methodical development of institutions, and in the progress of social ideas: in a word, we must make of France what Pascal called humanity, a great being which exists for ever'. Nationalism was, indeed, more successfully inculcated than democracy by French education—perhaps because it is more easily propagated and assimilated.

Jaurès, himself a product of the *école normale* and a university teacher at Toulouse, likewise believed that 'moral instruction should be the first thought of our teachers', and held that to awaken the spirit of justice, inquiry and social solidarity through education would inevitably promote the coming of a Socialist commonwealth. But in sharp contrast to the somewhat optimistic expectations of the ardent educationists, here is the verdict of Clemenceau, in 1894, on the excessive narrowness and unimaginative outlook which tended to infuse much primary education.

When I read the history of these wretched teachers, alternately scolded by the prefect for their indifference, rewarded by the deputy they have served, and reviled and disgraced by whomever they have

THE NATIONAL VISION 147

opposed, it has seemed to me that the unfortunate schoolmaster is truly the most pitiable victim of our glorious Republic. . . . In futile efforts the pitiful ambassador of the Republic to the inhabitants of the rural districts consumes his time and his strength. The parents are inaccessible to him; the country squires are his enemies. With the priest there is latent hostility; with the Catholic schools there is open war. The latter have at their disposal greater resources than the teacher. They steal his pupils. They crush him in a hundred ways, sometimes with the connivance of the mayor, usually with the co-operation of the big influences in the Commune. The government, which should defend him but which often abandons him, is far away. The Church, which persecutes him, is very close at hand. A law eats into his miserable salary on the pretext of increasing it subsequently. To-day's deputy defends him; to-morrow's sacrifices him. He is spied upon, hounded, denounced. One word too many, and he is lost.

Whatever the lot of the school teachers, which varied greatly from district to district and which improved considerably in the twentieth century, their accumulative influence on democratic spirit was enormous. The army of teachers—some 125,000 strong—formed the most powerful Left-wing *cadre* in the ranks of the *fonctionnaires*.

National Security

Military defeat, invasion and occupation of the northern provinces, the loss of Alsace and Lorraine, and the exaction of an indemnity of five thousand million (five milliard) francs as well as the costs of German occupation, all brought home very vividly to every Frenchman the new danger on France's north-eastern frontier. By mobilizing national spirit at home and national credit abroad, Thiers managed to pay off the indemnity in full by 1873; and by persuading Bismarck in 1872 to link instalments of payment with instalments of evacuation, he got the last German troops off French soil by September 1873. Already France had begun to overhaul her military machine.

Military service for five years for all men between twenty and forty was made compulsory by Thiers's law of 1872. Evasion of personal service, common under the Second Empire, was made much more difficult. Technical weapons and fortifications were vastly improved. Credits of 500 million francs for the improvement of national defence were readily voted annually by the National Assembly, and after it by the Chamber. France threw herself into a frenzy of military preparation. But was it only for national defence? Was it not rather for a war of *revanche*, a vast national reprisal on the traditional enemy beyond the Rhine, recently grown so monstrous and threatening? Both answers were freely given. And the efforts of Bismarck to keep France without allies, and incidents such as the great war scare of 1875 which inflamed opinion just when the Republic itself was being constitutionally defined, seemed to betoken another Franco-German struggle within a few years.[1]

Again, the present argument is concerned only with the effects of this constant, looming shadow of war on the working of democratic institutions, and the shaping of democratic ideas, in the Third Republic. Its first effect was clearly to rally opposing parties and classes, and to compel them to work together by reason of a common external pressure and a clear national danger. The Right-wing parties were ultra-nationalist. Men like Maurice Barrès and Charles Maurras were violently anti-German, and a common argument against parliamentary government was that it weakened France, obstructed real national unity, and made France (as Bismarck himself hoped) something of a pariah nation among the respectable dynastic monarchies of Europe. So, too, were the Left-wing parties ultra-nationalist. Gambetta's record of waging *la guerre à outrance* in 1870, and the enthusiasm of Republicans of every

---

[1] Cf. G. Hanotaux: op. cit., Vol. I, Chapters VI, VIII, IX; G. Bouniols: *Thiers au Pouvoir* (1921), pp. 157, 171; A. Thiers: *Notes et Souvenirs* (1903), p. 275 ff. Thiers in public and in private repudiated the idea of *revanche*, saying: 'We are not thinking of *revanche*, as our enemies are wickedly asserting; we only want France to resume her place in the world.'

On the war-scare of 1875, see G. Hanotaux: op. cit., Vol. III, Chapter IV, and the documents in E. T. S. Dugdale: *German Diplomatic Documents, 1871-1914* (1928), Vol. I, Chapter I.

THE NATIONAL VISION

shade for military reorganization, provided all parties with a basis of agreement. There was at first no pacifism on the Left, though there might be rather more thunder on the Right.

The chief thunder from the Right came in the decades 1890-1910 from Maurice Barrès, whose main novels appeared in these years. And his spell was exercised over men of all parties and affiliations, rehabilitating their patriotism and nationalist spirit. It was the spell of a new synthesis in which individualism merged into, and found its finest expression in, nationalism. Intellectually and culturally, *Barrèsisme* was the reflection of the common danger threatening all Frenchmen. The reflection was found, characteristically, in a man from Lorraine.[1]

The *Ligue de la Patrie française*, which Barrès and kindred spirits founded in 1899 to resist the anti-nationalistic tendencies of the Dreyfusards, gave place in 1902 to the more positive political movement of Maurras, the *Action française*. Its exclusiveness and factiousness register the disruption caused by the Dreyfus affair. Some men of the Left were now impelled, by sheer repulsion, into pacifism, in the sense of seeking a means of conciliation with Germany and abandonment of the notion of *revanche*. Such a man was Jules Ferry. He was leader of the Radical and anti-clerical movement for the 'laicizing' and Republicanizing of education in the eighteen-eighties, and the champion of colonial expansion as a deliberately chosen alternative to the vendetta with Germany. Others such as Clemenceau, and the men of Lorraine such as Raymond Poincaré, refused to renounce preparation for revenge. The result was a new disorientation of French groups and parties over issues of foreign policy and national defence, and the break-up of the original national concord about foreign affairs. In face of the resurgent danger, in the years before 1914, a new apostle appealing to the patriotism of all parties was to appear in Charles Péguy

---

[1] The Left—led by Gambetta—expressly repudiated pacifism or cosmopolitanism, and Gambetta accepted the principle of universal conscription for military service (*Lettres*, Nos. 54, 126, 127).

On Maurice Barrès see Henri-L. Miéville: *La Pensée de Maurice Barrès* (1934), and of the novels of Barrès see especially *Les Déracinés* (1897).

—corresponding on the Left to Barrès on the Right. But that voice died in 1914, and the appeal to pure patriotism above party divisions was not to be heard again, in such clarion tones, until the third resurgence of the German danger in 1940. But Charles de Gaulle had to make his appeal after defeat, and four years were to pass before the idea took concrete form in an all-party Provisional Government actually ruling France and her Empire.

The second half of this evolution, and the connexion between French democracy and problems of national security after 1918, will be more aptly considered later (Chapter V). Suffice now to note the weakening of the impulse to democratic unity in face of national danger. True, the main divisions of opinion in France were concerned less with whether or not France must defend herself in Europe against new dangers, than with the precise degree of persistence with which national grievances against Germany should be nursed. Dispute was only about how far they should dominate French foreign policy. There was, during the late nineteenth century, little absolute pacifism even on the Left. The policy of colonial expansion could be justified as much on grounds that it opened up new reservoirs of man-power for recruitment into the French armies in Europe, new naval bases and new sources of raw materials for use in a future war, as on grounds of seeking reconciliation with Germany. Pacifism crept into the outlook of the Left only in the form of internationalism and the Internationals: in emphasis on the union of workers of all countries to prevent imperialist wars, rather than on any conscientious refusal to fight under any circumstances. Pacifism too, when it came, was a political and social conception, rather than a moral and religious doctrine. This became evident when the final challenge came in 1914. French Socialists voted for war-credits, and men like Péguy died bravely in the field, fighting for nothing else than the defence of their own country. Communism alone opposed the war absolutely: but it mattered little in French politics until after the war.

Just as social or economic crises at home were met politically by the forming of particularly large coalitions—the *Bloc*

THE NATIONAL VISION

des Gauches in the Dreyfus crisis, the *Bloc national* of 1919, the *Cartel des Gauches* of 1924, the *Union nationale* of 1926, or the *Front populaire* of 1936—so the international crisis which threatened national security was met by a so-called *union sacrée*, or all-party coalition. The Bordeaux Pact between Thiers and the National Assembly in 1871 was virtually such a union, though Thiers chose his ministers only from the moderate men of the Centre parties. Like Gambetta in 1870, the Government appealed to French patriotism in all classes and parties, yet kept its own political principles and drew its personnel from only a few groups. This is one form of *union sacrée*—a general rallying to support a broadly acceptable government, and calling a truce to active attempts to overthrow the Government. In 1914, a similar movement took place. The Socialists agreed not to exploit the murder of Jaurès and the Right agreed not to conspire against the civil government of the Republic. It was agreement 'not to shoot the pianist'.

But now there began a drive for a broad-based, comprehensive ministry as well, ranging from symbolic figures of the Left, like Sembat, to equally symbolic figures of the Right, like Denys Cochin. A halt was called to pressure against clericalists and anti-militarists like Laval. This second conception of *union sacrée*—all-party union within the government itself—was frequently appealed to in later years, though never substantially repeated until the Provisional Government of 1944. Thus, in 1936, the cry was raised for a government 'from Louis Marin to Léon Blum', and in 1938 'from Reynaud to Thorez'—that is, excluding only the extreme Right. Again in 1944 demands were made for a government 'from Louis Marin to Marcel Cachin' (i.e. from Conservatives to Communists). The inclusion of two Communists in the Provisional Government, which also included not only Marin but Radicals, Christian Democrats, Socialists and resisters of all shades of opinion, was just such a union: although complaints were made that Communists and resisters were inadequately represented.

But, as Professor Brogan has pointed out, the alleged lessons of history concerning *unions sacrées* have usually been exaggerated. That of 1914 was short-lived, and the Clemenceau government of 1917-19 'excluded many leading Left-wing leaders like Albert Thomas and Briand; it prosecuted or persecuted Left-wing leaders like Caillaux and Malvy; and its chief did not recant his strong anti-clerical views and prejudices'. After the outbreak of the Russian Revolution, and even before, many issues were raised which divided parties: financial policy, trade union policy, and even the bias of foreign policy. Nor was any real attempt made in 1939 to form a government of *union sacrée* in either sense. Communist Deputies were expelled and imprisoned by Daladier. The subsequent reshuffles showed how many forces had not found expression in the early war ministries. In short, the French political system made possible just as much unity, but no more unity, than existed in French opinion. The parliamentary regime did nothing to give a bias towards greater solidarity or unity than was already provided by French nationalist sentiment.[1]

The greatest force driving a wedge between parties on the issue of national defence measures was Republican fear of Caesarism. Conscription laws which placed French manhood at the disposal of the General Staff for a total of twenty years during times of emergency, when that General Staff was so closely connected with clericalism and Monarchism by sympathy, family, and professional training, could never be regarded with equanimity by good Republicans. The obvious remedy was to Republicanize the military command. But efforts to do this never succeeded—and indeed the greatest of them precipitated the worst military-political crisis which the Republic had to face until the supreme crisis of Dreyfus. It was fear of Caesarism which produced the most sensational attempt at Caesarism—Boulangism. The circumstances of the dramatic rise and fall of General Boulanger show clearly the dilemma of the Republicans.[2]

In January 1886 Boulanger became Minister of War in the

[1] Cf. D. W. Brogan in *International Affairs*, Vol. XX, p. 103 ff.

[2] The conscription laws of 1870 provided for a period of five years' basic military service, followed by four years on the reserve: then a further period of five years in the territorial army, and six years in its reserve. They affected men between 20 and 40 chosen by lot. For

third ministry of Freycinet—the stoutest of Republicans and the former collaborator of Gambetta in the writing and publication of *La République française*. The appointment was made on the special recommendation of Clemenceau, with whom he was on excellent terms. The reforms of the Army, long planned and discussed but hitherto little practised, which Boulanger proceeded to carry out with energy, were admirably Republican. The change from the old professional army to the new democratic force based on universal conscription demanded more intelligent discipline, better material conditions, more care for morale. These demands he implemented fully. He even purged the Army of prominent Royalist officers like the Duc d'Aumale himself, uncle of the Orleanist pretender to the throne. At his first great review at Longchamps on Bastille Day 1886 he was acclaimed as a popular idol—the darling of the people, who was giving them a people's army and an inspiring example of Republican leadership. He became the hero of revues as well as of reviews, and the music-halls sang his praises. No one since Gambetta had succeeded so well in capturing the imagination and the hearts of the common people. A *mystique* of Boulangism grew up. He was popular partly because his new model army meant the chance of *revanche*. And there lay the sting.

The idea of *revanche* was dying, amidst the seductive colonialism of Jules Ferry. But it was dying only in certain minds, and amid positive distractions from the old obsession. Paul Déroulède and his League of Patriots existed to keep it alive. By 1886 they had come to despair of the old politicians, and turned to demanding the revision of the constitution as the prerequisite

subsequent alterations of the law, see below, Chapter V, p. 180n. and p. 208n.

The best account of the whole Boulanger episode in English is in D. W. Brogan: *The Development of Modern France*, Book IV. Among French histories, see especially Jacques Bainville: *La Troisième République* (1935) for a Right-wing bias, and Alexandre Zévaès: *Histoire de la Troisième République* (1938) for a Left-wing account. For a contemporary exposition of the Boulangist type of arguments, see Le Comte de Chaudordy: *La France en 1889* (1889).

for a prepared *revanche*. They also turned to Boulanger as their greatest hope. When Bismarck himself, in his Reichstag speech of January 1887 named Boulanger as the greatest obstacle to good relations between France and Germany, any remaining doubts were dispelled. General Boulanger became 'General Revanche'. And he was led to sponsor the cause of revision of the constitution: revision in the direction of a far stronger and more directly popular executive. Thrown out of office when the ministry fell, in May, he was relegated to a military command in Auvergne, and thenceforth was ready to conspire in order to regain his coveted ministry.

His chance came with the Wilson scandal of 1887—one of those sudden dramatic revelations of political graft in high quarters which so often precipitated political crisis in the parliamentary Republic. Daniel Wilson, the son-in-law of Jules Grévy, the venerable President of the Republic since 1879, was discovered to have carried on a prosperous traffic in decorations and honours from the Élysée itself. The scandal also involved General Thibaudin, one of the few sound 'Republican Generals' who had been a Minister for War and was still military governor of Paris. In the prolonged political crisis which ensued, and which involved the resignation of both ministry and President, the forces hostile to the Republic looked to Boulanger as an ally. Both Monarchists and Bonapartists began to pay court to him. When the Government dismissed him from the Army, he had but one course left by which to pursue his growing ambitions: popular agitation and the use of violence. Thanks to the eager support of both extreme Left and most of the Right, and to the lavish financial help of the Royalist Duchesse d'Uzès, he was elected in several constituencies at once.[1] The climax came in January 1889 when he

[1] Cf. *Souvenirs de la Duchesse d'Uzès* (1939), Chapter IV, for a most revealing account of her dealings with Boulanger. The memoirs reveal a lady of curious *naïveté* and vigour, ready to spend lavishly to restore the monarchy. After an initial advance of 25,000 francs towards Boulanger's election expenses, she placed three million francs at the disposal of the so-called 'National committee' of Royalist intriguers which included the Marquis de Breteuil, the Comte de Mar-

THE NATIONAL VISION

stood for Paris itself—traditional home of Radicalism and democratic Republicanism. He was elected by 245,000 votes, and a *coup d'état* was staged. But Boulanger's nerve seems to have failed at the last moment—or else his incorrigible frivolity and laziness gained the upper hand. He did not march on the Élysée, preferring the attractions of his mistress, Madame de Bonnemain. The Republic was saved by little effort or virtue of its own.

But the Government, given breathing-space as by a miracle, acted quickly. It abolished the electoral method of *scrutin de liste*, instituted only four years before, and prohibited multiple candidacies. This foiled the Boulangist plan of making the General stand in every constituency at the forthcoming general elections, and forced him to expend his personal strength and appeal in one constituency only. It meant a hasty revision of the orthodox Republican conception of democratic machinery. As Professor Brogan puts it: 'The abolition of *scrutin de liste* was the abandonment of a reform preached by great Republican leaders, and the prohibition of multiple candidacies was a direct attack on the free choice of universal suffrage, but the Republicans were, for the moment, cured of their mystical deference to that political God.' The new Prime Minister, Tirard, and his Minister of the Interior, Constans, took action against the League of Patriots, and planned to bring Boulanger to trial before the Senate, as the High Court. Boulanger, successfully scared, fled to Brussels on the appropriate date of April 1. Two years later he shot himself on the grave of his mistress, and provoked from Clemenceau the comment that he 'died as he had lived, like a subaltern'.[1]

timprey, the Marquis de Beauvoir, and Comte Albert de Mun (see p. 62 above). She blames Madame de Bonnemain for the loss of courage, and general demoralization, of Boulanger.

[1] On the debate about *scrutin de liste* as against *scrutin uninominal*, see above, Chapter III, p. 94.

The system of multiple candidacies—by which anyone could stand for several constituencies at once though he could sit for only one of them, was carried over into the Third Republic from the electoral laws of 1849, adopted in the 1871 elections and endorsed by the constitu-

Though Boulangism ended as a farce, it had been a force. It brought the whole parliamentary regime into the most dangerous crisis it had known since its creation: and the regime, it was clear, had done much to bring itself into this danger. Its real strength in 1889 was the diversity of its opponents and the weakness of the one man who had become a focal point for them all. Indeed the General had unwittingly done a great service to the parliamentarians. Not only had he shaken them out of their self-seeking complacency. By enlisting all their opponents behind so bogus a hero and so fraudulent a cause, he had concentrated them for political execution. They had been gathered up into a common ignominy and despair. It was not the Republic that he killed in 1889. It was the Monarchy and the Empire which he killed in 1891, as well as himself. Public opinion, too, had been shaken by the easy approach to an irresponsible dictatorship and perhaps a second Sedan. The tinsel of Bonapartism was tarnished, and plain, dull, civilian Marianne was hailed again with a certain relief. It was even fortunate for the Republicans that the Paris Exhibition of 1888 and the centenary of the great Revolution in 1889 gave them the chance to provide a timely counter-attraction and a convenient distraction.

But the problem of an Army which might produce a Caesar remained unsolved. The real paralysis of government on the night of the Paris election had been due to the virtual certainty that the Army of the Republic could not be counted upon to oppose the popular military hero. The parliamentary politicians, ever jealous of a rival power within the State challenging 'the Republic one and indivisible', had learnt that it was well to keep generals unpopular, and thoroughly divorced from Radical reputations which might put demagogic ideas into

tional law of 30 November 1875. For the laws repealing these former procedures, which were passed in February and July 1889, see Duguit, Monnier and Bonnard: op. cit., pp. 344 and 349. It was this rule which made it possible in 1871 for Thiers to be elected in twenty-six different constituencies and Gambetta in nine. As a kind of popular plebiscite it had been useful then: it had become obviously dangerous to a parliamentary Republic such as that of 1889.

their heads. Bonaparte himself had been a good 'Republican' general But how then could the High Command be Republicanized? Perhaps only by having an anti-militarist as Minister for War. But even this device was not to prove very effective, as events six years later were to show.

The Boulangist crisis was the first stage in the Right becoming peculiarly nationalist. Until then, it had even been accused of being anti-nationalist, of subordinating French national interests to those of the Church, and ultramontanism had lent colour to these charges. Now it had emerged as the supporter of a peculiarly aggressive form of nationalism, and the Left had moved into the posture of opposing militarist men and ideas, and had been led to attack even the idea of *revanche* when it appeared a weapon or an excuse for Caesarism.[1] The Dreyfus affair marked the main stage in this reversal of party positions as regards national security and the Army.

Meanwhile the influence of Barrès, already described, provided the nationalistic Right with a *mystique* and an ideology of nationalism and traditionalism different from their older creed of the days of Maistre and Bonald. The Dreyfus case was to turn this new creed again into the still more positive Caesarism of the *Action française*. The link between the nationalism of Boulanger and the nationalism of Maurras was the violent campaign of anti-semitism waged by Édouard Drumont in *La Libre Parole* from 1892 onwards. His book *La France juive* (1886) sold in tens of thousands, and mobilized Catholic discontent with the way in which anti-clericalism had granted high office in justice and administration to Jew and Protestant, and in which the new financial oligarchy was linked with international Jewish capitalism. The nationalism of those who fell under the spell of Drumont became racialist and violent, an emotional thing of blind prejudice. Anti-semitism as a systematic policy was kindled by Boulangism, fanned into life by the scandals connected with the squalid and sensational

[1] Cf. Jacques Bainville: op. cit., p. 151. The change back again of the Right to an anti-nationalist attitude after 1930 is examined below (Chapter VI): and cf. Charles A. Micaud: *The French Right and Nazi Germany, 1933-9* (1943). Abridged French version (1945).

Panama affair at the end of the century, and burst into open flame in the Dreyfus case. The link between anti-semitism and rabid militarist nationalism was the charge that the Jews served as the agents of foreign powers—especially of Germany—undermining the preparedness and security of France.[1]

The charge of espionage brought against Captain Dreyfus, a Jewish officer, was readily accepted by the military tribunal and he was duly sent to Devil's Island. This success was equally naturally followed by a concerted drive to expel all Jews and Protestants from the armed forces of France. It was a drive engineered and carried out by the clericalist, ultra-nationalist members of the General Staff. Only gradually did it become clear that the isolated case of Dreyfus was but one item in a vast conspiracy against the Republic: a truth which dawned only when the document which had condemned him came to be strongly suspected of being a forgery. The upheaval in the French Army, occasioned by charges and counter-charges, gradually attracted wider public attention. Each new revelation in the vast and sensational scandal roused public opinion to still more feverish unrest. The recent scandals connected with parliamentary politicians were forgotten in this greater and more intriguing scandal concerning the Army itself. And the issues raised soon clarified into fundamental issues regarding the very nature of democratic society itself. A new *mystique* was born: the *mystique* of civilianism.[2]

---

[1] Cf. D. W. Brogan: op. cit., pp. 274-84. By 1894, as Roger Soltau points out (op. cit., p. 338), 'the vast majority of French officers were avowedly anti-Semites', and see details in A. Zévaès: op. cit., p. 221 ff.

[2] No attempt has been made here to tell the story of the Dreyfus affair. It has already been admirably told in D. W. Brogan: op. cit., Book VII; and in French by Joseph Reinach: *Histoire de l'Affaire Dreyfus* (7 Vols. 1901-11); Louis Leblois: *L'Affaire Dreyfus* (1929); Daniel Halévy: *Apologie pour Notre Passé* (1910).

Among the many accounts by the leading participants, see for the Dreyfusards the documents and material in Pierre Dreyfus: *Dreyfus, his Life and Letters* (English translation, 1937); H. Dutrait-Crozon: *Précis de l'Affaire Dreyfus* (1924); Georges Clemenceau *L'Iniquité, Sur la Réparation, La Honte* (3 Vols.. 1903); Anatole France: *L'Île des Pin-*

THE NATIONAL VISION

As the Dreyfus affair dragged on, the issue of the guilt or innocence of Dreyfus sank into the background, and the general defence of the military and nationalist leaders came to rest not on the thesis that Dreyfus was guilty, but that even if he were innocent, it was better that one man should suffer than that the whole prestige of the French Army should be undermined in face of the enemy. This involved a challenge to the democratic creed, to the sacredness of individual rights and the sanctity of justice. It evoked, in reaction, a full-dress restatement of civilian ideas and the necessity for all order and security to be based upon justice and truth. The courageous act of the great novelist, Émile Zola, in publishing *J'accuse* in January 1896, raised the controversy to a level of dignity and moral greatness which it had not previously known. Setting forth his list of charges in detail, and explaining that he harboured no personal grievance or even knowledge of the military leaders accused, he deliberately incurred legal penalties as, in his own words, 'a revolutionary means of hastening the explosion of truth and of justice'. Jules Guesde, the Socialist leader, declared Zola's letter 'the greatest revolutionary act of the century'. The trial of Zola and his publisher in the *Cour d'assises*, defended by Clemenceau, became a political debate of the highest quality. In the country, faced with political crisis, street demonstrations, strikes in Paris, and incessant controversy in the Press, skilful journalists like Urbain Gohier began to expound the full doctrine of civilianism. His arguments, later accumulated in his *L'Armée contre la Nation* (1899), are worth examination.

Sweeping aside the Jewish question as irrelevant, he sets the

gouins (1908); Jean Jaurès: *Les Preuves* (1898); Charles Péguy: *Notre Jeunesse* (1916); Georges Sorel: *La Révolution Dreyfusienne* (1911); Alexandre Zévaès: *L'Affaire Dreyfus* (1931); Émile Zola: *La Vérité en Marche* (1901). For the anti-Dreyfusards, see especially Maurice Barrès: *Mes Cahiers* (1929-38); Charles Maurras: *Enquête sur la Monarchie* (1925), and *Si le Coup de Force est Possible* (1925). There is a characteristically tendentious account by Léon Daudet in his biography of *Clemenceau* (English translation, 1940), and a modern reassessment in Guy Chapman: *The Dreyfus Case* (1955).

whole affair in the context of the century-old battle between the Revolution and its opponents. 'The Revolution has not to be made again; it has not been made; it has to be made.' He attacks the conscription laws of 1889, which had made it possible for young men attending the *École centrale*, the *École forestière*, or the *Polytechnique*, to escape two out of their three years' prescribed military service—and to serve the one year as officers. He praises the rank-and-file soldiers, the people in arms, and confines his attacks to the privileged officer-class and the High Command. Barracks-life is a source of demoralization and a hotbed of tyranny, which the fortunate officer-class drawn from the *bourgeoisie* is spared: 'the only way of not becoming a soldier is to be an officer'. Military officials are like civil officials—the salaried servants of the nation. Yet their pretensions to power and privilege have raised them above the nation—even against the nation. He weighs the vast expenditure on the armed forces against the results—855 million francs in 1898, if pensions be included. The results—the imposition of military domination on Madagascar and other overseas territories. In this way, the anti-militarist tended to be naturally the anti-colonialist. Militarism led to imperialism, and both were incompatible with Republicanism and democracy.

The 'Military Power' is a State within the State, with its 'milliard budget, its uncontrolled and irresponsible disposal of nearly all national resources, with its laws, its justice, its special police'—and even its *bastilles* and its slave-galleys. The gloomy forebodings of Gohier did not come to pass before the Great War—thanks to the triumph of civilianism in the Dreyfus affair. But there is more than a foreshadowing of the Vichy regime in his definition of the militarists' programme: '*aux militaires, le pouvoir absolu: aux fripons, sous la protection du sabre, la liberté complète—liberté de la vengeance et liberté du brigandage. C'est ce qu'on appellera: le règne de l'Ordre*'. The rule of generals, admirals and higher functionaries, of Laval's minions and Joseph Darnand's Militia, in 1944, could not be better defined: though in 1898 none would have dared to predict this coming to pass in collaboration with German masters.

However exaggerated such language and such theorizing

THE NATIONAL VISION

may have been, it illustrates the challenge to civilian democracy thrown down by the affair. That the mingled forces which rallied to the defence of Dreyfus eventually directed their concentrated vengeance against the Church more than the Army was largely the responsibility of the Church itself. It rallied quite unnecessarily to fanatical defence of the Army and of the anti-Semites. The Archbishop of Paris became the patron of the 'Labarum League' of anti-semitic officers, while the Archbishop of Toulouse denounced 'the deadly campaign which is being waged against our military leaders'. The leading Catholic Dreyfusard organization—*Le Comité Catholique pour la Défense du Droit*—was a fiasco, and the Jesuits mobilized against the Jews.

The social forces which rallied to the defence of Dreyfus and of civilian democracy are significant: they reveal the nature of the fundamental social cleavage which the incidents of the affair exposed. In addition to leading Radicals like Clemenceau and Socialists like Jaurès; and in addition to prominent literary figures like Zola and Anatole France; the main classes from which the Dreyfusards drew their support were the teaching profession and the universities, already deeply imbued with the anti-clerical spirit of the *École normale*, the lower middle-classes, similarly anti-clerical and anti-militarist in outlook, and the industrial workers of the larger towns, whose Socialistic brand of Republicanism was aroused by the affair. To the negative emotions of anti-clericalism and anti-militarism was added the moral faith, so vital to modern French democracy, that no social order could endure unless it was based on justice to the individual and respect for human personality regardless of race or creed. When the forces of the older aristocracy, the service leaders and clericals, the authoritarians and the higher *fonctionnaires*, found themselves opposing this faith as well as defending clericalism and militarism, they were doomed. Yet the clash of forces, the clash of revolutionary and counter-revolutionary forces, was not resolved without prolonged political and parliamentary crisis, involving moments of real danger to the Republic itself.

In addition to several riots and plots in the earlier stages, there were two serious plots in 1898 and 1899, aimed at a *coup d'état*. The last, in August 1899, involved all the leading Monarchists, Bonapartists and anti-Dreyfusards, including Déroulède of Boulangist fame. It is probable that the most serious threat came in the familiar form of chronic ministerial crisis and parliamentary instability. Mr. Roger Soltau's summary is relevant:

> No less than three crises appear to us to have threatened the essentials of the existing order. The first of these was the elections of 1898: had the Conservatives gained a few seats, instead of losing a few, no Radical majority became possible; the Chamber would have tolerated none but cabinets in which the Catholic element preponderated and the Rennes court martial would either never have taken place or would have been followed by the maintenance of reactionary officers at the head of the army. . . . The same danger appeared on the fall of the Dupuy Cabinet in June 1899: had the Socialists then made impossible the formation of a Left Coalition Ministry . . . . the forces of the Right could have formed another coalition which might have made a successful appeal to a still uncertain public opinion. Finally, had Waldeck-Rousseau and his friends, because of the smallness of their majority and the apparent precariousness of their tenure, been timid and hesitant in their policy, refrained from arresting the August conspirators, from making sweeping changes in the General Staff and from boldly taking measures of 'Republican defence' in the following months, reaction might well have remained strong enough to make a successful appeal in the elections of 1902.

But these successive political crises were safely overcome, partly by good fortune and partly because of the change in public opinion and the skill of Waldeck-Rousseau. The combination of Radicalism and Socialism, symbolized by Waldeck-Rousseau and Jaurès, turned the tide in favour of the ideals of the revolutionary tradition, of which both formed an integral part.[1]

The Great War did much to reconcile Army and nation. The pre-war tendency to install an anti-militarist at the Ministry of War, which had been prompted by the experience of Boulanger

[1] Cf. Urbain Gohier: *L'Armée contre la Nation* (1899), and the account in Roger Soltau: *French Political Thought in the Nineteenth Century* (1931), Chapter XI.

and confirmed in 1906 when Clemenceau appointed the Dreyfusard Colonel Picquart to this office, had prevented any further challenge to parliamentary sovereignty from the direction of the General Staff. Yet the military leaders continued to be by origin, professional training and natural inclination authoritarian, and 'sound Republican' generals remained scarce. The issue was smothered rather than solved, on the one hand by the separation of Church and State which removed the stimulus of clericalism from militarist movements, on the other by the increasing menace of Germany which rallied nation and armed services more firmly than before. Meanwhile, the social classes which supported military power found an alternative outlet for their energies and ambitions in colonial development: and the interconnexion between this development and the national vision must be briefly considered.

Colonial Development

Just as Bismarck welcomed the Republic because it seemed likely to help him to keep France isolated in a continent of dynastic monarchies, so he encouraged her colonial expansion because it seemed likely to embroil her with Italy and Great Britain and would contribute to her isolation in Europe. But there were other and more solid reasons than German encouragement for that remarkable burst of colonizing energy which the French nation produced during the generation after 1870. Professor Brogan has put his finger on one—perhaps on the main—impulse behind it.

There was a natural connexion between the defeat of 1870 and the renewal of colonial activity. As the hopes of immediate revenge grew less, the more energetic Army and Navy officers became bored with a life of preparation for an ordeal and an achievement that never came. It was this boredom, frankly admitted, that drove one of the two greatest of French empire builders to seek service in Tonkin, and less brilliant and less vocal officers than Lyautey must have felt the same urge. In the colonies a young soldier like Marchand could rise from the ranks and enter world history. Africa and Asia were, to the men of the generation that followed 1870, what Algeria was to the men of the generation that followed 1815.

And just as the two great French military defeats of the nineteenth century were followed by outbursts of colonial activity, so the consequences of this activity were valued chiefly because of their relevance to the problem of national security in Europe. Deficiencies of man-power and colonial markets, considerations of strategy and prestige alike, were met by the acquisition of a vast overseas empire, stretching over some four and a quarter million square miles of Africa, and extending as far afield as Indo-China and New Caledonia. The administration of British India has been called a 'system of outdoor relief for the upper classes'. Much more clearly was the French colonial empire welcomed as a career open to the talents of ambitious soldiers and administrators, who brought back into French politics an outlook, experience and traditions which had a far-reaching effect on French political life and ideas. It is this backwash which is our chief concern here.[1]

The first generation of the Third Republic saw extension of the French colonial policy of giving overseas possessions direct representation in the national parliament. The test-case was Algeria—which the Third Republic inherited from Louis Philippe, and where the defeat of 1870 led to a great rebellion in 1871. In the person of Marshal Macmahon, its Governor-General, it provided France with a Conservative figure-head as successor to Thiers. When Albert Grévy, brother of President Jules Grévy, became Governor-General, he replaced the former authoritarian regime in Algeria by a system of 'attachment' to France. The separate centralized administration was broken up and each administrative department was attached to the appropriate ministry in Paris. The three *départements* were represented in both Senate and Chamber, as an integral part of metropolitan France, and they are still so regarded. The other main parts of the empire—the four colonies of Martin-

[1] Cf. D. W. Brogan: op. cit., Book V. On French colonial expansion in general see S. H. Roberts: *History of French Colonial Policy* (2 Vols. 1928), and H. I. Priestley: *France Overseas* (1938). The Tunisian campaign and its domestic repercussions are described in G. Hanotaux: op. cit., Vol. IV, Chapters IX and X. Cf. also E. Lavisse: *Histoire de France Contemporaine* (1920-22), Vol. VIII, Book III.

ique, Guadeloupe, Réunion and the French West Indies—were likewise given direct representation by the laws of February and November 1875, and in 1885 ten seats were allocated to the colonies in the Chamber of Deputies. The fiction by which colonies were treated as parts of France wore thin, in face of reality and of the electoral corruption which grew up in them. In 1896 the policy of administrative 'attachment' was reversed, and in 1898 local opinion was given more effective expression through 'financial delegations' with advisory functions. Financial decentralization to some extent offset political centralization. But their parliamentary representation was too firmly established to be reversed, and the principle was usually extended to the new colonies in Indo-China and French West Africa.

In Tunisia, with the entanglements with Italy, and Morocco, with the entanglements with Britain, Spain and Germany, a system of French protection afforded to a native ruler proved more expedient, and led to a new system of indirect rule. The Bey of Tunis and the Sultan of Morocco were preserved, and French Residents-General were implanted by their side. The Anglo-French Entente of 1904, following soon after the friction of the Fashoda incident, squeezed France out of Egypt and the Sudan but guaranteed her a predominant role in Morocco.

The Second Empire bequeathed her the colony of Cochin-China in the Far East, and opened the door to French military, commercial and missionary enterprise in Tonkin. The story of how Jules Ferry, as Prime Minister, captured for France the empire of Indo-China, is not our concern here: save that by presenting parliament and country with a series of *faits accomplis*, both military and diplomatic, he revealed unsuspected powers in the hands of the executive which enabled it to defy even a hostile and wildly angry parliament. He was able to do it because of the support of men on the spot: of naval officers in Tonkin, who set up a working administration in the conquered territories, and of Catholic missionaries, ever anxious and abundant, to carry French culture and Catholic religion into backward lands. Cardinal Lavigerie, Archbishop of Algeria, had readily moved his headquarters into Tunisia, and organized his missionary White Fathers: curious allies of the anticlerical Jules Ferry.[1] Before long, in Tonkin, civil governors replaced the naval officers and French law was imposed—often with unhappy results. Meanwhile Colonels Lyautey and Galliéni had gained colonial experience. Soon Paul Doumer, as Governor-General, was to develop the economic resources and opportunities of the new possessions, and Albert Sarraut was to increase the measure of native participation in their government. When Galliéni took over from General Duchesne, the task of conquering Madagascar, he was able to apply his 'splash of oil' principle which had proved so effective in Annam: that is, to pacify certain strategic areas, establish firmly law and order and French administration, and trust to the 'oilstain' spreading quietly and attracting other areas anxious for peace. The methods of the men on the spot were as undogmatic and opportunist as the political atmosphere at home in the same years was doctrinaire and extremist. The two fields of activity—the colonial and the domestic—were complementary in many ways, and attracted opposite kinds of personality.

It was the gradual acquisition of French West Africa and French Equatorial Africa in the last decades of the century which forced France to accept more openly her colonial responsibilities and to formulate a more systematic policy. Only in 1894 was a permanent Ministry of Colonies set up (with no authority over North Africa), but frequent changes of ministry negatived its influence over policy. Governorships too often became political consolation prizes. For lack of a clearly thought-out policy, colonial resources were wasted or abused, or else a wooden desire for uniformity and 'assimilation' served as a substitute for policy. Brazza, officially employed as an explorer by the Ministry of Public Instruction, became the high-souled agent of ruthless commercial exploitation. The incursion of France, as of most other European powers, into tropical lands produced periods of squalid commercialism and cruel administration. But such periods were less the result of deliberate policy than of negligence and indifference in Par-

[1] On Jules Ferry see A. Rambaud: *Jules Ferry* (1903). On missionary activities see above, Chapter II, p. 66.

liament: and the strong Roman tradition which has haunted all her colonial enterprise has tended to make the extension of French citizenship a more consistent aim than any other. However farcical it may often have become in practice, and however much it usually played into the hands of small oligarchies wielding local control, generous extension of citizenship has often served, too, to counteract brutality and exploitation. It has prevented the growth of a colour-bar; it has meant equality of payment between native and white administrators; and it led to modification of the policy of 'assimilation', which had proved a mixed blessing for the colonies.

The aim of 'assimilation' was that colonial people should absorb French culture and acquire French civilization so that they might become French citizens. It was in tune with the strong unitary and *étatiste* tendencies already described (Chapter II). But with the conquest of vast new tropical and sub-tropical lands, 'assimilation' in terms of the Rights of Man sank below the horizon and was replaced by the policy of 'association'. This policy had the more limited aim of transforming a native *élite* into full French citizens, and at taking this *élite* into partnership in administration. Both principles are opposed to the aim of colonial self-government as pursued by Great Britain: and the system of inspectors sent out by the central government made centralization a reality. At every stage, the development of the French Empire reflects less the Republican and democratic nature of modern France than the nationalist, authoritarian character of the social classes which have been most concerned with its creation.[1]

The nationalistic function of the empire is shown most clearly in its military role, mentioned already elsewhere. The black troops of Senegal have played a popular and honourable part in the French Army. By 1940, a tenth of the Army was recruited from the overseas colonies, and much progress had been made towards the boast of Lyautey that 'France is a nation of 100 millions'. Since 1940, the empire has served

[1] Although the policy of 'association', as formulated by Waldeck-Rousseau, was intended to encourage the natives 'évoluer, non dans notre civilization, mais dans la leur'

France well, and it was fitting that French North Africa should become one springboard for the liberation of metropolitan France. The naval bases of Dakar, Casablanca, Oran, and the material resources of Africa have done much to preserve France's importance in the world during her years of national submergence. But the nationalist interpretation of colonization has its permanent defects. Even the policy of 'association' has the effect, as Professor Eric Walker has pointed out, that 'the *élite* become Frenchmen, the native masses are deprived of their natural leaders'. The professional colonial administrators proved, in 1940, to be more often akin in spirit to Vichy than to the Republic. And the violent anti-militarists of the Dreyfus affair like Gohier, who saw in colonies a hotbed of authoritarianism, have not been proved entirely wrong.[1]

To sum up. The achievements of the Third Republic, judged relatively by the standard of the aims and social needs of France in the later nineteenth century, were great. Its constitutional and political arrangements were in accord with the highest common level of agreement among the great majority of Frenchmen. The Republic, despite many setbacks and weaknesses, vindicated its right to survive and successfully overcame the most concerted attempts of authoritarianism to overthrow parliamentary government. It also kept the French nation, in both its own military preparedness and its foreign alliances, strong enough to resist successfully the attacks of 1914-18. Its governments gave the country solidarity enough and unity enough to steer safely through a rapid succession of immense ordeals. Yet significantly the greatest achievements in overseas expansion were the work of a few enthusiasts and more the result of private enterprise and good fortune than of deliberate planning or even national ambition. Already financial, political and administrative corruption had beset the machinery of State. Old feuds and vendettas remained, and social divisions were little healed. And the pattern of future politics had been set by the *Bloc des Gauches* of 1905. The formation of *unions*,

---

[1] Cf. above, p. 160: and E. A. Walker: *Colonies* (1944), for an illuminating comparison of different national policies towards colonies.

blocs, *cartels* and *fronts* as devices to offset the splintering of groups was to shape the whole political working of French democracy. It was the basis of group-bargaining and ministerial coalitions, and from the loose-jointed, over-supple functioning of these *blocs* was to come the spirit of lukewarm compromise which has been already noted as a main characteristic of modern French politics. France remained an unstabilized society, for which her political system provided no real corrective.[1]

---

[1] Cf. above, p. 114 f. The lack of any adequate history of the Republic for the years between 1879 and 1900 has been noted and lamented by French historians. Cf. Daniel Halévy: *Pour l'Étude de la Troisième République* (1937), who suggested that the study of the great *cadres* of French life would be, for these years, more fruitful than parliamentary history: and who indicated Jules Ferry as the central parliamentarian of this period which is so confused in parliamentary affairs. Even the archives for it are deficient (ibid., p. 20 f.). Professor D. W. Brogan's work has done something (but not enough) to cover this gap. Vol. II of M. Jacques Madaule's *Histoire de France*, published in 1945, tells the complete history of the Third Republic in some 220 pages, and is probably the most satisfactory modern account in French.

V

THE MODERN CHALLENGE

Has Democracy Failed?

JUDGEMENT of the machinery and institutions of democracy in France by the standards of the French 'national vision' of democracy suggests that the democratic instrument seldom failed, before the Great War, in adaptability and flexibility. Its main characteristic was its immense elasticity: the ease with which it could be biased in favour of the prevailing wind of public opinion. Its parliamentary sails billowed and filled before the wind of Caesarism in the days of Boulanger—they deflated equally quickly when strong forces lost faith in or attacked Caesarism. Clericalist opinion could utilize the institutions of Church, Army and education to win power—until the reaction of anti-clericalism became powerful enough to destroy this power. One is driven to the conclusion that electoral, parliamentary and administrative arrangements in the Third Republic had less inherent conservative bias towards stability and the preservation of the *status quo* than the corresponding arrangements of the constitutional monarchy in Great Britain and the Dominions, or the federal constitutions of Switzerland or the United States. It has already been suggested that one reason for this might be that the 'revolutionary tradition' was identified with existing institutions far more completely in these countries than in the Third French Republic.[1]

That the French national tradition was one of revolutionary ideology whilst the constitution of the Third Republic was but a working compromise between Republican and anti-Republican forces, was a permanent underlying fact which determined its whole development. The system of parliamentary sovereignty which divided Frenchmen least was a neutral,

[1] Cf. above, Chapter I, p. 10 f.

negative thing which also satisfied them little. The Third Republic is an almost unique example of extremely positive political forces working through a negative instrument, which was in itself incapable of providing a government or an administration better or worse than the interplay of forces was able to provide. From the point of view of each separate political force—Conservatism, Radicalism, Socialism or Communism—the system worked badly and in the end failed. Yet in relation to the interplay of these forces at any given time it worked almost perfectly. If the function of democratic government is to be a mirror or a photographic negative—reflecting or reproducing accurately the conflicts of social and political forces—the Republic worked well enough. If the function of democratic government is something more positive than this; if it be to serve the good life and the general well-being of most citizens, to act as a 'hinderer of hindrances' to national prosperity and security, it worked less well.

In short, democracy in France has to be judged not only in terms of French standards and the mere interplay of conflicting internal social and political movements, but somewhat more absolutely in terms of its response to the modern challenge—to the great present-day problems of unemployment and social insecurity, of industrial despotism and world economy, of aggression and international disorder. The question which the world asks of France—and justifiably asks of a pioneer nation in democratic experiments—is what contributions her most durable experiment made towards the solution of the most pressing world problems of the twentieth century. What was the measure of her response to the modern challenge?

By about the year 1905, as has been shown above, all the main institutions and conventions of the Third Republic had been consolidated, and some of the most burning social and political issues had been fought out to a decision. Monarchism, if not dead, had been routed and relegated to the camp of lost causes. Bonapartism and Caesarism of every kind had been fought and beaten in open combat and thrown into sullen acquiescence. The Church and the Army, acting in fatal alliance during the first generation of the Republic, had been rendered impotent to overthrow the Republic. The rights of organized Labour had been recognized, and both C.G.T. and Socialist parties had planted their feet firmly in French social life. The system of national education had been formally completed, and the State had asserted its power to determine the structure, substance and spirit of training in which the great majority of its citizens were to be brought up. The new empire overseas had been acquired and consolidated, too, and the general shape of France as a Great Power in the modern world had become clear. In 1893 and in 1904, by her alliance with Russia and her Entente with Great Britain, France had frustrated German designs to keep her isolated and helpless in Europe, and the broad lines of her foreign policy had been laid down for the next generation to come. The Republic had been saved—both from its own weaknesses and from the attacks of its enemies. The age of formation and definition was past, and the age of construction was begun. Democracy was able to move from the defensive to the offensive; and move it must if it was to survive, for the challenge of the twentieth century was already thrown down.[1]

It is here, more than anywhere else, that French democracy failed. The full reasons for its failure are still difficult to define. Perhaps it was the exhaustion caused by the bitter fight for survival in the previous generation, or the undue optimism engendered by the triumph of State over Church and Army; perhaps the fatal irreconcilability between the political and the social strands of the revolutionary tradition (for French politics remained incorrigibly dominated by the past) or an excessive devotion to the outlook and individual independence of peasant proprietors and provincial interests; perhaps a more fundamental demographic weakness (for the size of French population had failed to keep pace with her international prestige and importance) or the mere historical working-out of the great new forces which had been started by the nexus of events in 1870.[2] Perhaps it was a combination of all these and other

[1] Cf. above, Chapters III and IV, *passim*.

[2] Cf. above, Chapter IV, pp. 134-9. Cf. D. W. Brogan: op. cit., pp. 406 and 417. The populations of France and Germany were

THE MODERN CHALLENGE

reasons. But whatever the reason, it is clear in retrospect that French democracy and the national policy which it produced failed to meet adequately the social, economic and political challenge of twentieth-century conditions, both at home and abroad. As will be shown, this challenge left without effective answer by the Third Republic has been taken up with vigour by the Fourth: and certain lessons can be drawn from the experience of past failures. They may be examined in four stages —her social failure prior to 1914; her military misfortune between 1914 and 1918; her political and economic weaknesses between 1918 and 1940; and her international position between 1918 and 1940.

The Challenge of the Positive State

At the dawn of the twentieth century every nation which had known the industrial revolution was confronted with the choice whether the State should in future dominate and control economic activities and new social problems, or be itself dominated by them. The first decade of the century saw a great increase of State interference in economic and social life in Germany, Great Britain and even the United States, no less than in France. These countries varied in the extent to which it was felt necessary or desirable for the State to assume greater responsibility for controlling and promoting economic progress and social welfare. Despite her spurt of activity, comparable to that of her neighbours, France did not go far in this direction. Again, there were both material and ideological reasons for this restriction of activity: but the restriction remained thereafter an important fact in the working of French democracy.[1]

---

very roughly equal in 1870. By 1914, Germany's was approaching 65 million while France's was only 40 million. The birth-rate fell rapidly in both countries between these dates, but in 1914 Germany's was still higher than France's had been in 1870. Only immigration was saving France from obvious de-population.

[1] Cf. Dr. A. D. Lindsay: *The Modern Democratic State*, Vol. I, pp. 245-8.

The decade before 1914 was a period of material prosperity combined with industrial unrest. The prosperity came partly from the stimulus of armaments—the greatest public-works expenditure in each large country. The new powers gained by organized labour and the scantiness of planned measures for social security resulted in recurrent strikes on a large scale, after 1906. Significantly enough George Sorel's *Reflections on Violence*, with its syndicalist arguments for a general strike as the central revolutionary weapon of the future, first appeared in 1906: but the conditions producing the result existed already. In the same year, too, the C.G.T. adopted its Charter of Amiens, which favoured the strike as the best method available for political action. One reason why organized labour eschewed direct political, parliamentary action and close alliance with the Socialist parties, as was becoming the procedure in Great Britain, was the apparent inefficacy of parliamentary action to produce satisfactory social results. The powerful Radicals like Clemenceau, representing peasants and small business folk, were wont to emphasize the gulf of property rights which lay between themselves and Socialism: and parliamentary Socialists seemed unlikely to be able to achieve anything without the Radicals.

Both the persistence and the scale of the strikes made them symptoms of a profound unrest and social sickness, which should have been heeded more. There had been hundreds of small local strikes in the eighteen-nineties, but in 1913 there were 1,073, involving nearly a quarter of a million workers. Although, after the law of 1892 setting up procedure for voluntary arbitration between workers and employers, the proportion of strikes settled by compromise tended to increase, so also did the number of 'sympathetic' strikes, showing the growing solidarity and class-consciousness of the workers fostered by the C.G.T. There were agricultural strikes, like that of 1906, many of which were protests against piece-work, and which led to riots, attacks on farm-houses, and intimidation of blacklegs. They raised the new problems of the landless labourers. There were strikes of postal and telegraph workers in Paris, like that of 1909, which brought to a crisis the question of how far State employees and *fonctionnaires* should have the right to band themselves together into trade unions and even to strike in protest against grievances. There was even a concerted attempt at a general strike, as in 1909, which was crushed by the new Prime Minister, Aristide Briand: although he had himself long preached the efficacy of the general strike. When the test-case came with the strike of the underpaid railway workers, Briand arrested the leaders and called up the strikers as army reservists—one of the earliest, but not the last, occasion when the executive used its military powers as a weapon of domestic policy.[1]

What were the substantial grievances underlying this unrest, and what did the parliamentary governments do to remedy them as distinct from mere suppression of the symptoms? During the years of political turmoil and parliamentary crisis, legislative change had lagged far behind social needs. The system of *métayage* and share-cropping, especially in the central region of France, perpetuated many grievances which had been grievances in 1789. Among the agricultural labourers, perhaps the most neglected section of French workers, wages were unduly depressed and conditions of work often appalling. There was widespread unemployment during the economic crises and slumps of the years after 1882 and 1892. Fluctuations in the prices of consumers' goods created a sense of insecurity among the workers. During the eighteen-nineties the bureaucracy had, indeed, created workers' delegations for the mines, and laws were passed limiting women's work to ten hours a day, regulating hygiene, pensions and accident insurance. These measures were sponsored by the conservative, moderate Republicans, under pressure from the Press and the Church, as well as from Socialist congresses and strikes. More legislation drawn up by the parliamentary Socialists before 1905 remained a dead letter, and in Halévy's words, the political world in a changing France, '*concentré dans une bureaucratie*

---

[1] For details of these events see E. Lavisse: op. cit., Vol. VIII, Book IV, Chapter IV, and Book II, Chapter XI; D. W. Brogan: op. cit., pp. 404-27; A. Zévaès: op. cit., Chapter XVI.

acceptée par les masses, deux forces lentes, tend à l'immutabilité'.[1] The social Conservatism of the peasants and the smaller *bourgeoisie* acted as a drag on social legislation. The divisions amongst the parties of the Left and the indispensability of the Radicals made this drag a powerful force opposing all State responsibility for providing social security. When Clemenceau formed his great ministry of 1906 he issued a seventeen-point programme of reforms, three of which concerned the Army, five workers' welfare, and four finance. The proposed reforms included provision for an eight-hour working day, retirement and pensions; government control of labour-contracts and the mines; workmen's compensation for accidents; trade-union status and organization; and income tax. Great Britain, in the same years, was putting through a corresponding programme of reforms. But in France they were obstructed at every stage, and the split between Radicals and Socialists brought the programme almost to nought. No similar concerted effort was to be made until the Popular Front programme of 1936—a generation later: a generation too late.[2]

Thus the experience of the pre-war years bred disillusionment amongst the working classes, and spread the conviction that social reform was, in the existing system and with the prevailing balance of parties, subordinated to the political mechanism of parliamentary manœuvres. It strengthened the extra-parliamentary forces—especially the trade unions—which had indeed been partly responsible for the failures of these years. Had they thrown their weight into support for the Socialist parties, and refrained from arousing fears amongst the Radicals which were too powerful for their own resources to overcome by force, more would have been gained in good time. Instead, many Left-wing energies were distracted into the channels of anti-militarism and opposition to the expenditure on national

[1] Cf. D. Halévy: *La Décadence de la Liberté* (1931), p. 47. He there gives a valuable analysis of the general elections held between 1871 and 1914, designed to show what questions were asked at elections, and what forces lay behind the political activity of the Third Republic.

[2] For details of Clemenceau's programme, see E. Lavisse: op. cit., Vol. VIII, p. 254.

security during the decade before 1914. These are the years when pacifism spread and deepened on the Left, and that old role of standing for national security and independence which had most distinguished the Left of Gambetta's day became now the role of the Right—the traditionalists and clericalist-militarists such as the *Action française*, and the Conservative Republicans. The doctrine that 'the worker has no country' was replacing the old Jacobin tradition of 'the country in danger'. Gustave Hervé, a follower of Déroulède and the Boulangists when young, became a leading pacifist. He edited the anti-militarist *Piou Piou de l'Yonne*. He came to represent the extreme pacifist wing of the Socialist Party, embarrassing to Jaurès and the moderates: until he became a noisy patriot again in the war and post-war years. In August 1914 his pacifist weekly *La Guerre Sociale* became overnight the fire-eating daily *La Victoire*, urging 'an authoritative Republic'. He published, in 1935, the curiously prophetic pamphlet *We need Pétain*. So does the link between wartime nationalists and postwar defeatists become apparent. The counterpart is Jacques Doriot, most vehement of Communists before 1934, most muscular of Fascist collaborators after 1940. Extremes of Right and Left, nationalist and Marxist, could meet and join hands in the face of imminent defeat and in common dislike of the parliamentary Republic.[1]

One significant issue was, however, settled in these years. It concerned the relation between those two agencies of middle-class predominance already described, parliament and administration. Developments in trade unionism raised the fundamental question: how far should the *fonctionnaires* be allowed to

---

[1] Gustave Hervé is a significant and unduly neglected figure in the transitions of opinion in these years. His pamphlet of 1935 (which some have argued reveals the hand more of Alibert, friend of Maurras and Pétain's first Minister of Justice in June 1940) was widely read at the time. It includes the ominous remark: 'In peace time it is not possible to upset a regime by a *coup d'état*, unless that regime is acquiescent and has no supporting elements in the armed forces, the civil service, or the population. Only in wartime and especially in a moment of defeat, when every citizen is armed, can the operation succeed' (p. 60).

form trade unions, and what should be the rights of such combinations as against the State? There were well over half a million *fonctionnaires* by 1906. The elementary school-teachers and postal and telegraph workers, especially, voiced grievances against the terms of their employment. Associations among State employees had been legalized by the Associations Law of 1901. But the teachers wanted to make these associations into full trade unions and join the C.G.T. Their immediate grievances concerned the conditions of promotion, and they accused the authorities of discrimination against Socialists. They were joined by the lesser civil servants, who complained that within the service wage scales, promotion and terms of service were chaotic, and that political influence was rampant. The *cabinet* or personal staff of each minister grew in size and was recruited from aspiring young politicians appointed as much to oblige other politicians as on personal merit. When the minister went out of office these protégés were often planted out in the higher ranks of the bureaucracy. The professional *fonctionnaires* demanded legal definition of their rights, security of status, and abolition of arbitrary powers within the hierarchy. A civil service career was open not to talents so much as to political graft. Here was a fine Republican cry—against discrimination, favouritism, arbitrary power—raised from within the very heart of the State itself. Radical governments had to listen, however responsible the Radicals themselves had been for producing this state of affairs.

But Clemenceau, then Prime Minister, took a stubborn stand against these demands. He refused to admit 'an anonymous organization of irresponsible *fonctionnaires* which . . . would deprive the Chamber of control over the government'. His attitude led to the general strike of 1909. The conflict was won by Clemenceau and the Chamber: but at the cost of splitting Radicals from Socialists, and frustrating all the rest of his programme of social reforms. The immediate grievances of the strikers were answered: but they were granted no 'Statute of *Fonctionnaires*' defining their status, as they had desired. In the event, parliamentary sovereignty was once again asserted, this time over its own employees.

Yet the effect of the victory was little more than a delaying action. In subsequent years, and especially after 1918, trade unions and associations of every kind were to go on growing, even within the administration. In time every branch of the administration had a powerful union, grouped into the *Fédération des fonctionnaires* and the *Cartel des Services Publics*. In 1930, they secured membership of the Central Council of French Trade Unions, the Government permitted the development, and adjusted wages to the price rise. Nor has the change meant strikes: it was resistance to the change which had produced the strikes. Although the status of *fonctionnaires* was not recognized and codified into one Statute, security was given piecemeal, and recruitment, promotion, dismissal and disciplinary action were all regulated by fixed rules. The long delay and the unsystematic treatment of the problem are expressive of all French government and politics in the twentieth century. The positive State was accepted with great reluctance.[1]

The Impact of War

No student of the French war-effort between 1914 and 1918 can help being filled with admiration. Against heavy odds—a dwindling population and inferior military preparation; within a generation of Sedan and the extortions of the Treaty of Frankfort; still weary from the exertions and disruptions of the Dreyfus affair and the pre-war social unrest: the people of France braced themselves for invasion, disaster and total war, with high courage and impressive solidarity. 'The country in danger' again asserted its spell: and national solidarity proved superior to party spirit.

The outbreak of war was preceded by a heated debate on the desirability of raising the period of compulsory military service from two to three years, as it had been between 1889

---

[1] Cf. Leroy: *Le Droit des Fonctionnaires* (1906); E. Lavisse: op. cit. Vol. VIII, Book II, Chapter IX; documents in L. D. White (ed.), *The Civil Service in the Modern State* (1930), with an introductory essay: by Aubert Lefas.

and 1905. The proposal was vigorously attacked by Jaurès on the grounds that the military theory underlying the proposal was false: that French generals clung too tightly to their faith in a highly trained and disciplined 'active army', and had too little faith in the mass of the nation trained, within a period of two years, to be spirited fighting men in time of need. He wanted a democratic army, and in 1910 outlined its basis in his amazingly prophetic book *L'Armée Nouvelle*. It was a plea for reliance on the deep human and spiritual reserves of the nation. To pin all hope—as most official strategists of the time were doing—on a first great initial clash between highly tempered and barracks-disciplined forces, and to neglect the great power of the reserves, would be fatal. He argued for 'a strong, democratic militia, reducing barracks to the function of a training school and turning the whole people into an immense and vigorous nation-in-arms at the service of national democracy and peace'. Switzerland was his model—a citizen army, avoiding all tendency to separate the army from the nation. He even looked to General Foch as the man to plan such a force. But the three-year law was passed by Barthou in 1913, and since the change was effected by calling up men of twenty along with those of twenty-one, there was an extra class of trained men in existence in 1914. The old invidious dispensations from service were also by then abolished.[1]

The result was that when mobilization was completed in 1914—and it was achieved quickly and smoothly thanks to the preparatory work done by General Joffre after 1911—nearly two million trained men could be called to the colours. This force, and the skilful strategy of Joffre, were the main reasons for the 'miracle of the Marne' in 1914. There was not to be a

---

[1] Cf. J. Hampden Jackson: *Jean Jaurès* (1943), pp. 137 ff.; E. Lavisse: op. cit., Vol. VIII, p. 284 f.; and cf. above, Chapter IV, pp. 152 f., and below, p. 208n. The law of 1913 provided for three years' service in the active Army followed by eleven years in its reserves; then for seven years in the territorial army followed by seven years in its reserves. Thus the High Command had some direct control over all Frenchmen between twenty and forty-eight. This arrangement prevailed until 1923.

THE MODERN CHALLENGE

second Sedan—until 1940. France had survived: but only just, and with immense losses of both blood and soil, of which only the soil could be recovered.

It is not within the scope of this study to examine the events of the war years, but only to estimate their impact on French government and French political life. Her northern provinces were invaded, her industrial areas ravaged by fifty-two months of unbroken warfare. Mines, factories, cities and farms were left in ruins. Her direct war-expenditure was estimated at some 150,000,000,000 francs. She lost nearly one and a half million men. Her birth-rate was still further diminished by war's upheaval. In short, all her pre-war problems, industrial and demographic, had been intensified and none of them had been solved. Yet even these losses and the consequent exhaustion would have been deemed worth it, if one thing had been gained: absolute national security—irrefrangible guarantees that she would not be in danger of such calamities again. To ensure this, no less than speedy reparation of the ravages of serving as the main western battlefield, all her post-war policy was inevitably directed. French politics and policy during the inter-war years have been too often misunderstood by interpreting them mainly or even entirely in terms of the peace-settlement. It is one evil consequence of studying history in periods which begin with a peace-settlement. They are comprehensible only in terms of the war as well as of the peace—of the experience baldly outlined above, and the consequent resolve that the same should never happen again, as well as of the national obsession with preserving the 1919 *status quo* in Europe and zenophobic hatred of the *Boche*.

But what, meantime, of the political repercussions of the ordeal inside France? How was the Third Republic affected in its spirit, working and conventions by the necessities of fighting the war?

The changing internal balance of social forces was, as in most other belligerent countries, speeded up by the war. Because France was not liable to starvation by naval blockade, and the demand for feeding the country had to be met primarily by French agriculture despite great shortage of labour, it was a period of prosperity for the peasants not within the battle-zone itself. But heavy industry and mining developed fast, and France emerged from the war, and from post-war reconstruction, a more highly industrialized nation. A hundred milliards of francs were spent on reconstruction of the devastated areas, and the recovery of Alsace and Lorraine augmented France's industrial resources and her industrial population. Her industrial man-power, even more than her farm labour, was supplemented by foreign immigrants, on the scale already described.[1]

With the growth of industry, the inner tension between industrial oligarchy and industrial workers assumed more front-rank importance in French politics. At the same time, the position of the middle and professional classes was depressed by the war. The broadest contrast between pre-war and post-war France was the replacement of dynastic and clericalist issues by economic and financial issues. The growing power of the banks and trusts on one hand, of the Socialist, Communist and trade union movements on the other, forced problems which had previously been latent or secondary enough to be ignored or tackled piecemeal, into the centre of the political stage. The reluctance or inability of the parties given power by the existing constitutional arrangements to tackle these problems led to a long series of proposals for the reform of the constitution—some of them a revival of pre-war schemes. They also led to consideration of new principles of taxation and financial policy, which brought into the open forum of public debate the underlying conflict of economic interest between property-owners and wage-earners. At every stage these issues linked up closely with issues of foreign policy; and the second main feature of post-war France is the constant interaction between domestic and foreign affairs. This had been not uncommon be-

---

[1] Cf. above, Chapter II, p. 46. On the economic and social effects of the war on French life, see D. W. Brogan: op. cit., pp. 511-34; and the specialist studies of Arthur Fontaine: *French Industry during the War* (1927), and of W. F. Ogburn and W. Jaffé: *The Economic Development of Post-War France* (1929).

fore 1914. It became a dominant characteristic after 1918.[1] The climax of this convergence of threats—the internal threat to civil order and political stability from social tensions, and the external threat to national security from the resurgence of Germany and the breakdown of international peace—was reached in 1936. The foreign-aided *Cagoulard* conspiracy was symbolic. For these reasons, just as the turn of the century had been the climax of conflicts in the first half of the Republic's history, so 1936 was the climax of conflicts in the second half.

There is even a similarity of pattern between the events of these years of crescendo, 1905 and 1936. Each begins with a political scandal—the Panama scandal and the Dreyfus case corresponding to the Stavisky scandal of 1934. Each crisis produced street riots and demonstrations, especially in Paris. Each was tackled by a belated rallying of the parties of the Left to 'save the Republic'—the *Bloc des Gauches* in 1905 and the *Front Populaire* in 1936. Each domestic crisis coincided with a climacteric in foreign affairs—the Anglo-French Entente in 1904 and the German re-militarization of the Rhineland in 1936. Each was accompanied by the formulation (again belatedly) of a comprehensive programme of social and economic reforms, doomed to fragmentary fulfilment. The whole history of the Third Republic was dominated by the curious rhythm of one supreme crisis every generation—in the five years before 1875, before 1905 and before 1940.

The nature of the 'modern challenge' to French democracy can best be examined by considering the circumstances and the response to the last beat of this rhythm, in 1936. But it can only be fully understood in the light of the connexions and transitions between these three great crises. The ground common to all is the challenge of war to national security, and the repercussions of the experience of war on the national outlook and institutions. The transition from one crisis to the other is due to the changing balance of social forces inside France—this bal-

---

[1] These constitutional and financial reforms are discussed below, pp. 184 ff. and 192 ff. Cf. Pierre Renouvin: *The Forms of War Government in France* (1927); and G. Jèze and H. Truchy: *The War Finance of France* (1927).

ance itself being deeply affected by the preparation and ordeal of war. Parliamentary institutions survived in France by means of a perpetual tight-rope performance. The sudden swings from Right to Left, the lurches and hesitations which so alarmed her friends, were often but the signs of the skill of Marianne in keeping her balance. The defensive posture into which French democracy was so often thrown was a consequence of the same necessities. The Maginot Line was but the military version of a wider mental outlook and a general set of national conditions, of which the 'form of government that divided Frenchmen least' was the political expression and the neglect of timely social reforms was the economic expression. It is less remarkable that *la gueuse*—as her enemies called Marianne—should have been at last strangled by them when she fell in 1940, than that she should have been able to sustain her performance for so long, and after each stumble had been able to dust herself down and continue on her precarious way.

Political Problems 1918-40

Given a world of growing industrialism, fresh tensions between capital and labour, a speedier tempo of events, what self-adjustments did democracy in France attempt? It was *a priori* unlikely that constitutional arrangements made in the peculiar circumstances of the eighteen-seventies and only slightly revised since, should be appropriate to the new conditions of the post-war years. This was apparent to many leading French thinkers and politicians, and from time to time proposals for constitutional, political and administrative reform were mooted either in parliament or in public discussion. Extremely few of these ever reached the statute book.

Extension of the vote to women was frequently proposed. There was a small suffragette movement. The Chamber even agreed on occasions, but the Senate regularly voted against it. It was left to the Provisional Government of 1944 to give votes to women in the first French general elections after the defeat of Germany. So long as the Right had little faith in universal suffrage, the Left feared clericalist influence over women voters, and all party organizations were inclined to resist any change which might upset their constituency committees, little could be achieved. French devotion to the family and the legal traditions of the Roman paterfamilias equally militated against separate political power for husband and wife.

Schemes for proportional representation were likewise frequently put forward, and in 1919 one half-hearted experiment of the kind was attempted. It was combined with the second experiment in *scrutin de liste* rather than *scrutin uninominal*. The larger unit of the *département* was made the voting area, in which electors chose not merely between rival candidates for their own *arrondissement* but instead for rival lists of candidates drawn up by the party organizations. In 1911 a parliamentary committee of the Chamber had been set up to make recommendations, and the change was supported by groups on the extreme Right and extreme Left. The arguments used in its favour were that it would drive the smaller groups into forming party organizations, that it would tend to emphasize issues of general national policy as against local and sectional interests and pressures, and would obviate the bother and possible corruption of a second ballot. It was opposed on the grounds that it would unduly strengthen the grip of party caucus over the candidate, and by consolidating groups would make a governmental majority still more difficult to attain and to keep. The following year Poincaré adopted a draft law, based on the scheme of transferable votes suggested by the mathematician-politician, Painlevé The Opposition, headed by Jaurès, defeated the proposal in the Chamber by 497 votes against 91. The attempted compromise was so complicated that the scheme was shelved when the Senate voted against it.

In 1919 a very restricted version of the scheme was put into practice, whereby proportional representation only began to apply at the second ballot, that is when there was no clear party majority in a *département* on the first ballot. Where there was, that party got all the seats. The result was to give a great advantage to electoral discipline—which happened at the time to be much stronger on the Right than on the Left. The fissure of Communism was developing within the Socialist Party, and the Radicals feared close co-operation with the Socialists. The elections gave a large majority to the *Bloc National*, including most parties to the right of the Socialists, of which the common motives were fear of Communism after the Bolshevik Revolution of 1917 and severity towards Germany. The elections of 1924 gave a similarly sweeping majority to the *Cartel des Gauches*, because by then the party organization of the Left was the better. Experience seemed to show that the existing arrangement might group parties for elections but not for the forming of governments. Its complexity made it unpopular, and after several tinkerings it was swept away with *scrutin de liste* in 1927.[1]

Even the procedure of voting was questioned and reconsidered from time to time. It was 1913 before really secret ballot was ensured. Only after the law of that year could the voter retire into a cubicle to place his paper in an envelope. This change had been repeatedly blocked by the Senate. The system of second ballot, to which French democracy remained remarkably faithful, was nearly abolished in 1932 by the parties of the Right. It enabled the formation of electoral 'cartels', whereby groups could bargain beforehand to support at the second ballot whichever was the more successful at the first, in order to preclude their common rivals. The Radicals and Socialists frequently used this device: but since the bargain was again limited to electioneering and did not involve mutual support later inside parliament it was argued that it helped to produce a hiatus between the wishes of the electors and the party manœuvres in parliament. But where so many small

---

[1] For further details of the debates on proportional representation, see E. Lavisse: op. cit., Vol. VIII, pp. 269-71, 275-84; A. Ésmein: op. cit., Vol. II, pp. 330-52. For the text of the Law of 12 July 1919, establishing proportional representation, see Duguit, Monnier and Bonnard, op. cit.: pp. 368-71. It was modified by the Laws of 15 March 1924 (ibid., p. 380), and of 8 April 1924 (ibid., p. 383), and was repealed by the Law of 21 July 1927 (ibid., pp. 386-9). A form of proportional representation was adopted for the first general elections after liberation—the elections to the National Constituent Assembly in October 1945.

THE MODERN CHALLENGE 187

groups existed, the stimulus it gave to even partial coalition probably produced more good than harm.[1]

Apart from these slight changes, the drift of all constitutional adjustment reaffirmed rather than weakened the power of the elected assemblies against both the executive power on one hand and the electorate on the other. The President's power was progressively weakened during the first half of the Republic by the Macmahon crisis of 1877, the Wilson scandal connected with Jules Grévy which led to Grévy's resignation in 1887, and the election of Carnot to succeed him. The first three Presidents had been forced out of office, and Carnot was chosen on Clemenceau's advice—'Vote for the stupidest'—as a deliberate rejection of Jules Ferry who was too positive a character to suit the parties or the country. 'Thiers had been chosen as the greatest living French statesman; Macmahon as the most honourable French soldier; Grévy had been elected in 1879 because of what he had said in 1848; Carnot was elected in 1887 because of what his grandfather had done in 1793.'[2] Weak successors like Loubet and Fallières had reduced the office to an impotence from which it was only temporarily saved by the sensational election of Poincaré in 1913. Once more expressive of the foreign situation as much as of domestic politics, his election in spite of Clemenceau's opposition and the Radical majority in power, meant that in future the President would represent a compromise choice between parties rather than the party majority at the moment of election. Poincaré's resolve to strengthen the power of his new office was

---

[1] The constitutional Law of 30 November 1875 (Article 5) had laid down 'Le vote est secret'. The Law of 29 July 1912 laid down new and much more elaborate provisions for ensuring absolute privacy and complete secrecy for the voter: cf. Duguit, Monnier and Bonnard: op. cit., p. 354 ff. for its text; and A. Ésmein: op. cit., Vol. II, p. 354 ff. for a commentary on it. The Law of 31 March 1914 (ibid., p. 362 ff.) made still more provisions to prevent corruption during elections. On the 'second ballot'. cf. above, Chapter II, pp. 93 f.; and see A. Ésmein: op. cit., Vol. II, p. 327 ff.

[2] Cf. D. W. Brogan: op. cit., p. 198. See also ibid., pp. 445-6, 568-9, 584-5.

expressed in his message to the two chambers. 'The diminishing of executive power is in accord with the wishes of neither the Chamber nor the country.' But although he was accused of interfering over-vigorously in the government of Briand who succeeded him as Prime Minister, his example was followed by only one of his successors—Millerand—with decisive results. He compelled Briand to resign in 1922, openly opposed the *Cartel des Gauches*, and supported the *Bloc National* in the general elections of 1924. When Herriot, as leader of the triumphant Cartel, refused to assume responsibility with Millerand in office, he was forced out in the same way as the first four Presidents of the Republic. Doumergue and Doumer who followed exerted considerable influence on governmental composition because of the frequency of ministerial crises and their own personal tact. But the positive leadership and executive strength which French democracy so much needed could not consistently come from the man in the *Élysée*.

Proposals to strengthen the Presidency by direct popular election on the American model, instead of by the two chambers, met with no response. More frequent and persuasive arguments that the President (or the government) should be given the power to dissolve the Chamber and appeal to the country, on the English model, were equally rebuffed. M. André Tardieu pleaded for such a change—which would indeed have been revolutionary in the Third Republic, since it would have undercut the very basis of parliamentary sovereignty and control over the executive. Doumergue, in September 1934, put the proposal for giving the Prime Minister the personal right to dissolve the Chamber in the forefront of his schemes for strengthening the executive power and preventing so many cabinet crises. Raymond Poincaré lamented the lapsing of the Presidential right of dissolution. Léon Blum argued, in his *La Réforme gouvernementale* and elsewhere, for the strengthening and stabilizing of the executive power. So men of experience of all parties were aware of the defects of the working system: yet no definitive move was ever made to remedy them.[1]

[1] Cf. A. Tardieu: *L'Heure de la Décision* (1934), and the abbreviated version of it, *La Réforme de l'État* (1934), and *Métier Parlementaire*

If one reason for this is the interest of most practising politicians and most political parties in evading any venture into the unknown which might prejudice their existing powers, another is the facility with which governments could resort to rule by decree instead of by formal legislation. In times of emergency—which were so frequent after 1914—the constitutional *pouvoir réglementaire* of the President, and the juristic doctrine of his wielding the power to make *règlements de nécessité*, combined to make virtual government by decree familiar enough to Frenchmen. Parliament was prorogued from August to December 1914, and even when it met regularly, decrees went on being issued freely to speed up necessary and urgent measures. The habit lasted through the inter-war years, and was extended by parliamentary willingness to grant plenary powers for specific purposes: although when Blum in 1937 and Chautemps in 1938 asked for such plenary powers to issue

(1937); A. Werth: *The Destiny of France* (1937), p. 80; L. Blum: *La Réforme Gouvernementale* (1936), Chapter II and *passim*; R. Poincaré: *How France is Governed* (1913), p. 180; A. Ésmein: op. cit., Vol. II, p. 180 ff.

Prévost-Paradol, in his *La France Nouvelle* of 1868, described (p. 142 ff.) the right of dissolution as the necessary counterpoise to parliamentary government, but regarded a constitutional monarch, raised above parties, as the best repository for this right, and an upper chamber as a valuable check on its exercise by the Government. In 1875 the Senate was given this function of, as it were, arbitrating between President and Chamber in the event of a deadlock leading to dissolution (Law of 25 February 1875, Article 5). When the Senate tended more and more to side with the Chamber against the President, this provision in fact helped to block the President's use of his power of dissolution and so helped to increase Presidential impotence. A further check (instituted in 1878) was that certain powers of the President lapsed during the interval between a dissolution and the first session of a new Chamber, as a guarantee against a *coup d'état*. But all such checks were in practice unnecessary, since no President after Macmahon in 1877 ventured to dissolve the Chamber.

Tardieu suggested, in addition to giving Government and Senate the right of dissolution, equal political rights for women and a system of referendum (*La Réforme de l'État*): these ideas were adopted only in 1945.

financial decrees, they were defeated. The chief reason was the extent to which Laval had abused the power in 1935—issuing some 500 decrees aimed at economies and deflation.[1]

But before 1937, parliament on occasion willingly gave authority to the President to make rules for certain purposes, as in 1926, to enable the overhaul of the administration. Jurists argued at great length as to the constitutional theory and implications of such action: but in general all such powers were supposed to be controlled by parliament either through a specific grant for a fixed period, and for a special purpose; or through later ratification of the rules so made; or ultimately through normal parliamentary control over the ministry. This last was so effective, with interpellations and the regular facility for overthrowing a ministry, that even drastic powers could never be said to carry the government beyond the reach of parliamentary authority, as did the famous Article 48 of the constitution of the German Weimar Republic.

If parliament as a whole amply preserved its powers against both electorate and executive, what of the relations between the two halves of parliament itself, Senate and Chamber? Here the basic fact was normal agreement between the two houses. Despite the original intentions behind the Senate as an institution, and the very different modes of election of the two houses, there was seldom any real clash between them. When measures passed by the Chamber were turned down by the Senate, it was as often as not because the Chamber had allowed the measure to pass knowing that the Senate could be relied upon to block it. Leading figures flitted easily from Chamber to Senate, and party formations were broadly akin in both houses, despite differences of label.

It is true that the very existence of a second house served as an additional obstacle to new legislation. It is true that the

[1] Many of Laval's decrees had in fact little to do with finance: such as the decree prohibiting foreigners living in France from keeping carrier pigeons! Conversely, he showed little enthusiasm in applying by decree the laws against the Fascist and semi-Fascist leagues, and suppressed only one—the *Camelots du Roi*; cf. A. Werth: op. cit., p. 152 and Chapter XII.

THE MODERN CHALLENGE

Senate in many ways served as a Conservative force, as it had always been intended to do. It is true, above all, that the Senate before 1884 represented the peasants and the villages in absurd excess over the larger towns, and that after 1884 it represented most favourably the small market towns of 10,000 to 15,000 inhabitants. By its nature it emphasized provincialism. Yet the system worked as most Frenchmen, or at least most politically effective French people, wanted it to work. The best evidence of this is the moderate change effected in 1884 and 1919, the absence of serious clashes between the two houses until 1936, and the almost total lack of any vigorous movement to reform or abolish the Senate in modern times. The tact of Senators explains much and reveals much. As Professor Vaucher puts it: 'Senators were given privileges equal to those of the Deputies, except that they must take no initiative in matters of finance. However, they refrained from using them fully, applied the brake with moderation, avoided entering into open conflict with the other house, and submitted to the will of the country whenever it was clearly expressed.' Moreover, where the popular theoretical assumption is that the 'sovereignty of the people' and 'universal suffrage' must prevail, the more democratically elected house inevitably triumphed over the house which was indirectly and less frequently elected. Nevertheless, in the two questions of finance and foreign policy the Senate took an increasing interest and assumed greater importance during the inter-war years.[1]

This general complacency about the existing system and this general preference for changelessness, compromise and half-measures, go far towards explaining the inertia of the Third Republic in dealing with the social and economic changes of the inter-war years. As that shrewd commentator, Paul Guérin, expressed it, 'The regime is paradoxical, Conservative in purse, revolutionary at heart; extremist and idealist in its programmes, opportunist and moderate in its action; admiring great men but refusing them power; captivated by eloquence and words,

[1] Cf. Paul Vaucher: *Post-War France* (1934), Chapter I, p. 29. Léon Blum and many Socialists were in favour of abolishing the Senate, but did not make it a prime issue.

but freely changing its orators in a dizzy merry-go-round; little preoccupied with essential problems but generally solving them at the last minute: the Republic *à la française* has nothing quite like it in the world. . . . It lives by suppleness and adroitness. It is a regime of perpetual deals; one might say of compromise, if this word were not too "compromising". It is the system of government of an independent, rich and happy people.'[1]

Economic and Social Problems, 1918-40

The most controversial of these post-war economic issues was that of currency and finance. Before the war, Caillaux had proposed a moderate income tax—a sensational innovation in Republican France. It came to nought then, and France went through three years of war before she at last instituted this method of paying for the war which to most other countries had long seemed obvious. The tax imposed in 1917, complicated and mild in application, affected little the actual financing of the war. What divided parties most in the post-war years, when the tax was kept on, was whether it should be moderated or made steeper in incidence. The Socialists and Communists favoured it as against the indirect taxation so beloved of the more orthodox, and even proposed a capital levy as well. The more Conservative parties opposed it on grounds of 'fiscal inquisition'—the old fear of excessive government power and the State's gaining overmuch control over the family and individual income. Evasion of taxation, among all classes but especially by the peasants, became widespread and rampant. Again, the practical effect was a half-hearted compromise typical of the parliamentary Republic at its least virile —retention of income tax but weak application of it against the most powerful *blocs* in the electorate.[2]

This humanly comprehensible but nationally reprehensible

[1] Cf. Paul Guérin: *Le Problème Français* (1939), p. 43 f.

[2] Cf. D. W. Brogan: op. cit., p. 516 ff.; Paul Vaucher: op. cit., p. 104 ff.; and the specialist studies of R. H. Haig: *The Public Finances of Post-War France* (1929); and J. H. Rogers: *The Process of Inflation in France, 1914-27* (1929).

aversion to income tax, combined with affection for indirect taxes such as customs, excise, estate and stamp duties, dominated French finance during the inter-war years. Since the war could be paid for only by taxation, loans, inflation or reparations, the less reliance that was placed on taxation the more frequent had to be recourse to the second and third methods, and the more insistent were demands for the fourth. In this way financial policy was doubly connected with foreign policy: for not only did insistence on Germany's full payment of reparations force a rift between France and her main ally, Britain, and result in the French occupation of the Ruhr in 1923; but also the excessive recourse to short-term loans and unbalanced budgets linked public confidence, and therefore the franc, with governmental prestige at home and national prestige abroad. Even financial stability was a function of national security, and not vice versa.

Commercial policy reflected similarly the internal balance of social interests, and was closely linked with foreign policy. Largely because of her financial policy and her reliance on indirect taxation for revenue, but also because of the strength of peasant and agricultural interests, France remained a strongly protectionist and even mercantilist country. Before the war there had been two distinct tariffs, a general and a minimum. Governmental control of imports during the war made it possible for duties to be imposed by ministerial decree, and the level of tariffs varied a great deal in the immediate postwar years. In 1926, parliament decreed a general increase of 30 per cent. Again out-of-date methods and crude adjustments were preferred to systematic overhaul, because of the conflict of groups and classes. Industrial needs for freer imports were subordinated to agricultural protection and even subsidy. Commercial agreements with other countries for the lowering of tariffs became frequently a diplomatic instrument.[1]

---

[1] Cf. George Peel: *The Economic Policy of France* (1937); Paul Einzig: *France's Crisis* (1934), which is an appeal for a timely economic overhaul as part of urgent national regeneration, and which acquires poignancy in the light of later events; cf. also J. H. Rogers: op. cit.

Problems of labour organization and social security for the workers raised their heads immediately after the war. During the war trade unions had been growing fast. In Tours, for example, the number of unionists rose from 2,000 to 10,000 between 1914 and 1920, and total membership was about two million by 1920. New national federations had been formed, such as the federation of railwaymen. The metal-workers' unions throve on the munitions industry. The numerous strikes were fought mainly over wage-increases and working conditions. Apart from incidents like the large and serious strike in the Paris munitions factories in March 1918, which was anyhow started in spite of many of the unions, the unions were on tolerably good terms with the Government. Again a working compromise was reached in face of the enemy. In 1917, arbitration of strikes was made compulsory. In return, Clemenceau passed an eight-hour bill. Workers' delegates (shop-stewards) served as a link between Government and workers in the factories. By 1919 collective bargaining had been legalized. The greatest new force of cleavage and disruption came from without—again a matter of foreign affairs: it was the reverberations of the Bolshevik Revolution in Russia in 1917. Here was the 'modern challenge' in its most acute social form.

Its effects on the Left have been already noted. Its effects on the Right and the Centre were no less disruptive. The idea of a *cordon sanitaire* against Bolshevism in eastern Europe was largely French in origin, and it was Clemenceau in December 1919 who spoke of *un fil de fer barbelé*. Left-wing and organized Labour movements at home were now regarded with a new horror, and the large loans which French financiers and *bourgeoisie* had sunk in the Tsarist government left these classes permanently fearful of the spread of Bolshevism to France. Indeed all French parties save the extreme Left now felt that they had two enemies in Europe—the traditional national enemy, Germany, and the new social enemy, the Third International or Comintern, operating from Moscow. Political attitudes and policies tended to swing from one bias to the other, according to whether Germany or Bolshevism was regarded at that moment as 'Public Enemy Number One'. Before the rise

THE MODERN CHALLENGE

of Hitler to power in Germany, this ambiguity mattered little in foreign policy. After his rise, French policy as guided by the Right-wing and Centre governments of Barthou and Laval, made the Franco-Soviet Treaty. Republican France had as little in common, ideologically, with Bolshevik Russia as she had had with Tsarist Russia: and all her relations with Russia were dictated ultimately by her position *vis-à-vis* Germany.[1]

But internal politics were another matter. Anti-Republican forces which had learned to put up with the parliamentary regime so long as it had a natural bias towards Conservatism and the strict protection of private property now merged their anti-Communism into their anti-Republicanism, and began to clamour for a more authoritarian regime. To the old Royalist, anti-Republican movements such as the *Action française*, dating from 1905, was added the *Croix de Feu* movement of Colonel de la Rocque (an ex-service men's organization founded in 1927, which 'during 1934 became the rallying-point for the Conservative youth of France'): with it were linked the *Volontaires Nationaux* and the *Camelots du Roi*. There was the *Jeunesses Patriotes*, formed in 1924 under Pierre Taittinger out of the post-war remnants of Déroulède's old *Ligue des Patriotes* which played so important a part in the Boulanger and Dreyfus affairs. Its official aim was declared to be 'to defend the National Territory against the dangers of internal revolution, to increase public prosperity and to improve our public institutions'. Even more openly Bonapartist in sentiment was the *Solidarité Française*, founded significantly in 1933 by the perfumier Coty. Its paper, *Ami du Peuple* and its slogan 'France for the French' purported to appeal to a combination of ultra-democratic and nationalistic sentiment as against parliamentary Republicanism, the Jews and the Communists. Its leader after Coty's death in 1934 was Jean Renaud, and its recruits came chiefly from the rowdy younger members

---

[1] Cf. above, Chapter II, pp. 51–53, and Chapter III, pp. 71–74; Arnold Wolfers: *Britain and France between two Wars* (1940), p. 132 ff.; D. J. Saposs: *The Labour Movement in Post-War France* (1931), *passim*.

of the *petite bourgeoisie* and a few discontented workers.[1]

The leagues have been mentioned in descending order of intelligence and importance, the latter two being important only as potential 'storm-trooper' formations, which together probably numbered between 6,000 and 8,000 in Paris and could thus have provided the physical force element for a *coup d'état*. But the brains and guidance came from the first two—the *Action française* of Charles Maurras and Léon Daudet, and the *Croix de Feu* of la Rocque. Taken altogether, they provided all the elements of propaganda, private army and *mystique* which in Germany, Italy and elsewhere produced Fascist revolutions. And between 1934 and 1936, all the circumstances favourable to a Fascist revolution co-existed in France. They are the supreme crisis-years of the Third Republic—even more critical, probably, than the days of the Dreyfus affair.

The Stavisky scandal which broke in the winter of 1933-4 brought the crisis to a head. Since the end of 1930 France had had ten different ministries, and the musical-chairs atmosphere of parliamentary politics had become absurd. The economic slump had hit France later than other countries, and unemployment-figures were increasing alarmingly. Government had seemed paralysed, and did little to counter the slump. Hitler had come into power in Germany. There were reasons enough for popular unrest and disorder apart from the Stavisky exposures of corruption in the very heart of government itself. It became apparent at once that Stavisky could not have carried on his shady and crooked financial operations for the previous six years with impunity had he not been protected by authority —and this authority included politicians, judiciary, police, as

---

[1] The best analysis and account of these leagues and their share in French politics during the inter-war years are in Alexander Werth's two books: *France in Ferment* (1934), and *The Destiny of France* (1937). They were later reprinted along with *The Last Days of Paris* as *The Twilight of France, 1933-40* (1942). See also a Communist's account in Maurice Thorez: *France To-day and the People's Front* (1936); a brief summary in D. W. Brogan: op. cit., pp. 669-722; or A. Zévaès: *Histoire de la Troisième République* (1939), Chapter XIX. Every student of France owes a great debt to Mr. Werth.

well as the business world itself. The result was the organization of demonstrations against both government and parliament by the Right-wing leagues—especially the *Croix de Feu*—on 6 February 1934.[1]

The only remedy which the Daladier government could find was to resign: which it did on 7 February. Doumergue formed his ministry which was to tide France over for the rest of the year. On 9 February the Communists staged protest demonstrations, and three days later the C.G.T. and C.G.T.U. combined to call a twenty-four hour general strike, to rouse the working class against 'the Fascist menace', and to warn off the Fascist and semi-Fascist leagues. The strike extended beyond Paris to most of the other big towns and many of the smaller towns. It marked the drawing together of Socialists and Communists against the common danger, and by July they had signed a United Action Pact 'to defend democratic liberties' by launching a joint campaign of public meetings. At the same time the Radical Gaston Bergery organized a *Front Commun*, designed to appeal to the 'non-proletarian elements of the population', and to attack the 'industrial and financial oligarchy'. There had been an abortive *Front populaire* of the Radicals and Socialists in the general elections of 1932, partly as a result of which the Radicals had gained forty-eight new seats and the Socialists seventeen. This success was remembered in 1936, and again the two parties made an electoral pact to withdraw their candidates in the second ballot in favour of the most favoured Left candidate: and this time the pact was joined by the Communists as well. After the experience of the February riots, and the authoritarianism of the Doumergue, Flandin and Laval governments of 1934 and 1935, the whole Left was able to rally and make a concerted effort at last, to 'save the Republic'. In the demonstrations on Bastille Day 1935 the forces lined up in almost symbolic shape: a joint procession of Radicals, Socialists and Communists, some 300,000 and more strong, took place at one end of the town: a *Croix de Feu* parade, some 30,000 strong, at the other. The general

[1] On the Stavisky case, see A. Werth: *France in Ferment*, Chapters IV-VI.

elections of 1936 were held two months after Hitler had marched into the Rhineland. They were fought on the main issue of the Popular Front.

The programme of the *Front Populaire*, which claimed to be in the direct revolutionary tradition and to be 'directly inspired by the watch-words of 14 July', was grouped under four heads. First, the 'defence of freedom', which meant the dissolution of the Fascist leagues, purification of the Press and public life generally, and defence of trade-union liberties. Secondly, the 'defence of peace', which meant support for the League of Nations and the principles of collective security, and for disarmament. Thirdly, 'economic demands', which included systematic tackling of unemployment, reduction of the working week, old-age pensions, a programme of public works, a Wheat Marketing Board, and nationalization of the Bank of France. Finally, 'financial purification', which meant establishing a War Pensions Fund, a more steeply graded income tax, and more severe measures against tax-evasion. In a word —all the social and economic reforms which had been clamouring for attention since 1919 or earlier were to be tackled after the civil strife of 1934, and after Germany had seized the essential spring-board for her next attack on France.[1] If the Popular Front experiment failed, it was not and could not be entirely the responsibility of the Popular Front Government itself. The 'modern challenge' was taken up at five minutes to twelve, thanks to the dilatory politics which were the product of a divided national community and a compromise parliamentary regime. That the challenge was taken up with such fine spirit at so late an hour is indicative of the life that still survived in the French democratic ideal. The Popular Front failed, in the sense that it lasted barely two years and gave way, by uneasy stages, to the Radical Government of Daladier in April 1938. It did not fail, in the sense that every reform carried out by it—except the institution of the forty-hour week which had not been specified in the Popular Front programme,

[1] On the Popular Front Programme and how much of it was achieved, see A. Werth: *The Destiny of France*, Chapters XIV-XX. And cf. below, Appendix II, B.

but only in the C.G.T. plan—survived in France, far into the Vichy regime.

What were these reforms? First, in time and even in importance, was the Matignon Agreement between the C.G.T. and the employers' federation, the *Confédération générale de la Production Française*. Blum himself presided over their joint conference at the Hotel Matignon on 6 June, to settle the stay-in strikes which had broken out that month 'to push the Government'. The main points of the Agreement were recognition of collective bargaining contracts, an all-round wage-increase ranging from 7 per cent to 15 per cent, and the setting up of workers' delegations to deal direct with factory managers. Léon Jouhaux, General Secretary of the C.G.T., hailed it as 'the greatest victory which the working class has won in its whole history'. The Agreement was confirmed by the Collective Contracts Act of June 1936. Secondly, labour conditions were improved by legislation: the forty-hour week and compulsory holidays with pay.[1] There was much substance in the criticisms of these measures, that they further aggravated France's industrial weakness and shortage of man-power *vis-à-vis* Germany, at a time when the relative strength of the two countries was becoming of urgent relevance in foreign affairs. Thirdly, the *Office du Blé* was set up, to eliminate speculation and achieve stability of prices in wheat, by acting as a kind of marketing-board administered by representatives of all the main interests concerned, including consumers. Finally, the Bank of France was brought more directly under Government control, as already described: and so too were the armaments works. The attempts to dissolve the Fascist leagues and purify the Press were only partly successful: the leagues tended to form again under new names, and the Press laws did not eliminate corruption and violent scurrility from the Press. But both attempts showed a concentration on the right problems which was something new and refreshing in French politics between the wars.

The Popular Front experiment neither failed nor was it over-

[1] On the C.G.T. attitude to Matignon and its 'Plan' for the 'Renovation of French economy', see Léon Jouhaux: *La C.G.T.* (1937).

thrown. It was smothered by the looming clouds of international crisis. The Rhineland, Abyssinia and Spain raised in turn problems of policy which transcended and distracted attention from domestic reform. The drift to war overwhelmed everything else, and forced France, in a different field, into her old *débrouillage*—her bad habit of hand-to-mouth half-measures which introduced so much ineffectiveness and frustration into her national response to the 'modern challenge'. Half a Maginot Line was not necessarily better than no Line: nor 'non-intervention' and 'appeasement' an adequate substitute for aeroplanes and tanks.

The International Position of France 1918-40

As the neighbour of a probable enemy country which was stronger than herself, France was driven after 1918 to an incessant search for alliances. The 'official' theory of the Covenant of the League, as expounded by President Wilson and favoured by Great Britain, was that it replaced the pre-1914 system of great alliances and 'balance of power' by a system of collective security and an all-embracing 'concert of Powers'. France valued the League chiefly as a preventive of war, in the sense of preserving intact the Treaty settlement of 1919. She had little faith in it as a solvent of international grievances, and all parties agreed that France should seek more concrete support in a system of 'buttressing' alliances. France, like Britain, was concerned to prevent war if she could: unlike Britain, she was equally concerned to ensure victory in war if war should come to pass. She wanted security not only *against* war but *in* war.[1]

---

[1] I owe the gist of the present argument to the admirable work of Arnold Wolfers: *Britain and France between two Wars*. On the earlier stages of foreign policy after 1919, see F. L. Schuman: *War and Diplomacy in the French Republic* (1931); and on the special conflicts between Britain and France over the German problem, W. M. Jordan: *Great Britain, France and the German Problem, 1918-39* (1943).

On the forces most influential in moulding French policy from inside, see F. L. Schuman: op. cit.; W. d'Ormesson: *France* (1939); and Paul Allard: *Le Quai d'Orsay* (1938), and cf. above, Chapter II, pp. 55-59.

L'Organisation de la Paix remained her national, all-party objective throughout: and the differences in foreign policy between her successive governments depended on differences of emphasis as regards means, not on differences of direction or aim. Even Laval, in seeking appeasement of Italy and Germany, and de Brinon, in seeking positive *rapprochement* with Germany, were seeking the common aim of national security by means different from the predominant anti-German policies. It is not far from Geneva to Locarno or from Locarno to Stresa: and little further still, diplomatically, from Stresa to Munich.

In order to assess the connexion between French democratic ideas and her national policy in foreign affairs, the general structure of international relations after 1919 must be viewed as a whole. The pre-war dual system of alliances had gone, and neither a truly collective system nor a French diplomatic network had fully taken its place. Instead, there grew up a triangular structure of diplomatic relations, from which three different alliance-groups could at any time appear. It was this, more than any one national policy, which determined the constant uncertainty and tensions of the inter-war years in Europe.

In the West were the two democratic Powers of Britain and France, anti-revisionist in interests but not in concord as to foreign policy, save for a short period after 1924. In central Europe were Germany and Italy, each for different reasons a revisionist Power, hostile in spirit to the League and to the western democracies, after 1933 both Fascist and after 1936 in alliance. In the East, the Soviet Union, at first ostracized and hostile to all her western neighbours, but later emerging into open participation in European affairs. Relations between any two of these three groups inevitably affected the third. Any drawing together of the first two, as at Stresa or Munich, looked like an anti-Soviet bloc. Any *rapprochement* between the western democracies and Russia, as when Russia joined the League in 1934, meant 'encirclement' for Germany and to a less degree Italy. Any sign of German-Soviet co-operation, as at Rapallo in 1922 or in the Nazi-Soviet Pact of 1939, made the democracies fear a union of single-party states against democracy. Although each shift of these alignments was due to particular national policies, it equally meant that the foreign policy of the third side in the triangle was at that moment dictated by events. The result was twenty years of extreme political instability in Europe, and the emergence of a system of great alliances even more nerve-racking than in the years before 1914.

The situation was still further complicated—and here with particular effect in France—by the co-existence, alongside these national conflicts, of a social and ideological conflict. Each of the three groups came, by the nineteen-thirties, to represent a specific kind of political, social and economic regime, even a *Weltanschauung*, either Liberal, Fascist or Communist. These differences of social structure and outlook were not distinct, but overlapped, so that any two could contend that they had certain features in common. Thus arose 'ideological fronts', usually negative in label—the 'anti-Comintern Pact' for the 'defence of European civilization against Bolshevism': the 'anti-Fascist' coalition against aggressor nations: the denunciations of the 'imperialist pluto-democracies'. Each was a tune played according to the drift of affinities at any one moment. The result was peculiarly disruptive to the democracies: especially to that which was already internally split on other lines, the Third Republic. This nexus of continental and even world forces alone explains the acuteness of political conflicts in France of the nineteen-thirties.

Within this general framework French foreign policy passed through characteristic phases. In so far as the years 1919-23 were a phase of consolidation and attempted enforcement of the peace settlement, and the war against Bolshevism went on until 1921, and the final treaty between belligerents was the Treaty of Lausanne with Turkey in 1923, these first four years after the war may be regarded as essentially part of the period of peace-making. In France they saw the ascendancy of the *Bloc National* and the Right-wing nationalism of Poincaré. French policy remained, in many ways, indistinguishable from that followed by Clemenceau at the Paris Conference: the policy of 'making Germany pay' and 'keeping Germany down'.

But in another way the exit of Clemenceau in January 1920 is a crucial date in French foreign policy.

At the Conference of Paris Clemenceau had been placed on the horns of a dilemma. He had to choose between either exchanging the material fruits of victory over Germany—symbolized by French control of the Rhineland—for British and American guarantees: or holding on to material benefits at the cost of diplomatic isolation. He chose the former, and had he remained in power he would doubtless have continued to choose the former. He understood Great Britain and her policy in Europe much better than most Frenchmen, and he understood the alternative policies confronting France. Poincaré, whilst ostensibly continuing French policy towards Germany, fell between two stools as regards French relations with Britain. He could not retrieve the material benefits which Clemenceau had surrendered: and he lost contact with Britain, which he alienated by his policy of immediate alliances in eastern Europe—with Poland and the Little Entente—and above all by his occupation of the Ruhr in 1923. French policy was anxious not to 'sell out' to British—until 1936: but by choosing the British horn of the dilemma in 1919, Clemenceau had already virtually 'sold out' to British policy. That the American and British guarantees had been meanwhile repudiated does much to explain the self-help policy of Poincaré: but it made it no more possible for him to retract Clemenceau's choice.

The failure of Poincaré's policy, and the tremors it produced in British opinion and international confidence, bred the financial crisis of 1923-6. From these years emerged a new phase of French policy: the policy of Briand. The shift was represented in home affairs by the victory of the *Cartel des Gauches* in 1924, in Germany by the leadership of Stresemann, and diplomatically by the Locarno agreements. It was one of attempted reconciliation between the western and central blocs within the framework of a 'buttressed' League, during the period of Russian preoccupation with internal reconstruction. It was dictated as much by reaction against the Poincaré policy and by fear lest Britain should drift into the camp of the revisionists, as by any belief that Germany could be indefinitely placated without drastic revision of the settlement. Such a policy of cooperation harmonized with the growing internationalism of the Left and the coincidence that Left or moderate governments were also in power in Britain. Germany was allowed and even induced to enter the League in 1926.

It is during these years that the League itself had a profoundly disruptive effect on French opinion by sharpening the new divisions between Right and Left. The romantic hopes aroused by the League and the *mystique* of internationalism acted like a narcotic on the Left and disgusted the Right. Those sections of opinion which were now 'internationalized' were not easily won back to national effort and sacrifice. Those who were antagonized by the League were attracted more by the ultra-nationalist temper of the Fascist movements. French statesmen, more than those of any other nation, seized upon the lime-lit forum of Geneva to make speeches intended for home consumption. This *penchant*, to which Briand succumbed more than most, damaged the prestige of their own institutions at home—particularly the Chamber and Senate, where such speeches would often have been better made. When they were not made for home consumption, they tended to be vaguely idealistic and even mystical, as was described by André Maurois in his Foreword to Robert de Traz's book *The Spirit of Geneva*:

> Every year, during the first week in September, a great and sacred orator (such as was the late Père Briand or as is the Reverend Arthur Henderson) preaches before the Assembly of Nations a solemn sermon on the text of the Covenant. Then the Congregation sings its favourite psalms: Psalm 159, Disarmament-Security; Psalm 137, Must Politics, Gentlemen, have precedence over Economics? It is an excellent thing for the disbeliever to undergo Church discipline, for ceremonial of any kind lulls to sleep and calms the passions. . . . At Geneva the art of saying nothing has almost reached perfection.

In Geneva—the city of Calvin and Rousseau before it was the city of the League—the French Left found a spiritual home, where its own traditions were at ease.

Except for one day, Briand was at the *Quai d'Orsay* from April 1925 until January 1932. It was the counterpart to the reign of Delcassé a generation before. Briand was willing to go far, even in concessions to Germany, in order to harmonize French policy with British. He saw the problem of French national security in a world setting and not merely in a European setting: as witness the Briand-Kellogg Pact of 1928, his support for the League system as a whole, and his proposal of of what was erroneously called 'European Federal Union' in 1930. But if the policy ever had a chance of succeeding, it was certainly too late by 1930. In September of that year 107 National Socialists were elected to the German Reichstag, and the world economic crisis, bringing mass unemployment in its train, had already burst upon Europe.

The disorientation of French policy is shown by the rapid swings it took in face of the new crisis. It alternated between appeasement and defiance, between the policy to which Clemenceau and after him Briand committed France, and the alternative policy which Poincaré had tried to pursue. France pursued alternatives alternately. Laval held power throughout 1931, and resumed power after the assassination of Louis Barthou at Marseilles in 1934. Barthou stood for consolidation of France's network of alliances. Again he looked to Poland and the Little Entente; and to alliance with Soviet Russia, now becoming again a world power, through her entry into the League in 1934 and the Franco-Soviet Pact. He 'set out to forge a new and more powerful ring of Continental alliances around Germany with which to supplement the now insufficient "small ring" in central Europe and to balance the effects of Germany's impending rearmament'. Laval, on the other hand, sought solidarity with Italy through the 'Stresa Front' of 1935 and appeasement of Mussolini's ambitions in Abyssinia and Spain. Blum, confronted with the dilemma of the Spanish Civil War, clung to his last straw of co-operation with Britain and to the policy of 'non-intervention' in Spain.

The main feature of French foreign policy from 1936 onwards was its complete subservience to British policy. Her basic weakness was Hitler's control of the Rhineland. This not only gave him access to France's most vulnerable frontier, but prevented France from implementing her support for her eastern allies, Poland and the Little Entente, by direct action against Germany. Instead, she was driven to concern herself so much with her own defence that little effective help could be given elsewhere. She came therefore to depend on British support as the keystone of her foreign policy. The *Quai d'Orsay*, whatever its inclinations, could make no major move that was not correlated with the policy of the British Foreign Office. This became obvious at Munich, when the virtual merger of French and British policy was completed. France had separate and quite specific obligations to Czechoslovakia by her treaty of 1925. When the Czechs were first menaced in May 1938, M. Daladier assured them that France would fulfil these obligations. But in July Lord Runciman was sent to Prague without the prior agreement of the French, and Daladier, fearful of war, of internal divisions at home, and of doing anything to forfeit British support, followed the initiative of Mr. Neville Chamberlain. It was characteristic and almost symbolic that the French declaration of war on Germany in September 1939 came six hours after the British. In 1914 she had been at war with Germany a day earlier than Britain.[1]

But this post-1936 characteristic of French policy was only the most conspicuous manifestation of a fact which had haunted her since 1919: a fact which Sir Edward Grigg in his study of *British Foreign Policy* has called 'the overburdening of France'. France was driven by circumstances often beyond her own control to follow a policy and assume undertakings which were beyond her own capacity to fulfil. This overburdening was quite distinct from internal political weakness or social divisions: it was inherent in the whole structure of European relations after 1919. 'The main point is that France was not equal either in spirit or in military strength to the task of keeping Europe at peace, and that neither Britain nor the United States (the only powers which had the necessary resources)

---

[1] For a detailed account of the diplomatic relations of France with the other Powers in the period immediately before war, see F. L. Schuman: *Europe on the Eve, 1933-9* (1939); *The French Yellow Book (Diplomatic Documents, 1938–9)*. And cf. Sir Edward Grigg: *British Foreign Policy* (1944).

was ready to prevent German expansion and rearmament... and if anything was more ominous of trouble than the overburdening of France after 1919, it was the lack of Russian participation in the diplomatic arrangements designed to keep Germany disarmed.'

With the Nazi-Soviet Pact of 1939 and the Russian policy towards Poland, Finland and the Baltic States during the first two years of war, the triangle of diplomatic alignments turned one way up: it became a war of revisionist powers against the anti-revisionist. With the German attack on Russia in 1941, it turned quickly on to its other base and became a war of satisfied and peace-loving powers against Fascist aggression. The twin Anglo-Soviet and Franco-Soviet Treaties of 1942 and 1944 perpetuate that alignment, and attempt to project it far into the future.

All judgment of French policy, all criticism of the hesitations and fluctuations of parliamentary and national attitudes, and of French military weakness and errors of strategy between the two wars, must be made within the given limitations of this broader triangle of forces. Perhaps no Foreign Minister is ever a free agent, however secure his tenure of office and however unanimous the parliamentary support for his policy. But in the peculiar circumstances of European relations in these years, no Foreign Minister of France could enjoy even the normal amount of free agency. To her primarily, and at times alone, was left the task of preserving the peace settlement in Europe: the settlement on which not only her own security but the very existence of Poland, Czechoslovakia and the other succession states depended: and the security, too, as events were to prove, of Britain and the United States. If she failed it was not the failure of democracy or of the Third Republic.

But even if France could not have avoided German resurgence and rearmament, might she not have avoided defeat so rapid and complete as she suffered at Germany's hands in 1940? This further and secondary question raises the issue of responsibility for France's relative unpreparedness for modern war which was explored in great detail at the Riom Trials of 1942. The trials—originally demanded by Germany as a device for presenting France as a war-monger—were delayed until 1942. They were framed by Vichy to place responsibility for French defeat on the shoulders of the Republican politicians—Blum, Daladier and their colleagues in government between 1936 and 1939. The vigorous and eloquent defence put up by the accused showed that to a very large extent the blame rested on the General Staff and the High Command, of which Marshal Pétain and Admiral Darlan had been leading members. Riom became a dramatic battle between civilians and service chiefs, parliamentarians and militarists: a competition in mud-slinging, of which the civilians got so much the best that the trials were called off and left undecided. The main contentions of the Republicans—that the government had never failed to supply the service chiefs with all the men and material they asked, and that the social reforms carried out in 1936-7 had not interfered with the programme of rearmament laid down by the experts in defence, seemed to be amply borne out by the facts and figures. Perhaps the final truth is that for a nation of forty millions to have avoided defeat by a nation of seventy millions, it would have had to be extremely well prepared and equipped: and whatever the reason, France undoubtedly fell very far short of these requirements.[1]

Military and naval preparedness—conspicuously in an overburdened power such as France—cannot be intelligibly considered apart from policy and diplomacy. Had the Soviet Union been won as an active ally by 1939, or had the Rhine-

[1] Cf. Pierre Tissier: *The Riom Trial* (1942), and *Léon Blum before his Judges* (1943). In 1923, the period of compulsory military service was reduced from three years to eighteen months, and in 1928 to only one year. In 1928 the number of professional soldiers was increased by 50 per cent (to 106,000), and the conscription age raised again from twenty to twenty-one. Thus more reliance came to be placed on the standing Army than before 1914 (see above, p. 180). The first special credits for the Maginot Line were voted in December 1929. It was scheduled to be completed by 1935, to compensate for the shortage in French man-power between 1934-9 when the age-groups born between 1914-18 would be called up for service. These were computed to be only half the normal annual call-up of over 250,000.

land and the Czech fortresses been preserved as French outposts, the deficiencies of man-power and equipment might have been offset. And there is abundant testimony to the spirit of resolve with which the people of France grimly moved into the war in 1939. She was able to mobilize five million trained men, and her Maginot Line fortifications, so much maligned, were circumvented but never really broken through. 'If she had been well led', writes Gordon Waterfield of Reuter's, an eye-witness of the tragedy, 'France would have shown as much vitality as she has done during previous national emergencies.'[1] 'The rank and file of the French Army and the French nation were not rotten from within, but the political system was rotten and it produced leaders, with a few exceptions, who were not fit to lead a great nation.' It is probable that after German remilitarization of the left bank of the Rhine in 1936, the defeat of France was inevitable if war should break out. Military neglect of fortifications along the Franco-Belgian frontier ensured that defeat would be rapid and decisive. It is arguable (though not plausible) that had France not been a parliamentary democracy—had she been a dictatorship or even a presidential or cabinet democracy—her preparedness would have been greater, her alliances firmer. But the ifs of history are always stillborn.

In view of the concerted efforts to malign the Third Republic after 1940, one final *caveat* is necessary. In the post-war years, parliamentary politics were shabby and often sordid, many politicians were corrupt, the Press and the police were notoriously bribable and open to sectional or personal influence. It is doubtful whether corruption was greater than during some of the pre-war days: Stavisky was no worse a scandal than Panama, and in many ways less significant than the Dreyfus case. But the connexion between political corruption and military weakness and defeat has to be proved and not merely assumed. Corruption does not necessarily involve inefficiency. There is little doubt that the most graft-ridden state of modern times was Nazi Germany: yet it produced no obvious or speedy consequences in military weakness. England

[1] Cf. Gordon Waterfield: *What Happened to France* (1940), p. 105.

of the eighteenth century was a by-word for political bribery and corruption at every level of public administration: yet it was a period of great military and naval conquests. Feebleness and inefficiency there undoubtedly were in Third Republic France: especially as regards the bureaucratic red-tape, which often demanded forty or even sixty-five copies of the most trivial of documents. But there was little if any connexion between this kind of inefficiency and either the 'Republic of Pals' or the 'Cabinet of Mistresses' in the latter days of Reynaud and Daladier. Similarly, many of the incidents which looked like treachery and the work of a 'fifth column' were often due to this administrative muddle and *paperasserie*. Treachery, corruption, inefficiency existed side by side: one did not necessarily derive from the others.[1]

---

[1] Of the many colourful accounts of the fall of France and attempted explanations for it, see especially Élie-J. Bois: *Truth on the Tragedy of France* (1941); André Maurois: *Why France Fell* (1940); Oscar Paul: *Farewell, France!* (1941); Jacques Lorraine: *Behind the Battle of France* (1943); A. Werth: *The Last Days of Paris* (1942). All suffer somewhat from being written soon after the event and during the war, so that undue importance is often given to the immediate circumstances, and perspective is lost. D. Barlone: *A French Officer's Diary* (1942) gives some eloquent examples of administrative red-tape in 1939-40. Marc Bloch's *Strange Defeat* (1949) is in a category of its own as a moving contemporary analysis by a great scholar. For an English account see Major-General Sir Edward Spears: *Assignment to Catastrophe* (2 vols., 1954). There is a mass of relevant material in the lengthy report of the *Commission chargée d'enquêter sur les événements survenus en France de 1933 à 1945* (rapporteur, Charles Serre), entitled *Événements survenus . . . Témoignages et Documents* (9 vols., 1947).

VI

THE OPEN SCHISM

The Armistice of 1940

THE sequence of events between May and July 1940, which is loosely called 'the fall of France', was in reality three distinct events. They were the invasion and military defeat of May; the making of an armistice with Germany and Italy in June; and the constitutional revolution of July. Each of the three might have happened without necessarily leading to the others. The transition from one set of events to the next did not happen inevitably; it had to be engineered, and rested on the decisions of certain leading men. Had the French Government, as the Prime Minister M. Paul Reynaud at first desired, decided to move to London or to North Africa, defeat need not have led to a separate armistice. Had Marshal Pétain and Pierre Laval not secured a grant of emergency powers from the National Assembly, even the armistice need not have led to the overthrow of the Third Republic. Had the enemies of the Republic not used defeat to gain power, some sort of provisional Republican regime might have survived both defeat and the armistice.

But to emphasize the extent to which the course of events depended on a series of human decisions, and not on any inevitable fate, is not to imply that the whole 'fall of France' was the result of a far-reaching conspiracy, wherein the men who eventually set up the Vichy Government had from the first worked for the military defeat of France and the early conclusion of an armistice with Germany. This theory, that the fall of France was the successful outcome of a plot, was widely believed by many Frenchmen during the war and was officially adopted by the Free French Movement led by General de Gaulle. It is true that the same men who pressed for the making of an armistice in June were also mainly responsible for setting up the Vichy Government in July. But there is no evidence that they exercised the degree of foresight and control over events which would imply an elaborate conspiracy. On the contrary, events might have taken a very different turn at several moments, and the whole policy of Vichy is marked by constant improvisation and opportunism.[1]

The military defeat of May does not need any far-fetched explanation to make it comprehensible. France's lack of preparedness to shoulder the great over-burdening to which she was subjected by 1940 has already been considered. She was intensely war-weary and had suffered permanent exhaustion after 1918. Internal social conflicts had sharpened during the years between the wars. Many of the Right were defeatist, many of the Left were pacifist. The Communists, whose representatives were excluded from the Chamber by M. Daladier in February 1940, denounced the war as a struggle of rival imperialisms which could only enslave the worker. The High Command, anxious to be thrifty with French lives, were obsessed with defence and with the notion that time would be on France's side. In spite of the warnings of France's greatest expert in tanks and mechanized warfare, Charles de Gaulle, both the High Command and the Government neglected the implications of mobile warfare until it was too late. France went down in defeat before an overwhelming weight of men and machines and military power, having already forfeited most of her strategic advantages in the decade before war began. Compared with this supreme responsibility of the Germans for the defeat of France, all other responsibilities are secondary.

As soon as the fact of defeat was obvious—and as early as 25 May the French Government was forced to consider the

[1] For the conspiracy theory, see *Pétain-Laval: The Conspiracy* (Anon., 1942); H. R. Knickerbocker: *Is Tomorrow Hitler's?* (1941), Chapter IV; Élie-J. Bois; op. cit. For the contrary view, see my *Two Frenchmen: Pierre Laval and Charles de Gaulle* (1951), pp. 55–73. For a day-to-day narrative of the events, see A. Kammerer: *La Vérité sur l'Armistice* (1944).

THE OPEN SCHISM

possibility of seeking an armistice—there were only two possible courses for the Government to take. It could adhere to its promise to Britain never to withdraw from the war, and that meant its withdrawing either to North Africa or to England to continue the war. Or it could seek release from this promise, and sue for an armistice on the most advantageous terms possible. M. Reynaud clung to the former plan, but regarded it as calling for a military capitulation in order to spare the country irreparable destruction. General Weygand, whom M. Reynaud had appointed Commander-in-Chief in France on 20 May, refused to capitulate. He maintained that he would either fight on to the bitter end, or would resign, but that for a soldier to capitulate in open country would bring total dishonour to the French Army. The cessation of hostilities was a matter for the Government to decide.[1] Faced with this *impasse*, and with heavy pressure from within his cabinet that he should seek armistice terms, M. Reynaud resigned on 16 June. Marshal Pétain, the 'Hero of Verdun' now aged 84, formed a new government with the prime purpose of concluding an armistice. The next day Pétain asked Hitler for terms, and these became known on 20 June.[2]

The armistice with Germany was signed on 22 June. It divided France into two parts, with the demarcation-line running from the Franco-Swiss frontier near Geneva westwards to near Tours, and then southwards to the Franco-Spanish frontier near Pau. German troops occupied the whole

---

[1] General Weygand and M. Reynaud have stated their case subsequently; see *Recalled to Service: The Memoirs of General Maxime Weygand* (1952) and Paul Reynaud: *In the Thick of the Fight, 1930–45* (1955). Among other leading participants who have published their own version of these events are Paul Baudouin: *The Private Diaries of Paul Baudouin* (1948); F. Charles-Roux: *Cinq Mois Tragiques aux Affaires Étrangères* (1949); A. Lebrun: *Témoignage* (1946); Charles de Gaulle; *War Memoirs*, Vol. I: *The Call to Honour 1940–2* (1955).

[2] The text of the Franco-German Armistice of 22 June is printed below, Appendix III. The French texts both of this and of the Franco-Italian Armistice of 24 June are printed in A. Kammerer: op. cit., pp. 324 ff.

of the northern area, including the Atlantic coast, but the French Government kept control of the Mediterranean coast. It was also allowed to keep a small army of 100,000 men, the French fleet, and the overseas territories. Alsace and Lorraine were again, as in 1871, annexed to Germany. This partition existed until November 1942, when the Germans occupied the whole country. The prisoners of war, numbering nearly 2 million, remained in German hands. Germany thus secured control over the capital, the main industrial areas, and all the Channel and the Atlantic ports for prosecution of the war against Britain. But the French Government, though burdened with large numbers of refugees from the north to feed and house in a predominantly agricultural area, as well as with heavy occupation-costs, was left with certain important assets. Chief of these were the fleet and the African colonies, and considerable freedom of action in the western Mediterranean.

Meanwhile, Pierre Laval was busy helping to engineer the further stage in the whole process. He was a member of the Senate, but did not enter upon the scene until 15 June, when he joined the general flight to Bordeaux. He was wholeheartedly in favour of an armistice, and opposed to any continuation of the war from outside France. He had an interview with the hesitating President of the Republic, Albert Lebrun, and dissuaded him from leaving France. He lobbied and harangued the available deputies and senators, and helped to persuade a majority of them to ratify the armistice agreement. On 10 July he promoted in the National Assembly, summoned at Vichy to ratify the armistice, a bill investing the government of Marshal Pétain with provisional plenary powers until a 'new constitution' should be promulgated. He did not become a member of the Government until 23 June, after the armistice had been signed: and the fact that 569 members of the assembly voted for his bill, and only 80 against it, suggests that the last parliament of the Third Republic substantially agreed with his policy. It was over 100 more than the minimum majority needed. As Laval wrote later, 'the majority loudly demanded it, or it must be imagined that I had extraordinary powers of suggestion over the two Chambers'.[1]

Constitutionally, the Vichy Government survived for four years by simply never promulgating this 'new constitution', and by never again summoning the National Assembly. Even in form it was a stop-gap regime. Pétain's first 'Constitutional Act' was to repeal Article 2 of the Constitutional Law of 25 February 1875. It was the famous 'Wallon amendment', which stipulated that the President of the Republic must be elected by the National Assembly. Carried by a majority of one vote in 1875, it had contained the germ of the Third Republic. The Third Republic died on 10 July 1940. Born of one defeat, it failed to survive another.[2]

By a succession of eleven other 'Constitutional Acts' Marshal Pétain abolished the legislative powers of Parliament and the responsibility of ministers to it, adjourned the existing chambers *sine die*, appointed Laval as his successor, and required from civil servants and members of the armed forces an oath of fidelity to himself as 'Head of the State'. On this basis of emergency dictatorship, and the material assets secured by the terms of the armistice, the Vichy Governments sustained themselves for the next four years.

[1] *The Unpublished Diary of Pierre Laval* (1948), pp. 51–5. See the remarkable defence of his actions at his trial, reported in full in *Le Procès Laval* (1946), and A. Mallet: *Pierre Laval* (2 vols., 1955), Vol. I.

[2] On the 'Wallon amendment', see above pp. 89–90. The Free French consistently denied the legality of these proceedings, and Professor René Cassin wrote a full-scale *exposé* of their case (*La France Libre*, Vol. I for December 1940, and *Un Coup d'État: La soi-disant Constitution de Vichy* (1941)). But the technical arguments against its legality are very flimsy, and somewhat unrealistic. In any event the case for the legality of the Vichy Government is inherently stronger than that of the Free French Movement: and the plea of emergency measures which must be used to justify the behaviour of de Gaulle applies equally strongly to the behaviour of the men of Vichy. For the texts of the main Constitutional Acts of July, see *Documents on International Affairs, 1939–46*, Vol. II, *Hitler's Europe* (1954), pp. 119–23.

The Vichy Governments

What forces in French life did this new regime represent? A clear distinction has to be drawn between what Vichy set out to be and what it later became. It began as the convergence, in the moment of defeat, of all those forces which had long disliked the Republic. It represented the service chiefs, and Vichy became notorious for the prominence in its governments of dug-out generals, admirals and higher-grade *fonctionnaires*, and for the remarkable loyalty to it of the highest colonial administrators such as Admiral Decoux in Indo-China, Admirals Noguès and Estéva in North Africa, and M. Pierre Boisson in West Africa. It represented the more traditional and royalist authoritarian movements, and from the first the *Action française*, led by Charles Maurras, welcomed the rule of Marshal Pétain and created a cult and a mystique surrounding him. It represented the forces of defeatism, and men like Paul Baudouin and Laval took a large part in its early phases. It also represented men who, like General Weygand, regarded an armistice as inevitable but as something quite different from a peace treaty. It was an attitude shared by General Giraud later, and was probably essentially the view of Pétain himself: Germany remained the enemy, France remained in a state of war with Germany, and the armistice must be used to conserve and develop France's resources against the day when she might be able to hit back. This attitude, resting on slender hopes in 1940, grew as the progress of the war transformed the whole situation. The regime of Vichy was set up in the curious interlude between Dunkirk and the Battle of Britain, when most expert military and political opinion in France—and not only in France—believed that the war was nearly over, that Germany had won the war, and was about to establish the Nazi 'New Order' in Europe. France must, for the time at least, bring herself into line as a partner in this 'New Order' if she was to survive. But as soon as the Battle of Britain made it clear that the war was not ended, but was likely to go on for a long time with increasing disadvantage to Germany, the policy of Vichy shifted more and more towards a persistent

THE OPEN SCHISM 217

attentisme, alternating with periods when German pressures or successes produced moments of more anxious collaboration.[1]

For this reason the history of the regime falls into four main phases. The first, dominated by Laval, ended with his abrupt dismissal by Pétain in December 1940. Its keynote was defeatism—acceptance of the doctrine that some collaboration was inevitable. Its essence was the arrangements made in the Laval–Goering and Hitler–Pétain meetings at Montoire in October 1940. Pétain explained that it was in order to 'maintain the unity of France . . . within the framework of constructive activity in the New Order of Europe, that I enter to-day upon the path of collaboration'.[2] By December the conservative and authoritarian forces centred around the Marshal decided to eliminate Laval from his key post. They did so by a palace revolution which removed Laval from power for the next sixteen months.[3] He was replaced first by Pierre-Étienne Flandin, and then by Admiral Jean Darlan.

In the second phase, between February 1941 and April 1942, the dominance of Darlan reflected the enhanced value of the French fleet and the prevalence among the service chiefs of the wait-and-see opportunists. It was the phase *par excellence* of conservative, traditionalist, authoritarian rule in France. It reveals more clearly than any other the nature of the anti-democratic forces indigenous in France, because with Vichy's bargaining assets still intact and the Germans heavily

[1] The best detailed account of the Vichy Governments as a whole is Robert Aron: *Histoire de Vichy* (Paris, 1954), but their strange atmosphere is even better understood from Maurice Martin du Gard: *La Chronique de Vichy, 1940–4* (Paris, 1948). The best accounts in English are D. M. Pickles: *France Between the Republics* (1946); the section on 'Vichy France' by Alfred Cobban in *Hitler's Europe*, ed. Arnold and V. M. Toynbee; [*Survey of International Affairs, 1939–46* (1954)]; and Alexander Werth: *France, 1940–55* (1956), Part I.

[2] The text of the Montoire Protocol of 24 October, the supplement to the Armistice as the formal basis of Vichy's relations with Germany, is printed in *Documents on International Affairs, 1939–46*, Vol. II, pp. 125–6; and Pétain's broadcast on 30 October in ibid., pp. 126–7.

[3] For a detailed account of the *coup* of 13 December, see A. Mallet: op. cit., Vol. I, Chapter VIII.

preoccupied in the East, it was the period of relatively greatest independence *vis-à-vis* Germany. The changes that Vichy introduced at this time are particularly relevant to any examination of the nature of democracy in France, and are considered more fully below.

With the return of Laval to power in April 1942, German pressure was intensified. Her necessities were great, for now she was bogged in Russia and suffering heavy losses, and the entry of the United States brought much nearer the danger of renewed war in the West. From Laval the Germans hoped to get skilled French labour, either in French or German factories, and at the same time a more docile and submissive spirit in France: two demands which the growth of resistance made incompatible demands. This third phase, which lasted until January 1944, represented a perpetual battle of wits between Pierre Laval and on one hand the Germans, driven by military exigencies into ever more exacting demands, and on the other the militant forces of resistance, bitterly hostile to Vichy and impatient for liberation. These twenty months of severe tension are of special significance for the future. It was then that the social schism in France between the supporters of Vichy and the surging movement of resistance (permeated increasingly by Communism) took shape. It is a time full of significance for the moulding of the Fourth Republic, and as such will also be considered more fully below.

Until January 1944, Vichy did not represent the forces of pro-Germanism. The enthusiastic collaborators gathered not at Vichy but in Paris, and men like Marcel Déat, Jacques Doriot, and Philippe Henriot kept up from Paris an increasing fire of criticism and hatred against the *attentisme* of Vichy and the double game of Laval. In January 1944 the collaborators from Paris were forced upon Pétain and Laval as ministers at Vichy. Déat the neo-Socialist, Joseph Darnand the ex-Cagoulard conspirator, and Henriot the venomous journalist of *Gringoire*, were forced into the Vichy Government by German pressure. There followed six months of virtual civil war between collaborators backed by the Gestapo and resisters backed by the French Forces of the Interior, organized under

General Koenig. This final phase, the last six months before D-Day and the arrival of allied forces, introduced little that was new to the situation of December 1943, save even wider and deeper hatreds. It saw a hardening and crystallization of the opposing forces already aligned against one another. Whilst the Resistance formulated its programme for the future in the 'Resistance Charter' of March 1944,[1] Laval and the other men of Vichy became more closely associated and identified with the pro-German collaborators.

The foundations of the Vichy regime shifted, in this way, from year to year, and melted away as they shifted. There was a steady drift away of national opinion and feeling from defeatism and reluctant collaboration towards *attentisme*, and from *attentisme* towards resistance. After November 1942, when the Allies invaded French North Africa, Germany occupied the whole of France, most of the French fleet was destroyed, and the 'armistice army' of Vichy was disbanded, the men of Vichy were deprived of most of their material sources of power and were left more helplessly at the mercy of German demands. These demands became more insistent as Germany's needs became greater. The regime survived mainly by dint of the personal prestige of Pétain, the nimble wits of Laval, and the inherent limitations of Germany's power to compel obedience without provoking open rebellion on her vulnerable western flank. Apart from these resources, Vichy's only substantial advantage was the ever-tightening stranglehold of the Allies on Germany herself.

The 'National Revolution'

The essence of all Vichy politics after December 1940 was the survival of a provisional and improvised regime into conditions totally different from those for which it had been devised. The men, movements and social groups which rallied behind Marshal Pétain and Admiral Darlan were united only by the urge to use this opportunity to eradicate the remaining

[1] See below, Appendix II (C).

institutions and ideals of the parliamentary Republic. For these men the Republic—*la gueuse*—had been finally discredited by national defeat, and now national survival depended on equipping France with the right political garb to qualify for a place in Hitler's 'New Order' in Europe. There was a certain air of camouflage about this façade of Fascism, so hastily erected, so feebly implemented, and so generally unpopular. It was, perhaps, as much a sign of the policy of survival by manœuvre, a more elaborate extension of Laval's policy of 'cringe and wriggle', as of any very deep-rooted Fascist philosophy. It belongs especially to the year 1941—a time when none could foresee the speedy collapse of Italy, the decisive failures of Germany's attack on Soviet Russia, or the entry of the United States and the prolongation of the war by another four years.

But within the confines of this peculiar situation, the measures passed and the implementation of them attempted by Vichy represented a mixture of the traditionalist, ultra-conservative and even royalist forces of French life, with the somewhat mystical and guilt-ridden 'personalist' notions of the 1930's. Vichy's 'National Revolution' was the apotheosis of undemocracy in France, and not without reason was it called 'the revenge of the anti-Dreyfusards'. One writer openly rejoiced in defeat because it meant destruction of an 'ignoble parliamentarianism'.[1]

It was the lawyer, Raphaël Alibert, an extremist supporter of the *Action française*, who drew up the crucial constitutional acts of July 1940. These virtually created a presidential autocracy in place of the parliamentary Republic. The new regime rested on the surrender of both governmental and legislative power to Marshal Pétain as 'Head of the State', and unlike Thiers in 1870 he was untrammelled by the existence of a National Assembly. The opening phrase of the first

[1] Lucien Rebatet: *Les Décombres* (Paris, 1942), p. 467. The 'personalist' notions of men like Baudouin, Gaston Bergery, and the trade-union leader René Belin found expression mainly in the Labour Charter, the attack on the big trusts, and the clericalist changes in education. See Robert Aron: op. cit., pp. 200–2.

constitutional act, *Nous, Philippe Pétain*, emphasized how intensely personal was his authority: a position more akin to that of Louis Napoleon in 1850 than to that of Thiers in 1870. The rise to power of Laval in July 1940, and the rise of Darlan in February 1941, were marked by their nominations as *Dauphin*, as personal successors to the Marshal. This personal authority was exercised partly through Ministers and Secretaries of State, who were reshuffled almost as often as those of the Republican regimes, and partly through the bureaucracy, many of whose higher officials were given ministerial posts. Vichy, like the Republics, was heir to the centralized bureaucracy of Napoleon, and it merged the *fonctionnaires* still more closely into the executive power. Upon this single thread was hung the imposing, monolithic fabric of the new State and the 'National Revolution'—interesting for its pretensions rather than for its reality, for it concealed a ramshackle, makeshift government, compounded of jostling individuals and jealous factions and lacking any real political coherence.

General Weygand seems to have been among the first to put forward, in a memorandum of 28 June 1940, the characteristic ideas that were to be carried out by the new regime.[1] They included the standard accusations levied against the Republic by its traditionalist enemies. The old order of masonic, capitalist, and international deals has brought defeat; the class-war has divided the country and led to demagogic overbidding for votes; the fall in the birth-rate has meant mass naturalizations of aliens; 'the wave of materialism that has submerged France, and the craze for pleasure and ease, are the profound cause of our weaknesses and negligences'. What France needs is not a new deal, but a 'return to the cult and the practice of an ideal summed up in these words: God, Country, Family'. But this can be brought about only by new men, animated by the desire to serve.

These reflections of an old soldier were echoed a month later in the memorandum that Paul Baudouin, the Catholic banker

[1] See *Recalled to Service* (1952), p. 229; and *The Private Diaries of Paul Baudouin*, pp. 151–2. It was read with approval by both Pétain and Baudouin.

representative of a younger generation of Pétainists, also presented to the Head of the State.[1] The French people must bow before the German victory, 'which Germany has deserved'. France has suffered moral and physical degeneration and lost the spirit of sacrifice. She should 'see in her defeat, and in the suffering which it has caused, one of those great and periodical revolutions which destroy the material while liberating the spirit'. It was in this mood of recrimination and expiation that the men of Vichy approached the self-imposed task of carrying out the National Revolution. The slogan was *Travail, Famille, Patrie:* the old-fashioned conservative virtues were to undo the harm wrought by the French Revolutionary democratic ideals of *Liberté, Egalité, Fraternité.* Despite the wide differences of emphasis and purpose between the groups at Vichy, which ranged from the royalist, anti-democratic, Jew-baiting chauvinism of Maurras to the sentimental moralizing of Baudouin, the National Revolution was in aggregate a total reaction against the whole revolutionary tradition. As an American commentator has put it, 'in any broad view of France in the twentieth century, Vichy must take its place as one phase in the continuous inner crisis of modern France'.[2]

In place of Liberty, Vichy offered the regimentation of a police state. The Legion of Ex-Servicemen, reorganized in August 1940 as the guardian of the National Revolution, a year later became the only official political party when other parties were suspended. Press and radio were subjected to censorship, control, and suppression. Workers' organizations of all kinds were destroyed or reorganized into official bodies. A 'Peasant Corporation' set up in December 1940 purported to bring landowners, farmers, and farm workers into a single corporation with local and regional branches. It came to be dominated in practice by the big landowners and State officials. Employers' associations (including the *Confédération Générale du Patronat Français,* the *Comité des Forges,* and the *Comité des Houillères*) were dissolved. Both the main trade-union Confederations, the C.G.T. and the C.F.T.C., were also dissolved.

[1] Baudouin: op. cit., p. 182.
[2] Paul Farmer: *Vichy: Political Dilemma* (1955), p. 7.

In their place Organizing Committees, eventually numbering nearly 200, were set up for the main branches of industry and business: they, too, were soon dominated by the chiefs of big business and State officials. The National Union of Teachers, one of the most powerful professional organizations, was suppressed, as was the *École Normale*. Free secondary education was abolished, and the curricula of the elementary schools were reorganized to ensure indoctrination with the Pétainist ideals. The Labour Charter of October 1941 was modelled on the Italian and German patterns.

In place of Equality, Vichy offered discrimination. Jewish Statutes of October 1940 and June 1941 excluded Jews from the public service and most of the professions. Thousands of Jews were deported and all were persecuted. In Algeria the *Loi Crémieux* was repealed, and Algerian Jews deprived of full citizenship. A *Commissariat Général aux Affaires Juives* was set up, under the direction of the notorious anti-Semite Xavier Vallat, to enforce the anti-Jewish measures. Naturalized aliens of all kinds were subjected to severe discriminations and barred from most of the professions. Maurras's aim of *La France Seule*, of exclusive and arrogant nationalism, came nearer to attainment in 1941 than at any other moment in French history. French women, too, found themselves subjected to anti-feminist legislation intended to force them out of industry back into the home and the family. Divorce was made more difficult. Married women were banned from the public services. But with nearly 2 millions of the men absent and an acute labour shortage, economic necessities prevailed over ideology, and these measures had very little practical effect.

In place of Fraternity, Vichy offered the cult of leadership, hierarchy, authority. Youth movements, devised to include a new moral outlook and a docile submission to the State, were founded and encouraged. Attempts were made to enforce religious instruction in State schools, which inevitably awakened all the old anti-clerical bitterness and had to be speedily abandoned. Even more important, Vichy embarked upon recrimination as well as discrimination when it decided to stage the Riom trials of the former Republican leaders.

Nothing more perfectly expresses the spirit of Darlan's regime than the tragi-comic episode of Riom. Since the armistice the Germans had clamoured for the trial and execution of men like Blum, Daladier, and Gamelin as warmongers. The men of Vichy procrastinated until February 1942 when the trials were at last opened. But the accused were charged not, as Germany had wished, with being war-mongers responsible for the war, but as incompetent national leaders responsible for the defeat. Moreover, only political and not military responsibility was invoked, and the charges were restricted to the period between March 1936 and the outbreak of the war. The outcome of such trials could never serve German purposes, though clearly enough they might serve the purposes of the men of Vichy. The careful exclusion of military liability, and of the year 1934 when Pétain had been Minister of War, revealed their tendentious purpose. In the event the trials were turned into a spirited defence of the republican parliamentary leaders and a condemnation of the General Staff, most notably Pétain. They had to be brought to an end after seven weeks, because publication of the hearings did as much harm to Vichy as to German propaganda. Riom was a fitting climax to the muddled, mediocre, moralizing phase when Darlan was Dauphin. The Republican leaders lived on, to play a part in the parliamentary life of the Fourth Republic.

Throughout can be detected the political *naïveté* and ineptitude of service chiefs suddenly exalted to positions of policy-making and government. With a mixture of cynicism and sanctimoniousness they tried to destroy the national traditions of 150 years. Few of them, if any, were pro-German, though they were often anti-British. Evasion of the law was often connived at by Vichy officials. When in November 1942 the French sailors at Toulon sank their ships to prevent them falling into German hands, they did so in obedience to standing orders issued by Darlan even before the signing of the armistice. Weygand, whilst expressing his disagreement with and even distrust of Darlan, shows how determined Darlan was that the fleet should never fall into German hands. But Darlan's record was such that the bargain which the American

General Mark Clark made with him in November 1942 was foredoomed to failure.[1] The historic schism in French life that his policy now symbolized was too wide to be healed by even the most expedient emergency arrangements: to it were added the further acrimony and confusion engendered by the ambiguous policy of Pierre Laval.

The Legacy of Laval

Under the guidance of Laval, from April 1942 until the end of 1943, attempts to complete the work of the National Revolution continued, and in some ways were intensified. Still more severe measures against the Jews were taken in the summer of 1942, and Jews were forced to wear the yellow star. The propaganda about *Travail, Famille, Patrie* went on. But Laval himself never had much patience with the ideology of Pétainism, dismissing it sarcastically as 'the patent medicine expected to cure every ill'.[2] He disliked the title 'French State' on official proclamations, coins, and stamps, as much as he disliked the personal cult of Pétain as a great father-figure, a cult which became particularly prevalent and idiotic during his absence from power. He ridiculed the reactionary ideas of Maurras and the fanciful elements of the Labour Charter. Engrossed in the immediate problems of bargaining with Germany and defending himself against both extremist collaborators and militant resisters, the notion of spiritual regeneration through physical suffering and sacrifice held no attractions for this hard-headed realist. For this reason his twenty months of power after April 1942 reveal more about the widening schism in French national life than about the

[1] A point underestimated by William L. Langer in *Our Vichy Gamble* (1947) and by Admiral W. D. Leahy: *I Was There* (1950).

[2] *The Unpublished Diary*, p. 62. Even on the fateful 10 July 1940 Laval had insisted, in his speech to the National Assembly, that 'in France's present condition we cannot look backwards nor revert to the past', and the former revolutionary socialist had little in common with either the reactionary traditionalism of the *Action française* or the mystical paternalism of the Pétainists.

anti-democratic character of Pétainism. Even before November 1942 the demands of the Germans for the transfer of large numbers of French workers to German factories drove Laval into a more dynamic policy of manœuvre than Darlan had ever attempted: and after November, devoid of material resources of power and compelled to work under total German occupation, Laval's resourceful guile was taxed to the utmost.

His first and most formidable task was to deal with Gauleiter Sauckel, appointed by Hitler to supervise the flow of French man-power into German factories. Sauckel demanded 150,000 skilled workers by the middle of October. Laval seized upon the characteristic device of linking supply of workers with the release of prisoners and in June 1942 launched the famous scheme of *la relève*. The two main elements in the situation were that the Germans, increasingly suffering from Allied bombing of their industrial and transport centres and engaged in immensely heavy fighting on the Russian front, were in urgent need of large supplies of skilled labour, of which France remained the only considerable source: and that one of the most profound heartbreaks of French life since the armistice had been the prolonged confinement in Germany of the flower of French manhood taken prisoner in 1940. The prisoners of war by now numbered some $1\frac{1}{4}$ millions, and to restore even a proportion of them to their homes would be enormously popular. Convinced that the Germans would eventually contrive to take French workers anyhow, Laval tried to make some gain in return by persuading Sauckel to exchange prisoners for workers. The rate and conditions of exchange proved to be very unfavourable for France. In return for 150,000 skilled industrial workers, 50,000 agricultural workers would be released from the prison camps.[1] After three months 17,000 workers had been induced to go, but only some 5,000 prisoners—the most aged and most ill—had returned home.

It was the moral effects of the scheme, which Laval as

[1] *The Unpublished Diary*, p. 126.

always was prone to underrate, that proved the most disastrous. There was substance in Laval's realistic claim that, since Germany was able anyhow to take workers by force, it was better to get 5,000 prisoners released in exchange than to get no benefit at all. But the scheme involved hoodwinking French workers into working for Germany voluntarily, as a patriotic duty to get prisoners released. It aligned Vichy more closely with the collaborationists.

On the other hand, when Germany was compelled to conscript labour in France and take by compulsion what Laval had failed to give them by bargaining, the solidarity of national resistance to the forced-labour decrees was probably all the greater. By his own law of September 1942, instituting forced labour, Laval secured postponement of Sauckel's much more drastic decree which was enforced in all other occupied countries. The intervention of the Vichy administration slowed down the drafts and alleviated some of the worst hardships. Sauckel complained bitterly that all Laval's efforts 'appeared to be bent towards gaining political advantages for France'. Alone among occupied territories, France did not have women conscripted for work in Germany. By gaining exemption for railway workers, miners, police, and civil servants, the Vichy Government was able to enrol large numbers of eligible young men on the lists of these occupations. Many French factories were classed as 'S' factories, whose workers could not be drafted. By the end of July 1944, 341,500 workers had gone to Germany, some of whom had found their way back: and 110,000 prisoners had been returned. It is doubtful whether blank resistance would have produced, in material terms, a result less unsatisfactory for France.

The personal price Laval paid for his policy was to incur bitter animosity at the time, and eventually death. The price France paid was a deepening of the schism within the nation. The more Vichy came to be popularly identified with collaboration, and the more the labour laws drove young men into the woods and hills to escape conscription, there to fight as resisters of the *maquis*, the faster France moved along the path to open civil war.

Nor were Laval's tactics likely to heal the schism. Always something of the lone wolf in politics, he contrived to remain in power by balancing in the middle of every see-saw. Internationally, he came to believe that the most likely outcome of the war would be neither a German victory nor a German defeat, but a stalemate peace: his hope was to emerge as the middleman between the Axis and the Western Allies, reconciling both against the threat of Communist revolution and Soviet hegemony. Domestically, there was the conflict between the camp of the *attentistes* at Vichy and the camp of the collaborationists in Paris. Laval, agreeing completely with neither but flitting conveniently between the two, could manipulate the balance in order to achieve his own ends. The collaborationists set up para-military legions to rival Pétain's *Légion des combattants*. But before long both Doriot's Anti-Bolshevik Legion and Joseph Darnand's African Phalanx were being linked up with yet further legions formed under the aegis of Laval. By constantly seeking a symmetrical balance between the rival bodies of the two zones, by unifying them and inserting his own nominees into the key positions, Laval kept some grip on these dangerous movements.[1] Again, however, the price he paid was to be saddled with political and moral responsibility for the brutalities of Darnand's *Milice française*, and for the deaths of patriotic resisters in the skirmishes and pitched battles that took place increasingly during 1943 and the first half of 1944. Then Frenchmen fought and killed Frenchmen on a scale unknown since 1871.

A further consequence of Laval's methods, though not necessarily intended, was not necessarily unwelcome: the method of 'divide and rule' helped to perpetuate the chronic rivalries between his enemies, and so to prevent the establishment of the much-discussed *parti unique*. Until the end of 1942 the division of France territorially into the occupied and unoccupied zones prevented Pétain's Legion from filling its

---

[1] For fuller discussion of Laval's tactics, see the present author's *Two Frenchmen: Pierre Laval and Charles de Gaulle* (1951); A. Mallet: op. cit., Vol. II, pp. 159–61; and Alexander Werth: *France, 1940–55*, pp. 93–118.

promised role of becoming the 'single party' in the State. Thereafter relations between Vichy and the Paris collaborators were such that each aspired to be the only legitimate 'single party' and none would countenance fusion with any other. Jacques Doriot's *Parti Populaire Français* (P.P.F.) and Marcel Déat's *Rassemblement National Populaire* (R.N.P.) remained jealous rivals throughout, despite their ideological affinities and their common hatred of Vichy. Each had its own subsidiary youth organizations and women's sections, as had the Pétainist Legion. There were smaller groups, too, such as Bucard's *Francistes*, Eugène Deloncle's *Mouvement Social Révolutionnaire*, and Constantini's bonapartist *Ligue française*, to add to the diversity and the confusion. This persistent multiplicity of aspirants for the role of *parti unique* made the very notion of a single-party State in France ridiculous. To assist in producing this result was one of Laval's unwitting services to the cause of anti-fascism.

The rich profusion of variegated shades of opinion both at Vichy and in Paris is a particularly vivid warning against regarding the characteristics and problems of the Third Republic as springing from its political constitution or even from democracy. Political, social, and personal divisions, even among collaborators under the shadow of *la lanterne*, were as great as any in the Third or Fourth Republics. Maurras contended that collaboration was the penalty of defeat and the price of national survival; Belin, that it was penance for past errors and an opportunity for reconstruction; Déat, that it was morally right and politically wise; Doriot, that it was a duty in the fight against Bolshevism; Laval, that it was simply the best bargain in the market at the moment, but one to be haggled over as much as possible. Extreme individualism, deep division of opinion, and a shuffling group system are clearly endemic in French life, and not merely the by-products of an unsatisfactory parliamentary system. The truth of this was to become still more apparent in the history of the Fourth Republic.

The Provisional Governments

Just as the Vichy regime passed through a series of different phases, so did its rival, the movement founded in June 1940 by General de Gaulle. On the day after Marshal Pétain asked Germany for an armistice, de Gaulle broadcast from London an appeal for all French men and women who wanted to carry on the fight to get in touch with him in London. With the response to this appeal he formed the Free French Movement. In August it was recognized by the British Government as a fighting organization of Frenchmen which would be given financial help and military equipment. When French Equatorial Africa rallied to the movement de Gaulle set up an Imperial Defence Council at Brazzaville. This council claimed the right to exercise public power based on French legislation enacted before 23 June—that is, before the armistice came into force. It claimed no right, as yet, to enact new legislation, but only to be a *de facto* administrative authority.[1]

A year later, in September 1941, the French National Committee was set up in London, making a much wider claim to be a political authority as 'the provisional guardian of the national patrimony'. It claimed a direct link with the Third Republic, as against the regime of Vichy which it denounced as illegitimate: and de Gaulle now claimed, too, 'to represent a nation which has no other means of expressing itself and to prepare the framework within which it will be possible for the French people to exercise its national sovereignty'. The ordinance creating the Committee laid down that all its decisions should, as early as possible, be submitted for ratification by the representatives of the nation.[2]

---

[1] For further details of the origins of the movement and the text of the agreement of August, see my *Two Frenchmen*, pp. 157–62. The story of the movement is told in Félix de Grand'Combe: *The Three Years of Fighting France (June 1940–June 1943)* (1943). The speeches of General de Gaulle and a few important documents are published as *Discours et Messages du Général de Gaulle*, 2 vols. (1942–3). For further documentation, see Charles de Gaulle: *Mémoires de Guerre*, 2 vols. (Paris, 1954–6).

[2] *Discours et Messages du Général de Gaulle*, Vol. I, p. 69.

By the beginning of 1943 the position of the Committee was complex. Both Washington and Moscow had kept representatives at Vichy, until events forced Vichy to break with both of them. But although this weakened Vichy it did little to strengthen the Committee: and the Darlan-Clark agreements, made when the Allies landed in French North Africa, by-passed the Committee as the authority responsible for administering the greatest and most important parts of the French Empire. The assassination of Darlan and his replacement by General Giraud made compromise possible and, on 3 June 1943, the National Committee and the North African administration merged into a joint authority known as the French Committee of National Liberation. This new Committee, broader in base and with more military power at its command, could now make a more plausible claim to be the spokesman for France. But diplomatically it was still given very limited recognition, as merely the body 'administering French territories overseas which recognize its authority'.

The merger was an uneasy one, and after prolonged manœuvres Giraud was ousted from the Committee in April 1944. Henceforth General de Gaulle alone headed the authority which, with the addition of the Provisional Consultative Assembly set up in 1943 in Algiers, was to move to France as the Provisional Government. What explains his steady ascendancy? Partly, it was his own persistent faith that he had a mission to liberate France under the Cross of Lorraine; even more, it was that he steadily won the adherence and active support of the organized resistance movements inside France. On 23 June 1942 the National Council of Resistance inside France, representing the main underground movements of resistance, entered into a formal agreement with de Gaulle. His name was widely known in France through the British Broadcasting Corporation. The National Council of Resistance was represented on the Provisional Consultative Assembly in Algiers, where the opinions and aspirations of the internal resistance groups greatly affected the plans of the National Committee. Its President, Georges Bidault, was to become Foreign Minister in the Provisional Governments.

The elaborate plans of procedure for restoring Republican government in France after liberation were discussed at length and with considerable heat in Algiers. When the time came to implement them they were of little importance, for there had to be much improvisation. Municipal and general councils were reconstituted wherever possible, but purged of collaborationist elements. Equal deference was paid to the local 'committees of liberation', self-constituted bodies of local resisters. Efforts to establish rather tenuous and fictitious strands of legal continuity gave way to an admittedly Jacobin theory: that there must be early general elections to express the national 'general will' of the sovereign people. The revolutionary tradition was born anew; and the Fourth Republic, instead of being in form a continuation of the Third, was to emerge from a momentous, creative act of national will, exercised through universal free suffrage.

The immediate effect of liberation was a period of violence and of persecution of collaborators or alleged collaborators. In April and May 1945, the first municipal elections were held: and by October conditions had become settled enough, and enough of the prisoners of war and deported workers had been repatriated, for general elections to be held. Women were now, by the electoral law, given the vote on equality with men. The elections were preceded by a referendum, in which the electorate was asked to choose between electing a representative assembly which would be a continuation of the old Chamber of Deputies, or a new Constituent Assembly. If the latter, a draft Law concerning the Organization of the Public Powers was printed on the back of the ballot-papers for approval.[1] Nearly 18 million voters opted for a Constituent Assembly elected according to this Law: so 96·4 per cent of those who voted rejected the notion of reviving the Third Republic. The Constituent Assembly, charged with the drafting of a new Constitution within seven months, was elected forthwith.

Its composition revealed the eclipse of the Right and the old Centre, and an almost equal division of the majority between

[1] For text of this law, see below, Appendix I (I).

the three Left-wing parties of the Communists, Socialists, and Catholic Democrats (*Mouvement républicain populaire*, or M.R.P.). They gained between 140 and 150 seats each, whereas the Radicals won only 25 and the Republican groups only 70. On 13 November this new Assembly unanimously acclaimed General de Gaulle Head of the Provisional Government. The period of reconstruction and of return to constitutional government had begun.

Immediately after the liberation the urgent needs were to reorganize shattered transport, food-supply agencies, fuel and power resources and housing. France had not ceased to be a battlefield after the armistice of 1940. Allied aerial bombardment, partisan sabotage, and German reprisals had made it a battlefield still, until D-Day brought back conditions reminiscent of 1940. By the end of 1945 the Provisional Government had tackled the most urgent of these problems, though their complexity, the world shortage of supplies and political recriminations all acted as a serious drag on reconstruction. Throughout all plans for reconstruction ran the theme which had been so prominent in the history of the Third Republic: the urgent need to catch up on overdue legislative and administrative reforms, and to reconcile the political and social strands of the revolutionary tradition. The demand for 'more social and economic democracy' re-echoed through the liberated French Press no less than through the clandestine Press, the Consultative Assembly debates, and the countless preliminary discussions in Algiers. This demand found concrete form in the so-called 'Resistance Charter', drawn up in March 1944 by the main resistance movements.[1]

In 1945 all the main political parties sponsored this programme. Its aim was to supplement political democracy by social democracy, and to extend the traditional revolutionary principles of Liberty, Equality, and Fraternity from constitution-making and political institutions into the realms of economic and social life. The development of democracy in

[1] See Appendix II, below, for the text of the 'Resistance Charter', as well as texts of the Belleville Manifesto and the Popular Front Programme.

France since 1870 can be traced through the differences between Gambetta's Belleville Manifesto of 1869, the Popular Front Programme of 1936, and the Resistance Charter of 1944–5. Gambetta specifically separated the political and social strands of the revolutionary tradition, maintaining that 'the progressive achievement of these reforms depends absolutely on the political regime and on political forms'. He held that the right order of priority was to achieve liberty and equality first, in the form of universal suffrage and civil rights within a republican regime, and then the appropriate social and economic changes would surely follow. The Popular Front aimed at considerable extension of economic equality and social security through State action and legislative control. The Resistance Charter aimed at more fundamental 'structural reforms', involving more direct participation by organized labour in the direction and management of economic life. All three programmes gave priority to the establishment of republican, parliamentary government, and the securing of political and civil liberties. The eternal problem was to devise a political system which would be capable of achieving social democracy: and it was here that each experiment ran into great obstacles.

The Provisional Governments nationalized the mines, the main power industries, transport and credit. They visualized a three-decker national economy, with nationalization at one level, national control at another, and free enterprise at the third. German penetration of the main French industries, and the sequestration of the main collaborationist trusts, made some degree of nationalization almost inevitable. The parties differed about how much further nationalization and *dirigisme* should be pressed. The main outcome was the Monnet Plan for the re-equipment and modernization of French industries within a period of five years. By 1951 this plan, one of the most realistic and successful programmes of economic reconstruction ever achieved in French history, had restored French industrial output to its pre-war levels and had surpassed them. An extensive system of social security, including lavish family allowances and more adequate pensions, was introduced in implementation of the promises of the Resistance Charter. Its primary aim was to encourage the growth of population and to safeguard the future, but it also aimed at an immediate redistribution of national income. Financial and monetary policy was planned by the new *Conseil national du Crédit*, set up in December 1945. Attempts were made to create economic regions decentralized from Paris, but only the Lower Rhone project achieved any degree of distinct regional development.

The most noteworthy feature of all these plans was that they gained impetus and succeeded almost exactly in proportion to the extent to which they were entrusted to the bureaucracy and shook themselves free from the political *impasse* in which both the Provisional Governments and the early ministries of the Fourth Republic found themselves. The Monnet Plan was never formally approved by parliamentary legislation, and did not even rest on government decrees. The *Conseil national du Crédit* was a semi-professional body, given a large degree of autonomy. It was the *Inspecteurs Généraux de l'Économie nationale* who mainly sponsored economic regionalism. Again, the familiar features of Third Republican history were perpetuated. Reforms sponsored by forceful individuals and by the bureaucracy proved more successful than those sponsored by parliamentary parties. The 'Constitution of the year VIII' is stronger than that of 1946, just as it was stronger than that of 1875.[1]

The remaking of democratic government in France was conditioned by historic factors, both recent and remote in time. Given the democratic tradition examined in the earlier chapters of this book, the Constitution had to be in form a Republic. On that issue there was no dispute in 1945 and 1946. Given that it had to be a Republic, the formation and expectations of the majority of French parties required that it should be a parliamentary Republic. Given the well-established fears of a dictatorship, either of one party or one man, which were strengthened by the experience of a 'presidential

---

[1] Cf. above, pp. 55–6 and 175–6, and Daniel Halévy: *Décadence de la Liberté*.

State' under both Vichy and General de Gaulle and reinforced by the emergence of a strong Communist Party at liberation, it was inevitable that a parliamentary Republic should seek to make the government directly controllable by Parliament. For this reason Article 48 of the new Constitution became the most basic of all its provisions: 'Ministers are collectively responsible to the National Assembly for the general policy of the Cabinet and individually responsible for their personal actions.' Yet, with the existence of a large aggressive Communist Party and, within a few years, of active Right-wing movements hostile to parliamentary government, the new regime was destined to the fate of every previous regime since the time of Napoleon I: the need to fight for survival against large disloyal oppositions, seeking to overthrow it from within and without. Most of the conditions that predisposed the new regime to resemble the old in all its essentials were already present when the Provisional Governments of General de Gaulle began their work of political reconstruction.

VII

THE FOURTH REPUBLIC

The Constitution

THE political *impasse* which characterized the first parliament of the Fourth Republic was foreshadowed by the deadlock of the Constituent Assemblies. The first Constituent Assembly drafted a unicameral constitution and submitted it to referendum in May 1946. It was rejected by 10,583,724 votes to 9,453,675. A second Constituent Assembly was therefore elected forthwith, and contained much the same balance of parties. It prepared a draft of a bicameral constitution in which the second chamber had very slight power: and this draft was in turn submitted to referendum in October 1946. It passed by 9,120,576 votes to 7,980,333 votes, with another 7,938,884 voters abstaining from voting at all. The Constitution of the Fourth Republic was, therefore, accepted by an actual minority of the electorate, but by 53·3 per cent of those who validly voted.[1] The elections for the new National Assembly were held in November, and the Constitution came into force on 24 December 1946, when the second chamber, the Council of the Republic, first met. In January M. Vincent Auriol, a Socialist, was elected first President of the Republic.

These prolonged debates, accompanied by equally strenuous discussions in the Press, offer rich material for the student of political ideas and constitutional devices.[2] Only the practical outcome of the debates need concern the student of how democracy works in France.

---

[1] For the English text of this Constitution, see Appendix I (J) below.
[2] There is a brief summary of them in *A Constitution for the Fourth Republic* (Foundation Pamphlet No. 2) published by the Foundation for Foreign Affairs in Washington, in 1947; and in Gordon Wright: *The Reshaping of French Democracy* (1950).

The Preamble to the Constitution, which occasioned undue delays in formulation, deserves some attention, if only because of its self-conscious reversion to the principles of 1789 and the French revolutionary tradition. But it did more than reaffirm the principles of the Rights of Man and of the Citizen. It proclaimed the need to extend them to social affairs and economic life. It spoke of the 'duty to work and the right to obtain employment'; of trade union rights and 'the right to strike', of providing social security especially for the young and the old, and of the State's duty to provide 'free, secular public education at all levels'; of international obligations and of France's 'traditional mission' to guide colonial peoples for whom she has assumed responsibility towards self-government and democracy. It echoed many of the principles and aspirations of the 'Resistance Charter' of 1944.

In the mode of election and the constitutional functions of the Presidency it introduced no significant innovations, in spite of the frequent demands that the President should be less of a mere figurehead than under the Third Republic. By 1946 General de Gaulle had resigned from office and had waged a campaign for a Constitution which should abandon the parliamentary pattern of *gouvernement d'assemblée* for a presidential system, with a strong executive more independent of the legislature. Both the Vichy Governments and the early Provisional Governments had been, in fact, variants of such a system, and the General made no secret of who should, in his view, be head of such a constitution. This sufficed to condemn a strong Presidency in the eyes of the parliamentary parties. At the same time, the Communists demanded a single-chamber system, on the model of the Convention of 1793. Such an arrangement was distrusted both by the Right and the Centre parties as too demagogic and revolutionary in character. The pattern of parliamentary government which emerged from the series of compromises made necessary by the balance of parties within the Constituent Assembly, and by popular rejection of the first draft constitution, therefore avoided both these extremes. In doing so, it edged closer and closer to a repetition of the arrangements of the Third Republic, which had been so utterly rejected by the referendum of October 1945. The wheel came full circle: and after a short experience of the working of the new Constitution it could be said with truth that 'the Fourth Republic is already dead: it has given way to the Third'. There is no more striking expression of the continuities and permanence of the forces which mould French life and politics.

The most important substantial differences from the constitution of the Third Republic are only two: the great weakening of the second chamber (the *Conseil de la République*) in legislative power and in relation to the other chamber (the *Assemblée nationale*); and the abolition, by Article 13, of the former system of *décrets-lois*. Even so, the Council of the Republic is given a voice in the election of the President, and in constitutional revision, and its 'opinion' is required on legislation and for declarations of war. In December 1948 its members adopted the old title of 'Senators'. And although a government may no longer issue *décrets-lois* because the National Assembly is forbidden to delegate its right to vote laws, it has other resources for direct administrative action, including all the old *pouvoir réglementaire* of the executive in France.[1]

The other changes are more spectacular than substantial. The vote to women, guaranteed by the Preamble and already in 1945 embodied in the electoral laws, appears to have made no great difference to the working of the regime as compared with the Third Republic. The elaborate arrangements by which the National Assembly might be dissolved before the expiry of its full term (now fixed at five years instead of four) were not invoked at all during the first Assembly: though within five years it overthrew eight ministries and produced

---

[1] For discussion of these arrangements see J. Théry: *Le Gouvernement de la IVe République* (1949); O. R. Taylor: *The Fourth Republic of France: Constitution and Political Parties* (1951); and the excellent examination of the whole parliamentary system of government by D. W. S. Lidderdale: *The Parliament of France* (2nd ed., 1954).

several other still-born ministries. Articles 49–51 were first invoked by Edgar Faure in November 1955 and the second National Assembly was dissolved more than six months before its normal expiry. It had overthrown seven governments in four and a half years. The highly opportunistic manner of the dissolution, and Faure's use of a constitutional nicety to defeat the expressed wishes of both chambers, made even this use of the power controversial. The outcome of the ensuing elections, which brought unexpected gains to the two extremist opposition parties of the Communists and Poujadists, so strongly recalled the unhappy crisis of *Seize Mai* in 1877 that it served as a discouraging precedent for future use of this power.[1] The dissolution emphasized how little such a power is liable to achieve in a multi-party system, where elections do not clearly indicate a new government. Each government has to be found after the new Assembly meets, and it emerges from party compromises. The Fourth Republic conformed to the same pattern of *gouvernement d'assemblée* and ministerial collapsibility as the Third, not because of its written constitution but because of its multi-party system.

The ministries also showed the familiar features of continuity (or recurrence) of the same men in office. From liberation in September 1944 until June 1954, except for an interlude of one month, foreign policy was kept in the hands of either Georges Bidault or Robert Schuman, both members of the Catholic Democrat Party (*Mouvement Républicain Populaire*). The Socialist Jules Moch held office in every ministry formed during the first National Assembly, and held the Ministry of the Interior through four of them consecutively. Social-service posts, such as the Ministries of Agriculture, Education, Public Health and Labour, were all held by one man for considerable periods of time. It has been pointed out that 'of 16 premiers elected from 1947 to 1953, 12 came from the previous cabinet, and 10 joined the following one'. Rarely did less than half the members of one cabinet fail to reappear in the next. This was

---

[1] See above, p. 95.

THE FOURTH REPUBLIC

equally reminiscent of the regular practice of the Third Republic.[1]

There were no doubt many different reasons for this reversion to type. The document in which the constitution was laid down was silent on many points, and these gaps in the constitution were usually filled by simple continuance of the customary arrangements and accepted habits prevalent under the Third Republic. The place and the rules of procedure for the election of the President of the Republic were determined by custom in 1946 and 1953. The conduct of negotiations between the President and likely candidates for the premiership was prescribed, in Article 45, as involving 'the customary consultations'. The power of custom was strengthened by the reappearance of so many veteran parliamentarians in high office: President Vincent Auriol, Édouard Herriot as President of the National Assembly, Léon Blum as Prime Minister in 1946, and Paul Ramadier as his successor, Paul Reynaud as Minister of Finance in 1948. The revival of the Radical Socialist Party as an almost indispensable Centre party brought to the premiership such old-time parliamentary hands as André Marie and Henri Queuille. Queuille had sat in nineteen pre-war cabinets.

Even constitutional procedure reverted to type. Article 45 implied a three-stage procedure for forming a new ministry: designation of the new premier by the President of the Republic, acceptance of him and his policy by an absolute majority of the National Assembly, and finally the formal appointment of the premier and the ministers by the President. This procedure was followed in 1947 and served to strengthen the position of the premier *vis-à-vis* his ministerial colleagues, for it was he alone and not the government whom the Assembly approved.

---

[1] Philip Williams: *Politics in Post-War France* (1954), p. 380. See above, p. 112, and the detailed examination of the pre-war system in A. Soulier: *L'Instabilité ministérielle sous la Troisième République, 1871–1938* (1939). As M. Soulier remarks (p. 483), 'Instabilité du Cabinet, stabilité des ministres, telles sont les deux faces inséparables de la vie politique française, les deux manifestations concomitantes du régime parlementaire.'

But Marie and Queuille chose most of their cabinet before being accepted by the Assembly: and the inherent logic of composing the cabinet and agreeing its policy before, rather than after, seeking acceptance by parliament was in their favour.

It is debatable how far the electoral systems of the Fourth Republic contributed to any significant changes in the political system as a whole. The electoral laws of October 1946 were modelled closely on those by which the two Constituent Assemblies of 1945 and 1946 had been elected. They provided France, for the first time, with a full system of proportional representation. Each metropolitan *département* was given one deputy for every 100,000 inhabitants, with a minimum of two. Candidates had to stand as members of lists, and each list had to have as many names as the constituency had seats. Each elector could vote for only one list, though he could express preferences for candidates within the list. When votes had been counted seats were distributed among parties according to the highest average in each constituency: so that seats went in turn to whichever list would have the highest average of votes per seat if it received the seat about to be allocated. The system tended to favour the larger parties, especially in the smaller constituencies which were mostly rural ones. In 1946 by-elections were made unnecessary by the rule that any vacant seat should be taken by the next available unelected candidate of the list to which the former deputy had belonged; but they were restored in 1951.

The electoral law of 9 May 1951 was passed by the Centre parties to offset the inherent advantages enjoyed by their larger and better-disciplined rivals, the Communists and the Gaullists. For all constituencies except those of the Paris region, it provided that wherever one list gained an absolute majority of the votes cast it should get all the seats: and it enabled national parties (i.e. those presenting lists in at least thirty *départements*) to make alliances (*apparentements*) which could for this purpose count as one list. Thus each party's share of seats now depended not only on its own share of votes (which aided the largest parties) but also on the alliances it was able to form with other parties (which aided the Centre parties). Since Communists could find no allies and Gaullists few, they suffered a disadvantage. In the Paris region, however, consisting of the 8 constituencies of Seine and Seine-et-Oise which returned 75 deputies, the Communists dominated the working-class districts and the R.P.F. attracted many middle-class votes. There a different and more complicated system of proportional representation was instituted, again calculated to favour the smaller parties. In all constituencies the voter was now given the right of *panachage* (splitting his vote between two or more lists), as well as of expressing preferences among candidates within one list. Despite this greater freedom of choice given to the voter, the list system remained essentially one of party voting and was manipulated mainly by local branches of the parties. The elections revealed that the Centre parties gained 51 per cent of the votes and 62·5 per cent of the seats; the R.P.F. gained 21·7 per cent of the votes and 19·6 per cent of the seats; the Communists gained 25·9 per cent of the votes and 17·8 per cent of the seats. It has been estimated that the electoral system of 1946, if unchanged in 1951, would have given the Centre only 44·7 per cent of the seats for its 51 per cent of the votes, and so by penalizing the smaller groups would have enabled the two extremists parties to wreck the parliamentary system.[1]

Plans by both chambers to amend the electoral laws yet again before the elections of 1956 were frustrated. When Edgar Faure's government was defeated in December, he took the snap decision to invoke Article 51 and dissolve the National Assembly. Opinion was setting in favour of a reversion to single-member constituencies with a second ballot—the classical electoral procedure of the Third Republic still generally favoured by the Radicals. For lack of time the elections of January 1956 had to be held under the electoral laws of 1951. The results showed that even the devices introduced to favour

---

[1] See Peter Campbell: *French Electoral Systems and Elections, 1789–1957* (1958), pp. 102–27: an admirable account of these electoral technicalities. Cf. Philip Williams: op. cit., Appendix VI.

the Centre parties availed little, since the Centre was itself split between the parties supporting Faure and the *Front Républicain* led by Mendès-France. *Apparentements* won absolute majorities, and therefore all the seats, in only eleven constituencies, and affected results elsewhere only as regards marginal seats. The whole record of electoral changes, in the Fourth Republic as in the Third, suggests that both the fears and the expectations they arouse are usually much exaggerated, and that if the French parliamentary system is to find greater ministerial stability and stronger leadership, these blessings are unlikely to be achieved by tinkering with electoral devices. The roots of France's political ills lie deeper and elsewhere.

The Political System

The fundamental reasons for the reversions to type already noted and for the continuing *immobilisme* of French government lay in the nature of the French party system itself, and beyond that again in the structure of French public opinion and national life. The tripartite system of 1944–6, which prevailed in the two Constituent Assemblies and dominated the shaping of the new constitution, did not long survive into the Fourth Republic. In May 1947 Paul Ramadier eliminated Communists from his ministry and at the same time General de Gaulle formed his new *Rassemblement du Peuple Français* (R.P.F.),[1] destined to become in effect a new right-wing opposition. These events marked the end of *tripartisme*, and with the recovery of strength by the Radicals came the formation of the 'Third Force'—a succession of coalitions of Socialists, Radicals, M.R.P., and Independents—opposed on the left by the Communists and on the right by the Gaullists. When in the parliamentary elections of June 1951 the R.P.F. won

[1] The R.P.F. was formally constituted on 14 April and won its first electoral victories in the municipal elections of October. See Jacques Debû-Bridel, *Les Partis contre Charles de Gaulle* (1948), for a well-informed but highly favourable account of its beginnings, and Dorothy Pickles: *French Politics* (1953), Chapter V, for a more critical account.

some 120 seats whilst the Communists retained 100, the party spectrum assumed its more familiar symmetry. The governments during the second Assembly (1951–5) were coalitions of the Centre and Right Centre from which the Socialists held aloof.

In 1939 M. Soulier had noted, as an inherent tendency of the Third Republic, *le phénomène de la migration vers le Centre des grands partis*. Gambetta, with his Belleville programme, was ousted on the left by Clemenceau with his Montmartre programme; he in turn was pushed towards the Centre by the growth of the Socialist Party of Jaurès; and the Socialists in turn by the Communists.[1] A similar process now took place on the Right, with the rise first of the R.P.F. and then, in 1955, of the Poujadists, each of which disintegrated once it had registered its protests against previous disequilibrium. By 1951 the centre of gravity of the National Assembly had shifted fairly steadily towards the Right: witness the succession, to Socialist premiers like Blum and Ramadier, of M.R.P. and Radical premiers such as Schuman and Bidault, Marie and Queuille. The elections of 1951 produced a 'hexagonal' chamber, in which membership was evenly spread between Communists and Socialists on the Left, M.R.P. and Radicals in the Centre, and Independents, Conservatives, and R.P.F. on the Right. The governments of the second Assembly continued the drift towards the Right with René Pleven, Antoine Pinay, René Mayer, and Joseph Laniel. Between 1944 and 1954 the pendulum, both of electoral opinion and of party-coalitions in power, swung fairly persistently from Left to Right. When Pierre Mendès-France, leader of the Left wing of the Right Centre, formed his crucial ministry in June 1954, he was the most dead-centre figure imaginable in that hexagonal Assembly.

The party spectrum became still more complex as a result of the activities of Mendès-France. The Radical Party split into three groups, because although Mendès-France remained official leader of the party with 45 deputies, his rival Edgar Faure led a splinter-group of 13 calling themselves the

[1] A. Soulier: op. cit., p. 481. Cf. above, p. 121.

Rassemblement des Gauches Républicaines (R.G.R.) and the older Radicals, led by Queuille and André Morice, also separated. At the same time, the Gaullist R.P.F., having suffered severe reverses and inner schisms, survived in parliament as a small group of 21 *Républicains Sociaux*; and after the elections of January 1956 the violent Poujadist group, numbering at first 52 but eventually only 37, appeared on the extreme Right. The third National Assembly also contained a considerably larger Communist Party of 150 deputies and a still more splintered Centre. The Socialists, with 100 deputies, resumed their participation in government in January 1956 when Guy Mollet, their leader, formed a Left-Centre coalition depending for its survival on support from the conservative groups. By following a broadly conservative policy this government survived for longer than any government since 1928—a total period of slightly more than 16 months. Similar coalitions led by the Radicals Maurice Bourgès-Maunoury and Félix Gaillard succeeded it during 1957, with the M.R.P. edging back into a share of power from which they had excluded themselves after the elections of 1956.

In these ways, too, the political system of the Fourth Republic approximated more and more closely to the classical pattern of the Third Republic. The evolution from the three 'monolithic' Left-wing giants of 1946 to the kaleidoscopic fragmentation of 1957 was an even more significant evidence of reversion to type than the affinities of the two constitutions. A dozen years after liberation the only substantial novelty that remained in the party system was the subservience of deputies, even of ministers, to the directives of their party organizations outside parliament. The Communists had always known this discipline. But now the Socialists, too, showed it to a marked degree, and they assumed the role of the destroyers of ministries because their deputies and ministers had so often to oppose measures at the dictates of the party executive, rather than seek to compromise about them for the sake of preserving ministerial stability. The list system of the electoral laws tended to enhance the power of the party organization. It became abundantly clear that the reasons for such a political system, and for the ministerial instability that went with it, must be sought deeper than in mere constitutional arrangements or even political habits. They must be sought in the needs and urges of French national life, and in the conditions of public schism that the experience of war, defeat, invasion, occupation, collaboration, and liberation had overlaid and had in so many ways aggravated. Behind this changing party kaleidoscope lay a shifting balance of social forces.

The Social Balance

In 1945 it seemed that the traditional bias in favour of agricultural and peasant interests had diminished, and industrial labour was now more strongly organized with trade unions taking a more direct and active role in political life. So long as the experience, *mystique*, and memory of the Resistance remained fresh in men's minds, this more even balance between farming and industrial interests, countryside and town, seemed likely to be perpetuated. The peasants had, in general, done better out of the war than the industrial workers, and were suspect of having done too well out of the black market. The 'big three' parties of 1945 were all Leftist in social policy and the Right-wing peasant parties suffered eclipse. Ten years later it became apparent that this impression had been much exaggerated. The high hopes of more complete 'social justice', as understood by the clandestine press or the Resistance Charter, faded along with the *mystique* of Resistance itself.[1] Post-war economic conditions favoured the farmers. As the growers of food in a period of rising food prices they prospered, and because their wealth lay in real property they suffered

[1] It is probable that the moral solidarity of the Resistance had always, naturally enough, been exaggerated, though it was real among many of the younger generation. It was blighted mainly by the excesses of the Communists and the prolonged vindictiveness of *épuration*, even before the unheroic nature of the parliamentary Republic lost it the sympathies of idealists. See Ronald Matthews: *The Death of the Fourth Republic* (1954) and Catherine Gavin: *Liberated France* (1955).

least from inflation. The peasant's standard of living tended to rise whilst that of the wage-earning industrial worker, the salaried public servant, and the small *rentier* fell. The farmer could still, moreover, evade direct taxation much more simply than the wage-earner or salaried worker.

At first the C.G.T., fallen very much under Communist Party control, could claim a membership of more than 5 million. As a result of the split in organized labour, brought about by the secession of the *Force ouvrière* in 1947 and the continuance of the independent Christian and other trade unions, the total influence of organized labour soon diminished.[1] Whilst Communist abuse of their power in the C.G.T. unions led to a decline in the membership of these unions, the non-Communist unions also remained weak and disunited. These facts, combined with the divisions between the main parties for which industrial workers voted (Communists, Socialists, and M.R.P.), meant that electoral strength still lay, as in the Third Republic, with the bulk of voters in the rural and semi-rural constituencies. Given the distribution of population in France, most deputies sat for such constituencies, and every party had to adapt its electoral programmes and methods to win them. Thus for familiar historical reasons the balance of political power was tipped once again in favour of rural interests.

In spite of the success of the Monnet Plan, industry and trade also showed great imperviousness to the trends making for concentration and more large-scale units of production and distribution. It was estimated in 1950 that whereas there had been about 1 million shopkeepers in 1940, there were 1½ million by 1950. This remarkable tenacity of the 'little man' in business, accompanied by the prosperity of the peasant farmer, explains such political phenomena as the speedy revival of the Radical Party and those Independent conservative groups which traditionally claim to represent the 'little man'; the importance of such pressure-groups as the *Confédération Générale des Petites et Moyennes Entreprises* led by the

[1] See Val L. Lorwin: *The French Labor Movement* (1954), for an authoritative discussion of these developments.

enterprising M. Léon Gingembre;[1] the capacity of the 'alcohol lobby' of sugar-beet and wine-growing interests to defeat Mendès-France and coerce Edgar Faure; and the sudden rise, when the first check to inflation narrowed the profit-margins of the small shopkeepers, of the movement of excited violence led by Pierre Poujade.

The social restiveness and political unsteadiness of the Fourth Republic concealed remarkably solid improvements in health, wealth, and productivity. The population grew by natural increase in a way unknown during the Third Republic. For the first time in modern history France's birth-rate exceeded that of Britain or Germany or Italy. The death-rate, and especially the infant death-rate, fell impressively from the abnormally high figure of 112 per thousand in 1945 to 52 by 1950, and the downward trend continued to around 40 per thousand. During the post-war decade the total population increased by nearly 3 million. In the same years the recovery of the French economy was so great that industrial production was more than 60 per cent above pre-war level, agricultural output 25 per cent above the average of the 1930s, and gross national production some 40 per cent higher than in 1938. The economy, like the social and political systems, had its strength as well as its weaknesses. If housing remained bad and food prices high, unemployment was almost unknown. If too many inefficient units and methods survived, the French railways, hydro-electric generating plants, and motor industries ranked among the best in the world. The Marshall Plan helped the progress of the Monnet Plan. Modernization was made easier by the nationalization of the major industries and services after liberation. The discovery of rich resources of minerals, especially oil, in the Sahara desert opened new vistas of economic expansion. All that her scientists and technologists could do to save France was, it seemed, being done, and the achievements were impressive.

[1] See the remarkable analysis of this aspect of French life in Herbert Lüthy: *The State of France* (1955), Part II, and the somewhat similar discussion in David Schoenbrun: *As France Goes* (1957), Part III. Cf. Jacques Fauvet: *Les Forces Politiques en France* (1951).

But if the country as a whole was rich, the wealth was unevenly distributed and the State remained poor. An out-of-date fiscal system led to a most inequitable spread of the burdens of taxation. Because so many industrial workers felt under-privileged and outside the *pays légal*, Communism had a strong appeal. The economic and financial issues that beset the governments of the Fourth Republic—and so often destroyed them—had little novelty: depreciation of the franc, inflationary rise in prices, unbalanced budgets, extensive tax evasion, hoarding of gold, chronic deficits in the balance of trade and of payments, had a strong pre-war flavour.

The interaction of the political and economic systems of France varied in its effects throughout the post-war decade. In the early years the temporary solidarity of the Resistance and co-operation among the three Left-wing parties coincided with rapid economic reconstruction and progress. The political disintegration and great strikes of 1947–8 impeded economic progress as a whole. The emergence of the 'Third Force' in 1948–50 gradually brought steadier progress again, and coincided with the advances of the Monnet Plan. The emergence of the R.P.F. coincided with the growing strain of the war in Indo-China, social unrest, and a rising cost of living. The fact that the heavy electoral gains of both Communists and Poujadists in January 1956 followed three years of stabilized prices and two of rapid economic expansion suggests, however, that political changes have other than economic explanations.

Certainly party divisions rarely coincided, save for the Poujadists, with social pressures or economic divisions. Communists got an important measure of support in some areas from peasant proprietors, the M.R.P. and Radicals drew upon a socially varied clientele, and the variegated backing of the Gaullists became apparent in the speedy disintegration of the R.P.F. The very lack of correlation between party structure and social group was an important factor in the parliamentary behaviour, as well as the electoral tactics, of the political parties. It was perhaps all the more tempting for party leaders, obliged to equivocate and compromise in practice, to exaggerate their ideological differences and strike postures of theoretical intransigence: until, from time to time, one of them exploited public weariness of even these attitudes and, like Antoine Pinay in 1952, announced: 'The remedies are neither on the left nor on the right. They have no parliamentary label. They are technical steps which must be taken in an atmosphere of political armistice.' Then the ghosts of Vichy walked again, and dreams of technocracy blurred the true revolutionary tradition of democracy in France.

What was most conspicuously lacking in the social scene was national cohesion and a willingness to forgo sectional advantages for the national good. Could a people that was so atomistic and so sectionalized sustain the joint effort needed to keep France a great nation? In old-fashioned military terms, the need for concerted effort was well understood. Frenchmen fought bravely in Indo-China for eight years, for a cause that was not only forlorn but anachronistic. They fought in Algeria for a principle—the essential unity between France and Algeria—which no longer had much reality. The costliest failure of statesmanship in the Fourth Republic was the failure to adjust party attitudes and colonial policies to the world-wide colonial revolution of the mid-twentieth century. Here, more than anywhere else, adherence to traditions and habits proved an impediment to success.

France met the challenge of foreign policy somewhat more adequately than she met the challenge of colonial policy. The Coal and Steel Community created in 1953 sprang from the initiative of Robert Schuman in 1950. This imaginative arrangement for softening the economic and military rivalries of France and Germany was followed by a mutually accepted settlement of the Saar problem. Although the proposals for a European Defence Community (E.D.C.) foundered on French fears of rearming Germany, there appeared a substitute for it in Western European Union, linked closely with N.A.T.O. and resting on British participation. It was wherever foreign policy and colonial relations merged—in Tunisia, Egypt, and the Middle East—that the foreign relations of the Republic were most unhappy.

The effect of both colonial and foreign problems in domestic politics was, above all, to add yet further dividing issues to a body politic already fragmented by a medley of historic and contemporary divisions. Sometimes they reinforced divisions that already existed on other grounds: the Poujadists, like the Gaullists, urged a strong imperialistic policy in North Africa whilst also attacking the Centre governments for their social policy at home and denouncing the parliamentary form of the Republic. At the other extreme the Communists were intransigent on all issues. But the Centre parties, too, though driven to combine to keep parliamentary government working at all, remained separated by their own intransigences. Catholic Democrats remained at daggers-drawn with both Socialists and Radicals on the issue of clericalism in education. The Socialists, kept apart from the rest of the moderate Left by their *laïcité*, were compelled to bid against the Communists for working-class votes. Prevented from urging economies in government expenditure by their powerful clientele of public officials and schoolteachers, and their concern to maintain social services, they could not whole-heartedly back the policies of the Right Centre. Mollet, in office, outdid the Right in the imperialism of his policy, just as Mendès-France, in office, outdid the Left in his willingness to undertake radical reforms. Félix Gaillard, in his attempts to grapple with French financial difficulties in 1957–8, found himself in a dilemma familiar enough to his predecessors: inconsistent pressure from the Right to cut expenditure rather than raise new taxes, though not to withdraw subsidies from those economically privileged groups, such as the farmers and small producers, whose support he needed: and equally inconsistent pressure from the Left to check inflation yet to make no cuts in expenditure on public officials or social services.

The multiple fractures of French opinion, and the lack of firm correlation between party alignments and social divisions, meant that in a parliament designed to reflect, with considerable accuracy, the state of opinion in the country, a differently constituted majority had to be found for settling each issue that arose. Such a task either defeated the ingenuity of a premier, so that he relapsed into *immobilisme* and like Queuille shelved problems rather than tackling them; or it called for unusual agility and energy, such as were shown by Pierre Mendès-France in 1954.

His ministry of June 1954, like its immediate predecessors, excluded both Communists and Socialists, and was a Right-Centre coalition of Radical Socialists, former Gaullists, men from the U.D.S.R. of René Pleven, and from the Independents, and two renegade members of the M.R.P. It lacked even the political cohesion of most of its predecessors, and was composed of a high proportion of new men. It achieved the remarkable feat of gaining the votes of both the Communists and Gaullists for its policy in Indo-China and Tunisia. The vote of August which killed the project of E.D.C. showed how much this issue divided parties internally. The Socialists, Radicals, dissident Gaullists, and U.D.S.R. voted in almost equal numbers on either side. The Communists were unanimously, the Gaullists almost unanimously, against it, the M.R.P. almost unanimously for it. In September Mendès-France used the resignation of three ministers to strengthen the elements of the Right in his cabinet, and thereby secured support for the ensuing London Agreement which replaced E.D.C. In October he attempted to shift its centre of gravity back to the Left, inviting six Socialists to join the ministry in order to tackle the economic problems which he regarded as the supreme test of his stewardship. He sought, in short, to find for each sector of policy that particular 'majority of the majority' needed to approve it: a degree of mobility within a single ministry that even the tactical refinements of the Third Republic could hardly parallel. Nor did such methods become normal in the Fourth.

The response of the regime to the Algerian crisis of May 1958 was very different. If the circumstances of the crisis were a conjunction of all the main elements of weakness inherent in post-war France and in the regime of the Fourth Republic, so also the nature of the crisis drew together in the common cause of 'saving the Republic' all political parties save the extreme Right. The parliamentary crisis created by the defeat of M. Félix Gaillard's ministry on 16 April was from the outset regarded as the most serious deadlock of the third National Assembly, and it lasted a month. Hostilities in Algeria had lasted for some three and a half years, and by then had become a war of attrition engaging nearly half a million French troops. At the moment when the parliamentary deadlock was broken by the formation of a new government headed by M. Pierre Pflimlin, Generals Salan and Massu in Algiers challenged the authority of the Assembly and found vigorous backing from the extreme Right inside France. The menace of military defiance awakened enough echoes of Boulangism to rally most parties to the support of the new government. The Assembly invested M. Pflimlin first with wide emergency powers to meet the situation in France (by a majority of 461 to 114), and then with special powers to deal with the situation in Algeria (by 475 to 100). Both the width of the emergency powers and the size of the government's parliamentary majority were unprecedented in the Fourth Republic. Confronted with the most acute crisis of its existence, the first response of the regime was not mobility but solidarity.

To the classical challenge of the Army to the civilian authority[1] there was added the challenge of personal power in the attitude of General de Gaulle. Repeating the familiar condemnations of the Constitution which he had made since 1946, the General emerged as the candidate of the Army officers in Algiers and the Right-wing extremists in France. Although insisting that he sought office only by constitutional means, de Gaulle announced his 'readiness to assume the powers of the Republic', and hinted at the need for exceptional powers to be delegated by 'a procedure which would also be exceptional—for investiture by the National Assembly, for example'. Between the alternatives of a semi-constitutional personal power backed by the extreme Right, and a 'popular front' canvassed by the Communists and backed by the power of organized labour, the Centre parties found themselves once more a 'Third Force', striving to preserve in essentials the traditional pattern of parliamentary democracy

[1] See above, pp. 152-63.

in France. The position in May 1958 was a veritable summary of the predicaments of post-war France.

But the crisis, born of the impact of Army defiance in Algeria on the political *impasse* in Paris, was not to be settled in this conventional way. Events of the week 26 May–3 June produced one of the most dramatic reversals in French history. M. Pflimlin, despite his enjoyment of drastic emergency powers, warned the National Assembly that France was 'threatened by civil war' and tendered his resignation. President Coty, similarly convinced, invited General de Gaulle to form a new government and in a message to the National Assembly on 29 May threatened to resign unless it accepted de Gaulle's return to power. Two days later he formally designated de Gaulle as Prime Minister. On 1 June the Assembly accepted de Gaulle by 329 votes to 224, and on the following day granted him full powers for six months. On 3 June it gave him power to reform the Constitution and submit the reforms to referendum.

The surrender of so much authority to General de Gaulle was hailed as the formal death of the Fourth Republic. In so far as the Fourth Republic had been, in substance, a resurrection of the Third and a system of *gouvernement d'assemblée*, this seemed indeed its demise. And yet, so powerful are the forces of continuity in France, it would be rash to sign the death-certificate. The General's new government included—to the indignation of the Right in Algeria—both M. Pflimlin and M. Guy Mollet, who were closely identified with the previous governments and the regime of parties. De Gaulle spoke with studied moderation and ambiguity. There were signs that even a Fifth Republic might be less novel, in its personalities and modes of working, than many Frenchmen hoped or feared. Although its Constitution, adopted by referendum on 28 September, gave great power to the executive, it contained also possibilities of a future *reprise* of effective parliamentary power.

Conclusion

There is clearly nothing artificial in treating the history of the Third and Fourth Republics as a continuous record of the working of democracy in France. The Vichy Governments and the Provisional Governments are but interludes in a remarkably consistent and continuous story, and throw sidelights of their own on the nature of the larger development. It only remains to be asked whether it is possible to formulate any general principles, or to detect any permanent factors, which help to explain this unity of French historical evolution during the past ninety years.

The first and most obvious factor is the new meaning of Republicanism. When Bismarck was forming the *Dreikaiserbund* of 1873 he wrote to Von Arnim, his ambassador in Paris, 'A French Republic will with great difficulty find a monarchical ally against us.' When the Third Republic was being created 'the Republican Anarchy' was still a bogey to scare the dynastic rulers of Europe, and France was the traditional home and origin of that bogey. After 1789 it was she, more than any other country, who had made 'red republicanism' a challenge to the whole established order in Europe. Lord Tennyson was reflecting accurately the reputation of France in Europe when he wrote of 'the red fool-fury of the Seine'.[1]

When the Fourth Republic was founded the situation was exactly the opposite. Not only was republicanism the normal form of government in Europe and monarchy the exception, but France herself was no longer regarded as the traditional home of revolutionary ideas. Within a decade of Bismarck's expressed hopes of making her the republican pariah of Europe, republicanism in France had become a force of order, stability, and even bourgeois respectability. She was an ally of Tsarist Russia and a friend of monarchical Britain. In that short time republicanism lost its redness and its scarifying implications, and France was well on the way to reversing her nineteenth-century role in Europe. It was the achievement of the Third Republic to make republicanism as conservative and respectable

[1] An excellent survey of this 'red' tradition may be found in John Plamenatz: *The Revolutionary Movement in France, 1815–71* (1952); and see John A. Scott: *Republican Ideas and the Liberal Tradition in France, 1870–1914* (1951) for a similar survey of the changing yet continuous tradition after 1871.

in the old world as the United States had made it in the new. The 'Conservative Republic' of Thiers which crushed the Commune of Paris, the 'Republic of the Dukes' which succeeded it and devised so conservative a parliamentary regime, combined with the 'Opportunist' republicanism of a tamed Gambetta to transform the whole meaning of the word. For these reasons, the Third Republic was quite unlike either of its predecessors: and the Fourth was predestined to bear a close resemblance to the Third. For after 1870 the whole international position of France changed, as has already been described.[1]

The pattern of this new and respectable republicanism was compounded of three main elements. The first was a strange combination of durability with instability. Whereas the First and Second Republics had been short-lived, the Third lasted a whole lifetime. Ministerial instability was by no means an invention of the Third Republic. It was a feature of the July Monarchy of Louis Philippe and of the Second Empire throughout most of its history. It was the achievement of the Third Republic to end constitutional instability at the price of greater ministerial instability. The penalty of keeping the same formal regime for seventy years was a constant tension and mobility in parliamentary politics. The famous 'Hundred Ministries' became almost as notorious as the 'Two Hundred Families': but both had almost the same continuities of actual personnel and a similar continuity in policy.[2]

The second element was a combination of conservative institutions with revolutionary movements and ideas. There were recurrent demands for constitutional revision, but remarkably few of them ever materialized. It was as if the most dynamic movements in the nation were for ever straining at the leash, finding so little opportunity to achieve far-reaching reforms within the conservative regime that they sought, if no longer to overthrow the regime, at least to modify it. Despite

[1] p. 134 above.
[2] For a spirited and ingenious discussion of this continuity, and a vigorous defence of the Third Republic, see Maurice Reclus: *Grandeur de 'la Troisième'. De Gambetta à Poincaré* (1948).

the much discussed *sinistrisme* of French parties in the Third Republic, it applied to little more than their self-affixed labels. There was as a rule a sharp contrast between the doctrines they professed for electoral consumption and their conservative and defensive behaviour when they were in office. The reasons for this were complex: the prolonging of anti-clerical and anti-militarist disputes long after these issues had ceased to be important for French life; the domination of most ministerial combinations by the Radicals, representing all those who wore their heart on the left but their wallet on the right; the weaknesses and divisions among the socialist and organized labour movements which prevented them from exerting their proportionate influence in parliamentary life. Behind it all lay the legacy of a 'revolutionary' republican tradition which was no longer really revolutionary. The consequences of the paradox were popular cynicism about all parliamentary parties and personalities, and an often irresponsible impatience with constitutional procedures. Both these consequences helped to undermine the Republic itself.

The third element in the pattern was a combination of decisive parliamentary power with a weak and fluid party system. The closed arena of the parliamentary chambers, immune from elections for four years (and, in the Fourth, virtually for five) and able to control ministries by a large repertoire of devices, ensured a system of *gouvernement d'assemblée*. It did nothing to ensure ministerial stability. Strong party discipline and a unified standing opposition, as in Britain, would have modified this system drastically. In conjunction with the highly flexible multi-party system which grew up under the Third Republic, *gouvernement d'assemblée* inevitably produced infinitely collapsible cabinets, confusion of public life, and a habit of *débrouillage* which further weakened public respect for parliamentary government. The consequence was a further paradox, that in a nation devoted to heroic ideals and dogmatic ideologies, national policy was often a patchwork of cautious half-hearted compromises. There was almost a cult of the second-best. The regime itself, in 1875, was accepted *faute de mieux*, as the least objectionable. The second ballot encouraged a habit of 'second thoughts' and 'next-best preferences'. The Centre parties, so constantly the crucial elements in ministerial coalitions, thrived because each extreme preferred them to the other extreme. The Republic was throughout the form of government that divided Frenchmen least: and so, in its own way, was the Fourth Republic.

The pattern which evolved from the interaction of these three elements had great practical advantages but also great psychological weaknesses. Each of these elements could be in one set of circumstances a source of strength, in another a source of weakness according to whether practical or psychological assets counted more. Thus the combination of constitutional durability with government instability shelved the tiresome and disruptive question of the form of regime, but it did so at the price of making democratic government weak government. This mattered little in the *laissez-faire* State of the 1870s. It mattered greatly in the positive State of the twentieth century. The combination of conservative institutions with revolutionary ideas meant that the Republic was the first successful attempt to reconcile the conservative and the revolutionary traditions in France. But it also meant that in the twentieth century the forces of change were resisted and obstructed to the point of frustration. The combination of a system of *gouvernement d'assemblée* with the multi-party system meant that in a deeply divided society the Republic was able to provide a forum where the highest measure of general agreement could be reached without recourse to violence. It also meant that in a half-century of world wars, economic crises, and totalitarian threats, French national policy was often weak when it should have been strong, and hesitant when it needed to be decisive.

Perhaps every regime is, in this sense, a mixed blessing. But what characterized the history of the Third Republic was the fatalistic way in which all its original assets turned, in course of time, into liabilities. The increase in ministerial instability between the wars, the increasing violence of party conflict, and the increasing tendency before the war to govern by decrees, suggest that France was heading for a constitutional crisis anyhow by the 1940s, even if the last National Assembly of the Third Republic had not cut short its own life by self-immolation in 1940.

The history of the Fourth Republic during the dozen years of its existence was of an uphill struggle to re-establish republican parliamentary government—an undertaking still far from being achieved by 1958. In a country convalescent after the ordeal of defeat, occupation, and liberation, and scarred by the deep wounds of social schism and civil war, the Republic proved to have hidden sources of strength. It kept at bay the power of Communism without help from the anti-parliamentary forces of Gaullism. It presided over the economic recovery of France after extreme impoverishment and dislocation. It showed a capacity for survival that confounded its most severe critics and surprised even its friends.

Every year diagnosis of the ills of France is elaborated and refined, and among the best-informed observers there is remarkable unanimity about the reasons for the economic *immobilisme* and the political *impasses*, about the paralysing extent to which France remains haunted by her history and accumulates unresolved dilemmas, about the perils of the multiple fractures in French national life and of the intensified contrasts, technological as well as psychological, between the France of Jean Monnet that looks forward and the France of Léon Gingembre that so tenaciously clings to the past.[1] There is even considerable agreement about the only conceivable remedies that can be applied: not constitutional reforms, nor new political movements, nor novel combinations of parties in power, nor even a dictator; but above all a change of attitude among the bulk of the French people, greater readiness to forget the feuds of yesterday in order to tackle the dilemmas of today, and willingness to abandon sectional privileges in the cause of that most neglected of all ideals in the revolutionary tradition—Fraternity.

[1] Cf. the Swiss Herbert Lüthy: *The State of France* (1955), the English Alexander Werth: *France, 1940–55* (1956), the American David Schoenbrun: *As France Goes* (1957), and the French Jacques Fauvet: *La France déchirée* (1958).

APPENDIX I

CONSTITUTIONAL LAWS

(A) *Resolution of 17 February 1871* nominating M. Thiers Chief of the Executive Power of the French Republic.

The National Assembly, depository of sovereign authority, considering it essential, until the institutions of France are constituted, to make immediate provision for the necessities of government and the conduct of negotiations, decrees that: M. Thiers be named Chief of the Executive Power of the French Republic: he shall exercise his functions under the authority of the National Assembly, with the concurrence of ministers whom he shall choose and over whom he shall preside.

(B) *Law of 31 August 1871* declaring that the Chief of the Executive Power shall take the title of President of the French Republic.

Art. 1. The Chief of the Executive Power shall take the title of President of the French Republic, and shall continue to exercise, under the authority of the National Assembly for so long as it shall not have finished its tasks, the functions which have been delegated to him by the decree of 17 February 1871.

Art. 2. The President of the Republic promulgates the laws as soon as they are passed to him by the President of the National Assembly. He ensures and superintends the execution of laws. He resides where the Assembly is in session. He is heard by the National Assembly whenever he deems it necessary, after having informed the President of the Assembly of his intention. He appoints and dismisses ministers. The Council of ministers and the ministers are responsible before the Assembly. Every act of the President must be countersigned by a minister. The President of the Republic is responsible before the Assembly.

(C) *Law of 13 March 1873*, regulating the attributions of Public Powers and the conditions of ministerial responsibility.

The National Assembly, reserving in its integrity the constituent power which belongs to it, but wishing to extend the attributions of Public Powers, decrees:

Art. 1. The Law of 31 August 1871 is modified as follows:

The President of the Republic communicates with the Assembly by messages which, except for those which open sessions, are read at the tribune by a minister. Nevertheless, he will be heard by the Assembly in the discussion of laws when he deems it necessary, and after his having informed it by a message of his intention. The discussion on the occasion of which the President of the Republic wishes to speak is suspended after the message is received, and the President will be heard on the following day, unless by a special vote it be decided that it shall be on the same day. The session is adjourned after he has been heard, and the discussion is renewed only at a later session. The debate takes place in the absence of the President of the Republic.

Art. 2. The President of the Republic promulgates laws declared to be urgent within three days, and laws not urgent within a month, after the vote of the Assembly. During the three days following, where a law not submitted for three readings is concerned, the President of the Republic shall have the right, in a message stating his reason, to ask for a new debate. For laws submitted to the formality of three readings, the President of the Republic shall have the right, after the second reading, to ask that the third debate should be put on the agenda only after a delay of two months.

Art. 3. The terms of the preceding article shall not apply to acts by which the National Assembly shall exercise the constituent power which is reserved for it in the preamble of the present law.

Art. 4. Interpellations can be addressed only to ministers, and not to the President of the Republic. When interpellations addressed to ministers or petitions sent to the Assembly are concerned with external affairs, the President of the Republic shall have the right to be heard. When such interpellations or petitions have bearing on internal affairs, ministers alone shall reply for acts which concern them. Nevertheless if, by a special resolution, communicated to the Assembly before the opening of the discussion by the Vice-President of the Council of Ministers, the Council declares that the questions raised are connected with the general policy of the government, and thus involve the responsibility of the President of the Republic, the President shall have the right to be heard according to the procedure laid down by Article 1. After hearing the Vice-President of the Council, the Assembly fixes the day for the discussion.

Art. 5. The National Assembly shall not dissolve before having legislated (i) on the organization and mode of transmission of the legislative and executive powers; (ii) on the creation and the attributions of a Second Chamber not due to enter into its duties until after the dissolution of the present Assembly; (iii) on the electoral law. The Government will submit to the Assembly draft laws on the objectives here enumerated.

(D) *Law of 25 February 1875*, relating to the organization of the Public Powers.

Art. 1. The legislative power is exercised by two Assemblies: the Chamber of Deputies and the Senate. The Chamber of Deputies is chosen by universal suffrage, in conditions determined by the electoral law. The composition, method of nomination and attributions of the Senate will be regulated by a special law.

Art. 2. The President of the Republic is elected by an absolute majority of votes by the Senate and the Chamber of Deputies meeting as the National Assembly. He is appointed for seven years. He is re-eligible.

Art. 3. The President of the Republic has the initiative in proposing laws, concurrently with members of the two Chambers. He promulgates laws when they have been voted by the two Chambers: he superintends and ensures their execution. He has the right of pardon; amnesties cannot be granted except by a law. He has direction of the armed forces. He appoints to all civil and military posts. He presides at State occasions; envoys and ambassadors of foreign powers are accredited to him. Every act of the President must be countersigned by a minister.

Art. 4. Gradually, as vacancies occur after the promulgation of the present law, the President of the Republic appoints, in the Council of Ministers, Councillors of State on ordinary service. Councillors of State thus appointed can be dismissed only by a decree passed in the Council of Ministers. Councillors of State appointed under the Law of 24 May 1872 can be dismissed before the expiry of their powers only in the way laid down in this Law. After the dissolution of the National Assembly, dismissal can be effected only by a resolution of the Senate.

Art. 5. The President of the Republic can, with the agreement of the Senate, dissolve the Chamber of Deputies before the legal expiry of its mandate. In this case, the electoral colleges are convoked for new elections within a period of three months.

Art. 6. Ministers are collectively responsible before the Chambers for the general policy of the Government, and individually for their personal acts. The President of the Republic is responsible only in the case of high treason.

Art. 7. In the event of a vacancy by death or any other cause, the two Chambers meeting together proceed immediately to the election of a new President. In the interval the Council of Ministers is invested with executive power.

Art. 8. The Chambers shall have the right, by separate decisions taken in each case by an absolute majority of votes, either spontaneously or at the request of the President of the Republic, to declare that there is need to revise the constitutional laws. After each of the two Chambers shall have passed this resolution, they shall meet together as the National Assembly to proceed to the revision. Decisions carrying out revision of the constitutional laws, either in whole or in part, must be taken by an absolute majority of the members composing the National Assembly. Nevertheless, for the duration of the powers conferred by the Law of 20 November 1875 on M. le Maréchal de Mac-Mahon, such revision can take place only when proposed by the President of the Republic.

Art. 9. The seat of the executive power and of the two Chambers is at Versailles.

APPENDIX I

(E) *Law of 24 February 1875*, relating to the organization of the Senate.

Art. 1. The Senate is composed of 300 members: 225 elected by the Departments and Colonies, and 75 elected by the National Assembly.

Art. 2. (*Allocation of Senatorial seats to the various Departments.*)

Art. 3. No one can be a Senator unless he is French, at least forty years old, and enjoys all civil and political rights.

Art. 4. Senators of the Departments and Colonies are elected by an absolute majority, and when need be by *scrutin de liste*, by a college meeting in the chief town of the Department or Colony, composed of (i) the Deputies, (ii) the General Councillors, (iii) the Councillors of the *Arrondissement*, (iv) delegates elected, one for each Municipal Council, amongst the electors of the Commune. In the French Indies, the members of the Colonial Council or of the local councils are substituted for the General Councillors, Councillors of the *Arrondissement* and delegates of the Municipal Council. They vote in the chief town of each settlement.

Art. 5. The Senators appointed by the Assembly are elected by *scrutin de liste* and by an absolute majority of votes.

Art. 6. The Senators of the Departments and Colonies are elected for nine years and are renewable, one third at a time, every three years . . . (*details of initial procedure*).

Art. 7. The Senators elected by the Assembly are irremovable. In the event of a vacancy arising from death, resignation or other cause, replacement will be arranged, within two months, by the Senate itself.

Art. 8. The Senate has, concurrently with the Chamber of Deputies, the right of initiative and drafting in law-making. Nevertheless laws of finance must, in the first instance, be presented in the Chamber of Deputies and voted upon by it.

Art. 9. The Senate can be constituted a Court of Justice to judge either the President of the Republic, or ministers, and to take cognizance of attempts against the security of the State.

Art. 10. Election of the Senate will be proceeded with one month before the date fixed by the National Assembly for its dissolution. The Senate shall enter upon its functions and shall be constituted the same day that the National Assembly dissolves.

Art. 11. The present Law shall be promulgated only after the decisive vote on the law of the Public Powers (i.e. (D) *above*).¹

(F) *Constitutional Law of 16 July 1875* on the relations between the Public Powers.

Art. 1. The Senate and the Chamber of Deputies meet every year on the second Tuesday in January, unless convoked earlier by the President of the Republic. The two Chambers must sit for at least five months every year. The session of one begins and ends at the same times as that of the other. On the Sunday after the opening of Parliament, public prayers shall be addressed to God in the churches and Protestant chapels, to invoke His blessing on the work of the Assemblies.

Art. 2. The President of the Republic declares the session closed. He has the right to convoke the Chambers for an extraordinary session. He must convoke them if requested, in the interval between sessions, by an absolute majority of the members composing each Chamber. The President can adjourn the Chambers. Nevertheless, adjournment may not exceed the period of one month, nor may it take place more than twice in one session.

Art. 3. At least one month before the legal termination of the powers of the President of the Republic, the Chambers must meet as the National Assembly to proceed to the election of the new President. If the Chambers are not convoked, this meeting may take place with full legality on the fifteenth day before the expiry of these powers. In the event of the death or resignation of the President of the Republic, the two Chambers meet immediately and with full legality. In the event that, by application of Article 5 of the Law of 25 February 1875, the Chamber of Deputies should be dissolved at the moment when

---

¹ The Law of 2 August 1875, defining in detail the procedure for the election of Senators, is not given here, as it was later considerably amended. The text in French, and later emendations, may be studied in Duguit, Monnier & Bonnard: *Les Constitutions et les Principales Lois Politiques de la France.*

the Presidency of the Republic becomes vacant, the electoral colleges should be summoned at once, and the Senate should meet with full legality.

Art. 4. Any assembly of either of the Chambers held out of the period of common session is illicit, and not of full legality save in the event foreseen in the preceding Article and when the Senate meets as a Court of Justice: and, in this latter event, it may exercise only judicial functions.

Art. 5. The sessions of the Senate and those of the Chamber of Deputies are public. Nevertheless each Chamber may form itself into a secret committee, on the request of a certain number of its members fixed by regulation. It then decides, by an absolute majority, whether the session should be held again in public on the same subject.

Art. 6. The President of the Republic communicates with the Chambers by messages, which are read at the tribune by a minister. Ministers have entry to both Chambers and must be heard when they so ask. They may have the assistance of commissioners, appointed for the discussion of any given proposed law by the decree of the President of the Republic.

Art. 7. The President of the Republic promulgates laws within a month after the transmission to the Government of the law definitely adopted. He must promulgate within three days laws whose promulgation has been declared urgent by a specific vote in each of the two Chambers. Before the date fixed for promulgation the President of the Republic may, by a message giving his reason, ask the two Chambers to reconsider them, and they cannot refuse.

Art. 8. The President of the Republic negotiates and ratifies treaties. He makes them known to the Chambers as soon as the interest and security of the State permit. Treaties of peace, of commerce, treaties involving State finance, those which have bearing upon personal rights and the property-rights of Frenchmen abroad, are operative only after they have been voted upon by the two Chambers. No cession, exchange or acquisition of territory may take place except by virtue of a law.

Art. 9. The President of the Republic cannot declare war without the previous assent of the two Chambers.

Art 10. Each Chamber is judge of the eligibility of its members and of the regularity of their election; it alone can receive their resignation.

Art. 11. The *bureau* of each of the two Chambers is elected each year for the duration of the session, and for every extraordinary session which may take place before the ordinary session of the following year. When the two Chambers meet together as the National Assembly, their *bureau* consists of the President, Vice-Presidents and Secretaries of the Senate.

Art. 12. The President of the Republic cannot be proceeded against except by the Chamber of Deputies, and cannot be judged except by the Senate. Ministers can be proceeded against by the Chamber of Deputies for crimes committed in the exercise of their functions. In this event, they are judged by the Senate. The Senate can be constituted a Court of Justice by a decree of the President of the Republic, issued in the Council of Ministers, to judge every person charged with an attempt against the security of the State. If the preliminary investigation has started in an ordinary court, the decree convoking the Senate can be framed to include the decision to transfer the case. A law shall determine the method of procedure for bringing the charge, the preliminary investigation, and the judgement.

Art. 13. No member of either Chamber can be prosecuted or harassed by the police because of opinions expressed or votes given in the exercise of his functions.

Art. 14. No member of either Chamber can, during the period of a parliamentary session, be prosecuted or arrested for a criminal or minor offence except on the authority of the Chamber of which he is a member, unless he be caught in the act. The detention or prosecution of a member of either Chamber is suspended during a session, and for its whole duration, if the Chamber so requires.

(G) *Organic Law of 30 November 1875* on the Election of Deputies.

Art. 1. Deputies shall be chosen by the electors registered: (1) on the lists drawn up in conformity with the Law of 7 July

APPENDIX I

1874; (2) on the complementary list comprising those who have resided in the Commune for six months. . . .[1]

Art. 2. Regular soldiers and conscripts of all ranks and arms in the Army and Navy take no part in any voting when they are with their corps, on duty or carrying out their functions. Those who, at the time of the election, are on leave, not on active service, or in possession of a regulation pass, can vote in the Commune on the electoral lists of which they are regularly registered. This last rule applies equally to officers and conscripts who are on half-pay or in the cadres of reserves.

Art. 3. Throughout the period of elections, circulars and programmes signed by candidates, posters and electoral manifestoes signed by one or more electors can, after a copy has been sent to the Public Prosecutor's office, be posted up and distributed without previous authorization. The distribution of voting papers is not subject to the formality of their being sent to the Public Prosecutor's office. It is forbidden for any agent of a public or municipal authority to distribute voting papers, programmes and circulars for candidates. The regulations of Article 19 of the organic Law of 2 August 1875, on the election of Senators, shall be applicable to the elections of Deputies.[2]

Art. 4. The poll shall last only one day. Voting takes place in the chief place of the Commune; nevertheless, each Commune can be divided, by decree of the Prefect, into as many sections as local circumstances and the number of electors demand. The second ballot shall continue to take place on the second Sunday after the day when the result of the first ballot is announced, in conformity with the regulations of Article 65 of the Law of 15 March 1849.

Art. 5. . . . The vote is secret. . . .

Art. 6. Every elector is eligible to be a candidate, without property qualification, when he is over the age of twenty-five.

Art. 7. No soldier or sailor, forming part of the active armed forces on land or sea, can be elected a member of the Chamber

---

[1] Some portions of this Act which deal with small details or which were subsequently changed have been omitted from this translation.
[2] This provides for punishment of corruption or intimidation at elections.

of Deputies, no matter what his rank or his functions.... [This regulation] does not apply to the reserves of the active Army, nor to the territorial Army.

Art. 8. The exercise of public functions paid for by the State is incompatible with a Deputy's mandate. In consequence every *fonctionnaire* elected as Deputy shall be dismissed from his post unless, within eight days after the verification of returns, he makes it known that he does not accept the Deputy's mandate. The above regulations do not apply to the functions of a Minister, Under-Secretary of State, Ambassador, plenipotentiary, the Prefect of the Seine, the Prefect of Police, the First Presidents of the *Cour de Cassation, Cour des Comptes, Cour d'Appel de Paris,* the *Procureurs généraux* attached to the *Cour de Cassation, Cour des Comptes* or the *Cour d'Appel de Paris,* Archbishops and Bishops ... etc.

Art. 11. Every Deputy appointed or promoted to a salaried public office ceases to belong to the Chamber by the mere fact of his acceptance: but he can be re-elected if the office which he holds is compatible with a Deputy's mandate. Deputies who are appointed Ministers or Under-Secretaries of State need not be re-elected....

Art. 13. Pledges exacted beforehand from candidates are null and void.

Art. 14. The members of the Chamber of Deputies are elected for single-member constituencies. Each administrative *arrondissement* shall elect one Deputy. *Arrondissements* whose population exceeds one hundred thousand inhabitants shall elect one further Deputy for every hundred-thousand inhabitants or less....

Art. 15. Deputies are elected for four years. The Chamber is all renewed at one time.

Art. 16. In the event of a vacancy by death, resignation or otherwise, the election must take place within three months, starting from the day the vacancy began. Where vacancy is due to the exercise of option, the vacancy must be filled within one month.

Art. 17. Deputies are paid. This pay is fixed by the regulations in Articles 96 and 97 of the Law of 15 March 1849 and by those of the Law of 16 February 1872.

Art. 18. No one is elected on the first ballot unless he has won (1) an absolute majority of the votes given; (2) a number of votes equal to a quarter of the electors on the register. At the second ballot a relative majority is sufficient. When votes are equal, the eldest candidate is elected.

Art. 19. Each Department of Algeria elects one Deputy. . . .

Art 21. The four Colonies to which Senators have been allocated by the Law of 24 February 1875 concerning the organization of the Senate, elect one Deputy each. . . .

(H) *Resolution of 10 July 1940* conferring power on Marshal Pétain.

The National Assembly confers power on the government of the Republic, under the signature and authority of Marshal Pétain, with a view to promulgating, in one or more decrees, the new constitution of the French State. This Constitution should safeguard the rights of labour, family and fatherland. It will be ratified by the nation and brought into application by the Assemblies which it creates.[1]

(I) *Law concerning the Organization of the Public Powers, 21 October 1945.*

(In the Referendum submitted to the French people on 21 October 1945, the electorate was asked two questions. First, whether it wished the Assembly about to be elected to be a Constituent Assembly: and secondly, if the majority should answer yes to this first question, whether it wished the Public Powers to be organized according to the text of the law printed on the back of the ballot-paper.

Below is the text of this Law. As a great majority voted affirmatively in reply to both questions, this Law came into force as the first Constitutional Law of the Fourth Republic, governing the deliberations and powers of the National Constituent Assembly.)

Art. 1. The Constituent Assembly created by the elections of 21 October 1945 shall elect forthwith, by public ballot and by

[1] This resolution was carried by 569 votes against 80, with 50 abstentions, and became the basis of the Vichy Government. As the last act of the National Assembly, it marks the death of the Third Republic. Cf. p. 216.

an absolute majority of the members composing it, the President of the Provisional Government of the Republic. He shall form his government and submit it for the approval of the Assembly, at the same time as the programme of the government.

The government shall be responsible before the Assembly; but rejection of a bill or of a vote of credit shall not involve its dismissal. This shall be obligatory only after a separate motion of censure taken at least two days after it has been notified to the *bureau* of the Assembly, and adopted, by means of open ballot, by an absolute majority of the members composing the Assembly.

Art. 2. The Assembly shall set up the new Constitution.

Art. 3. The Constitution adopted by the Assembly shall be submitted by referendum for the approval of the electoral body of French citizens within a month after its adoption by the Assembly.

Art. 4. The Assembly shall have legislative power. It shall have the right of initiating legislation, concurrently with the government. After the one month allowed for the promulgation of laws, the government shall have the right to ask for a second debate. If after that the former vote is confirmed by an absolute majority of the members composing the Assembly, the law shall be promulgated within three days.

Art. 5. The Assembly shall vote on the budget, but shall not have the right to initiate expenditure.

Art. 6. The powers of the Assembly shall expire on the day when the new Constitution shall come into force, and at latest seven months after the first meeting of the Assembly.

Art. 7. Should the electoral body reject the Constitution drafted by the Assembly, or should the Assembly not have drafted one within the time-limit fixed by Article 6, election of a new Constituent Assembly shall take place forthwith, by the same procedure and with the same powers, and it shall meet with full legality on the second Tuesday after its election.

Art 8. The present Law, adopted by the French people, shall have constitutional force and shall be executed as a Law of the State.

(J) CONSTITUTION OF THE FOURTH REPUBLIC

The text drafted and approved by the National Constituent Assembly was submitted to popular referendum on 13 October 1946. According to figures in the *Journal Officiel* (28 October 1946), it was approved by 9,120,576 votes to 7,980,333 votes, but 7,938,884 abstained from voting. Thus it was carried by 53·3 per cent of those who voted validly; but 34 per cent of the total electorate abstained from voting, and the affirmative vote represented only 39 per cent of the whole electorate. The elections for the National Assembly were held on 10 November 1946, and the Constitution entered into force on 24 December when the Council of the Republic first met. It operated fully from 22 January 1947, when M. Vincent Auriol assumed office as the first President of the Republic. This English version of the text is based on that issued by the French Press and Information Service in the United States of America, with many corrections and verbal amendments by the present author. For the French text (with a few omissions), see M. Duverger: *Manuel de Droit Constitutionnel et de Science Politique* (1948), pp. 379–94.

PREAMBLE

On the morrow of the victory of the free peoples over the regimes that attempted to enslave and degrade the human person, the French people proclaims once more that every human being, without distinction of race, religion or belief, possesses sacred and inalienable rights. It solemnly reaffirms the rights and freedoms of man and of the citizen consecrated by the Declaration of Rights of 1789 and the fundamental principles recognized by the laws of the Republic.

It further proclaims as most vital in our time the following political, economic and social principles:

The law guarantees to women equal rights with men in all spheres.

Anyone persecuted because of his activities in the cause of freedom has the right of asylum within the territories of the Republic.

It is the duty of all to work and the right of all to obtain employment. No one may suffer in his work or his employment because of his origins, his opinions or his beliefs.

Everyone may defend his rights and interests by trade union action and may join the union of his choice.

The right to strike may be exercised within the framework of the laws that govern it.

Every worker may participate through his delegates in collective bargaining to determine working conditions, as well as in the management of business enterprises.

All property and all enterprises that possess or acquire the character of a national public service or a *de facto* monopoly must become the property of the community.

The nation ensures for the individual and the family the conditions necessary to their development.

It guarantees to all, and particularly to children, mothers, and aged workers, health protection, material security, rest and leisure. Every human being who, because of his age, his physical or mental condition, or because of the economic situation, finds himself unable to work, has the right to obtain from the community the means of a decent existence.

The nation proclaims the solidarity and equality of all Frenchmen in regard to the burdens resulting from national disasters.

The nation guarantees equal access of children and adults to education, professional training and culture. It is the duty of the State to provide free, secular, public education at all levels.

The French Republic, faithful to its traditions, abides by the rules of public international law. It will not undertake wars of conquest and will never take up arms against the freedom of any people.

On condition of reciprocity, France accepts the limitations of sovereignty necessary to the organization and defence of peace.

France forms with the people of its overseas territories a Union based upon equality of rights and duties without distinction of race or religion.

The French Union is composed of nations and peoples who pool or co-ordinate their resources and their efforts in order to develop their respective civilizations, increase their wellbeing, and ensure their security.

Faithful to her traditional mission, France proposes to guide the peoples for whom she has assumed responsibility toward freedom to govern themselves and to manage their own affairs democratically; rejecting any system of colonization based upon arbitrary power, she guarantees to all equal access to public office and the individual or collective exercise of the rights and liberties proclaimed or confirmed above.

THE INSTITUTIONS OF THE REPUBLIC

TITLE I: SOVEREIGNTY

Art. 1. France is a republic, indivisible, secular, democratic, and social.

Art. 2. The national emblem is the tricolour flag—blue, white and red—in three vertical bands of equal dimensions.

The national anthem is the 'Marseillaise'.

The motto of the republic is: 'Liberty, Equality, Fraternity'.

Its principle is: government of the people, for the people and by the people.

Art. 3. National sovereignty belongs to the French people.

No section of the people nor any individual may assume its exercise.

The people exercise it in constitutional matters by the vote of their representatives or by the referendum.

In all other matters they exercise it through their deputies in the National Assembly, elected by universal, equal, direct, and secret suffrage.

Art. 4. All French citizens and nationals of both sexes, who are majors and enjoy civil and political rights, may vote under conditions determined by the law.

TITLE II: THE PARLIAMENT

Art. 5. Parliament is composed of the National Assembly and the Council of the Republic.

Art. 6. The duration of the powers of each Assembly, its mode of election, the conditions of eligibility, the grounds of ineligibilities and incompatibilities are determined by law.

However, the two Chambers are elected on a territorial basis, the National Assembly by direct universal suffrage, the Council of the Republic by the communal and departmental bodies by indirect universal suffrage. The Council of the Republic is renewable one-half at a time.

Nevertheless, the National Assembly may itself elect by proportional representation councillors whose number shall not exceed one-sixth of the total number of members of the Council of the Republic.

The number of members of the Council of the Republic may not be less than 250 nor more than 320.

Art. 7. War may not be declared without a vote of the National Assembly and prior consultation of the Council of the Republic.

Art. 8. Each of the two Chambers is the judge of the eligibility of its members and the regularity of their elections; it alone can accept their resignation.

Art. 9. The National Assembly meets in full exercise of its rights every year on the second Tuesday in January.

The total duration of interruptions of each session may not exceed four months. Adjournments of more than ten days are considered as interruptions of the session.

The Council of the Republic sits at the same time as the National Assembly.

Art. 10. The meetings of the two chambers are public. Verbatim reports of debates, as well as parliamentary documents, are published in the *Journal Officiel*.

Each of the two Chambers may form itself into secret committee.

Art. 11. Each of the two Chambers elects its *bureau* each year, at the beginning of the session, by proportional representation of party groups.

When the two Chambers meet together to elect the President of the Republic, their *bureau* is that of the National Assembly.

Art. 12. When the National Assembly is not sitting its *bureau*, exercising control over the actions of the Cabinet, may convoke Parliament; it must do so at the request of one-third of the deputies or of the President of the Council of Ministers.

Art. 13. The National Assembly alone has the right to legislate. It may not delegate this right.

Art. 14. The President of the Council of Ministers and the members of Parliament have the right to initiate legislation.

Government and private members' bills introduced by members of the National Assembly are laid upon the Table of that chamber.

Bills introduced by members of the Council of the Republic are laid upon its Table and sent without debate to the *bureau* of the National Assembly. They cannot be received if they would entail reduction of revenues or increase of expenditures.

Art. 15. The National Assembly examines the government and private member's bills submitted to it in its committees, of which it determines the number, composition, and competence.

Art. 16. The draft budget is submitted to the National Assembly.

This draft may include only such provisions as are strictly financial.

An organic law will regulate the method of presentation of the budget.

Art. 17. The deputies of the National Assembly have the right to initiate expenditure.

However, no proposal which would entail an increase in the expenditure forecast or create new expenditure may be presented during the discussion of the budget, of anticipated and supplementary appropriations.

Art. 18. The National Assembly settles the accounts of the nation.

It is assisted in this task by the *Cour des Comptes*.

The National Assembly may entrust to the *Cour des Comptes* all investigations or examinations of public revenues and expenditures or the administration of the treasury.

Art. 19. Amnesty may not be granted except by a law.

Art. 20. The Council of the Republic examines, in order to give its opinion thereon, the government and private members' bills voted on first reading by the National Assembly.

It gives its opinion not more than two months after a measure is sent to it by the National Assembly. When the budget is under discussion, this time may be reduced, if need be, to such time as does not exceed that taken by the National Assembly for its consideration and vote. When the National Assembly has agreed upon an urgent procedure, the Council of the Republic gives its opinion in the same time as that provided for debate by the rules of the National Assembly. The time limit specified in the present article is suspended during interruption of the session. It may be extended by a decision of the National Assembly.

If the opinion of the Council of the Republic is in agreement with that of the National Assembly, or if it has not been given within the time limit specified in the preceding paragraph, the law is promulgated as passed by the National Assembly.

If its opinion is not in agreement with that of the National Assembly, the latter body gives the government or private members' bill a second reading. It disposes definitively and absolutely of the amendments proposed by the Council of the Republic, accepting or rejecting them in whole or in part. If these amendments are completely or partially rejected, the vote on second reading of the bill is taken by open ballot and by an absolute majority of the members of the National Assembly, when the vote on the whole has been taken under the same conditions by the Council of the Republic.

Art. 21. No member of Parliament may be prosecuted, sought by the police, arrested, detained or tried because of opinions expressed or votes cast by him in the exercise of his functions.

Art. 22. No member of Parliament during his term of office may be prosecuted or arrested for a criminal offence or misdemeanour except with the authorization of the Chamber of which he is a member, unless caught *flagrante delicto*. The detention or prosecution of a member of Parliament is suspended if the Chamber of which he is a member so demands.

Art. 23. Members of Parliament receive remuneration fixed in relation to that of a given grade of civil servants.

Art. 24. No one may be a member both of the National Assembly and of the Council of the Republic. Members of Parliament may not be members of the Economic Council nor of the Assembly of the French Union.

TITLE III: THE ECONOMIC COUNCIL

Art. 25. An Economic Council, whose statute is determined by law, examines, in order to give its opinion thereon, the government and private members' bills within its purview. The National Assembly sends such bills to this Council before it discusses them.

The Economic Council may also be consulted by the Council of Ministers. It must be consulted by that body on the adoption of a national economic plan for full employment and the rational utilization of material resources.

TITLE IV: DIPLOMATIC TREATIES

Art. 26. Diplomatic treaties duly ratified and published have the force of law even when they may be contrary to internal French legislation; they require for their implementation no legislative acts other than those necessary to ensure their ratification.

Art. 27. Treaties relating to international organization, peace treaties, commercial treaties, treaties that involve national finances, treaties relating to the personal status and property rights of French citizens abroad, that modify internal French legislation, as well as those that involve the cession, exchange or acquisition of territories, become final only when they have been ratified by an act of the Legislature.

No cession, exchange or acquisition of territory is valid without the consent of the populations concerned.

Art. 28. Since diplomatic treaties duly ratified and published have superior authority to that of French internal legislation, their provisions cannot be abrogated, modified or suspended without previous formal denunciation through diplomatic channels. Whenever a treaty mentioned in Article 27 is concerned, such denunciation must be authorized by the National Assembly, except in the case of commercial treaties.

TITLE V: THE PRESIDENT OF THE REPUBLIC

Art. 29. The President of the Republic is elected by Parliament.

He is elected for seven years. He is not eligible for re-election more than once.

Art. 30. The President of the Republic appoints in the Council of Ministers Councillors of State, the Grand Chancellor of the Legion of Honour, ambassadors and special envoys, the members of the Superior Council and the Committee for National Defence, rectors of the universities, prefects, the chiefs of the central administration, generals, and the representatives of the Government in overseas territories.

Art. 31. The President of the Republic is kept informed of international negotiations. He signs and ratifies treaties.

The President of the Republic accredits ambassadors and special envoys to foreign powers; foreign ambassadors and special envoys are accredited to him.

Art. 32. The President of the Republic presides over the Council of Ministers. He has minutes of meetings recorded and kept.

Art. 33. The President of the Republic presides with the same powers over the Superior Council and the Committee for National Defence, and takes the title of Commander-in-Chief of the Armies (*chef des armées*).

Art. 34. The President of the Republic presides over the Superior Council of the Judiciary.

Art. 35. The President of the Republic exercises the right of pardon in the Superior Council of the Judiciary.

Art. 36. The President of the Republic promulgates laws

APPENDIX I

within ten days after the text, as finally adopted, has been sent to the Government. This interval may be reduced to five days if the National Assembly declares it a case of urgency.

Within the time limit fixed for the promulgation of a law, the President of the Republic may, in a message stating his reasons, ask that it be reconsidered by both Chambers; this reconsideration may not be refused.

If the President of the Republic does not promulgate a law within the time limit fixed by the present Constitution, the President of the National Assembly shall promulgate it.

Art. 37. The President of the Republic communicates with the Parliament by means of messages addressed to the National Assembly.

Art. 38. Every act of the President of the Republic must be countersigned by the President of the Council of Ministers and by a Minister.

Art. 39. Not more than thirty days and not less than fifteen days before the expiration of the term of office of the President of the Republic, Parliament proceeds to elect a new President.

Art. 40. If in the application of the preceding article the election must take place during the period when the National Assembly is dissolved in conformity with Article 51, the powers of the President of the Republic in office are extended until such time as the new President is elected. Parliament proceeds to elect this new President within ten days after the election of the new National Assembly.

In this case, the President of the Council of Ministers is appointed within fifteen days after the election of the new President of the Republic.

Art. 41. If the President of the Republic is not able to exercise his function for reasons duly recognized by a vote of Parliament, or in the event of a vacancy caused by death, resignation or any other circumstance, the President of the National Assembly assumes temporarily the functions of the President of the Republic. He is replaced in his own duties by a Vice-President.

The new President of the Republic is elected within ten

days, except under the conditions specified in the preceding Article.

Art. 42. The President of the Republic is responsible only in cases of high treason.

He may be indicted by the National Assembly and arraigned before the High Court of Justice under the conditions set forth in Article 57 below.

Art. 43. The function of the President of the Republic is incompatible with any other public office.

Art. 44. Members of the families that once reigned over France are not eligible for the Presidency of the Republic.

TITLE VI. THE COUNCIL OF MINISTERS

Art. 45. At the opening of each Legislature, the President of the Republic, after the customary consultations, designates the President of the Council.

The latter submits to the National Assembly the programme and the policy of the Cabinet he intends to constitute.

The President of the Council and the Ministers may not be formally appointed until the President of the Council has received a vote of confidence from the National Assembly by open ballot and by an absolute majority of the deputies, except when *force majeure* prevents the National Assembly from meeting.

The same procedure is followed during a legislative session in the event of a vacancy caused by death, resignation or any other circumstance, except in the case set forth in Article 52 below.

No ministerial crisis occurring within fifteen days after the appointment of the ministers requires the application of Article 51.

Art. 46. The President of the Council and the Ministers chosen by him are appointed by a decree of the President of the Republic.

Art. 47. The President of the Council ensures the execution of the laws.

He appoints all civil and military officials except those specified in Articles 30, 46, and 84.

The President of the Council assumes direction of the armed forces and co-ordinates all measures necessary for the national defence.

The acts of the President of the Council mentioned in the present Article are countersigned by the Ministers concerned.

Art. 48. The Ministers are collectively responsible to the National Assembly for the general policy of the Cabinet and individually responsible for their personal actions.

They are not responsible to the Council of the Republic.

Art. 49. A question of confidence may not be put except after discussion by the Council of Ministers; it can be put only by the President of the Council.

The vote on a question of confidence may not be taken until one full day after it has been put before the Assembly. It must be taken by open ballot.

The Cabinet may not be refused a vote of confidence except by an absolute majority of the deputies to the Assembly.

Refusal to give such a vote entails the collective resignation of the Cabinet.

Art. 50. Passage of a motion of censure by the National Assembly entails the collective resignation of the Cabinet.

The vote on such a motion cannot be taken until one full day after it has been made. It must be taken by open ballot.

A motion of censure may be adopted only by an absolute majority of the deputies to the Assembly.

Art. 51. If in the course of an eighteen-month period two ministerial crises occur under the conditions set forth in Articles 49 and 50, the Council of Ministers, after consultation with the President of the Assembly, may decide to dissolve the National Assembly. Its dissolution will be proclaimed by a decree of the President of the Republic, in accordance with such decision.

The provisions of the preceding paragraph may not be applied before the expiration of the first eighteen months of the Legislature.

Art. 52. In case of dissolution, the Cabinet, with the exception of the President of the Council and the Minister of the Interior, remains in office to carry out current business.

The President of the Republic appoints the President of the National Assembly as President of the Council. The latter appoints a new Minister of the Interior with the approval of the *bureau* of the National Assembly. He appoints as Ministers of State members of political groups not represented in the Government.

General elections take place not less than twenty and not more than thirty days after the dissolution.

The National Assembly meets in full exercise of its rights on the third Thursday after its election.

Art. 53. The Ministers have access to the two Chambers and to their Committees. They must be heard when they request it.

In discussions before the Chambers they may be assisted by commissioners designated by decree.

Art. 54. The President of the Council of Ministers may delegate his powers to a Minister.

Art. 55. In the event of a vacancy caused by death or any other circumstance, the Council of Ministers charges one of its members to exercise provisionally the functions of President of the Council of Ministers.

TITLE VII: THE RESPONSIBILITY OF MINISTERS UNDER
THE PENAL CODE

Art. 56. Ministers are responsible under the penal code for crimes and misdemeanours committed in the exercise of their functions.

Art. 57. Ministers may be indicted by the National Assembly and arraigned before the High Court of Justice.

The National Assembly decides by secret ballot and by an absolute majority of its members, with the exception of those who may be called upon to participate in the prosecution, investigation or judgment of the case.

Art. 58. The High Court of Justice is elected by the National Assembly at the opening of each Legislature.

Art. 59. The organization of the High Court of Justice and the procedure to be followed before it are determined by a special law.

APPENDIX I

TITLE VIII: THE FRENCH UNION

Section 1. Principles

Art. 60. The French Union is composed, on the one hand, of the French Republic which comprises Metropolitan France and the overseas departments and territories, and on the other hand, of the Associated Territories and States.

Art. 61. The position of the Associated States within the French Union depends in each case on the act which defines their relationship with France.

Art. 62. The members of the French Union pool their resources to guarantee the defence of the whole Union. The Government of the Republic assumes the co-ordination of these resources and the direction of such policy as will prepare and ensure this defence.

Section 2. Organization

Art. 63. The central organs of the French Union are the President, the High Council and the Assembly.

Art. 64. The President of the French Republic is the President of the French Union of which he represents the permanent interests.

Art. 65. The High Council of the French Union is composed, under the chairmanship of the President of the Union, of a delegation of the French Government and of the representatives that each Associated State is permitted to accredit to the President of the Union.

Its function is to assist the Government in the general conduct of the affairs of the Union.

Art. 66. The Assembly of the French Union is composed half of members representing Metropolitan France and half of members representing the overseas departments and territories and the Associated States.

An organic law will determine the conditions of representation of the different sections of the population.

Art. 67. The members of the Assembly of the Union are elected by the territorial assemblies for the overseas departments and territories; for Metropolitan France, they are elected two-thirds by the members of the National Assembly representing the home country and one-third by the members of the Council of the Republic representing the home country.

Art. 68. The Associated States may appoint delegates to the Assembly of the Union within the limitations and conditions determined by a law and an internal legislative act of each State.

Art. 69. The President of the French Union convokes the Assembly of the French Union and closes its sessions. He must convoke it upon the request of half its members.

The Assembly of the French Union may not sit during interruptions of the sessions of Parliament.

Art. 70. The rules set forth in Articles 8, 10, 21, 22, and 23 are applicable to the Assembly of the French Union under the same conditions as to the Council of the Republic.

Art. 71. The Assembly of the French Union considers the government or private members' bills submitted to it, for advice thereon, by the National Assembly or the Government of the French Republic or the Governments of the Associated States.

The Assembly has the power to express its opinion on motions submitted to it by one of its members and, if it decides to consider them, to instruct its *bureau* to send them to the National Assembly. It may submit proposals to the French Government and to the High Council of the French Union.

In order to be admissible, the motions referred to in the preceding paragraph must relate to legislation concerning the overseas territories.

Art. 72. In the overseas territories, the legislative power belongs to Parliament with regard to criminal law, civil liberties and political and administrative organization.

In all other matters, French law is applicable in the overseas territories only by virtue of an express provision to this effect or if it has been extended to the overseas territories by decree after consultation with the Assembly of the Union.

Moreover, as an exception to Article 13, special provisions for each territory may be decreed by the President of the

APPENDIX I

Republic in the Council of Ministers after prior consultation with the Assembly of the Union.

Section 3. The Overseas Departments and Territories

Art. 73. The legislative regime of the overseas departments is the same as that of the metropolitan departments save for exceptions determined by the law.

Art. 74. The overseas territories are given a special statute which takes into account their particular interests within the framework of the general interests of the Republic.

This statute and the internal organization of each overseas territory or group of territories are determined by law, after the Assembly of the French Union has expressed its opinion and after consultation with the territorial assemblies.

Art. 75. The respective statutes of the members of the French Republic and of the French Union are subject to modifications.

Modifications of statute and passage from one category to another in the framework established in Article 60 can result only from a law passed by Parliament after consultation with the territorial assemblies and the Assembly of the Union.

Art. 76. The representative of the Government in each territory or group of territories is the depositary of the powers of the Republic. He is the administrative head of the territory.

He is responsible for his acts to the Government.

Art. 77. An elective assembly is instituted in each territory. The electoral regime, composition, and powers of this assembly are determined by law.

Art. 78. In the groups of territories, the management of matters of common interest is entrusted to an assembly composed of members elected by the territorial assemblies.

Its composition and its powers are determined by law.

Art. 79. The overseas territories elect representatives to the National Assembly and to the Council of the Republic under conditions determined by the law.

Art. 80. All nationals of the overseas territories have the status of citizens, on the same basis as French nationals of

Metropolitan France or the overseas territories. Special laws shall determine the conditions under which they will exercise their rights as citizens.

Art. 81. All French citizens and nationals of the French Union have the status of citizens of the French Union, which ensures to them the enjoyment of the rights and liberties guaranteed by the Preamble of the present Constitution.

Art. 82. Those citizens who do not have French civil status retain their personal status so long as they have not renounced it.

This status can in no case constitute a ground for refusing or limiting the rights and liberties pertaining to the status of French citizen.

TITLE IX: THE SUPERIOR COUNCIL OF THE JUDICIARY

Art. 83. The Superior Council of the Judiciary (*Conseil Supérieur de la Magistrature*) is composed of fourteen members:

The President of the Republic, President;

The Keeper of the Seals, Minister of Justice, Vice-President.

Six persons elected for six years by the National Assembly, by a two-thirds majority and chosen outside its membership, and six alternates elected under the same conditions;

Six persons designated as follows: four members of the magistrature elected for six years, representing each category of the magistrature, in the conditions laid down by law, and four alternates elected under the same conditions; two members appointed for six years by the President of the Republic and chosen outside the membership of Parliament and judiciary, but from among members of the legal profession, two alternates being designated under the same conditions.

The decisions of the Superior Council of the Judiciary are taken by majority vote. In case of a tie the President has the casting vote.

Art. 84. The President of the Republic appoints the judges, whose names are submitted to him by the Superior Council of the Judiciary, with the exception of those in the office of Public Prosecutor.

The Superior Council of the Judiciary, in conformity with the law, ensures the discipline of these judges, their independence and the administration of the courts.

These judges are irremovable.

TITLE X: LOCAL ADMINISTRATIVE UNITS

Art. 85. The French Republic, one and indivisible, recognizes the existence of local administrative units (*collectivités territoriales*).

These units are the *communes*, the *départements*, and the overseas territories.

Art. 86. The framework, the scope, the eventual regroupings and the organization of the *communes*, the *départements*, and the overseas territories are determined by law.

Art. 87. Local administrative units are governed freely through councils elected by universal suffrage.

The execution of the decisions of these councils is ensured by their mayor or their president.

Art. 88. The co-ordination of the activities of Government officials, the representation of the national interests and the administrative supervision of these units are ensured within the departmental framework by delegates of the Government appointed by the Council of Ministers.

Art. 89. Organic laws will extend the liberties of the *départements* and municipalities; they may provide, for certain large cities, rules of operation and an administrative structure different from those of small towns, and include special provisions for certain *départements*; they will determine the conditions under which Articles 85 to 88 above are to be applied.

Laws will likewise determine the conditions under which local sections of the central administration are to function, in order to bring the administration and the administered closer together.

TITLE XI: REVISION OF THE CONSTITUTION

Art. 90. Revision takes place in the following manner:

Revision must be decided upon by a resolution adopted by an absolute majority of the members of the National Assembly.

This resolution stipulates the purpose of the revision.

After at least three months this resolution is submitted for a second reading under the same rules of procedure as the first, unless the Council of the Republic, informed by the National Assembly, has adopted the same resolution by an absolute majority.

After this second reading, the National Assembly draws up a bill to revise the Constitution. This bill is submitted to Parliament, and voted by a majority and according to the rules established for any ordinary act of the legislature.

It is submitted to a referendum unless it has been adopted on second reading by a two-thirds majority of the National Assembly or voted by a three-fifths majority of each of the two assemblies.

The bill is promulgated by the President of the Republic as a constitutional law within eight days after its adoption.

No constitutional revision relative to the existence of the Council of the Republic may be made without the concurrence of this Council or resort to a referendum.

Art. 91. The Constitutional Committee is presided over by the President of the Republic.

It includes the President of the National Assembly, the President of the Council of the Republic, seven members elected by the National Assembly at the beginning of each annual session by proportional representation of the political groups, and chosen outside its own membership, and three members elected under the same conditions by the Council of the Republic.

The Constitutional Committee determines whether the laws passed by the National Assembly entail a revision of the Constitution.

Art. 92. In the period allowed for the promulgation of the law, the Committee receives a joint request from the President of the Republic and the President of the Council of the Republic, the Council having decided by an absolute majority of its component members.

The Committee examines the law, tries to bring about agreement between the National Assembly and the Council of the Republic and, if it does not succeed, decides the matter within five days after it has received the request. This period is reduced to two days in cases of urgency.

The Committee is competent to decide only on the possibility of revision of Titles I to X of the present Constitution.

Art. 93. A law which, in the opinion of the Committee, entails a revision of the Constitution is sent back to the National Assembly for another reading.

If Parliament adheres to its original vote, the law cannot be promulgated until the Constitution has been revised according to the procedure set forth in Article 90.

If the law is considered to be in conformity with the provisions of Titles I to X of the present Constitution, it is promulgated within the period provided in Article 36, this period being prolonged by the addition of the period provided in Article 92 above.

Art. 94. In the case of occupation of all or part of the metropolitan territory by foreign forces, no procedure of revision may be undertaken or continued.

Art. 95. The republican form of government cannot be the subject of any proposal for revision.

TITLE XII: TEMPORARY PROVISIONS
(No longer operative)

APPENDIX II

PARTY PROGRAMMES

(A) *The Belleville Manifesto*

The Programme with which Léon Gambetta triumphed over Hippolyte Carnot in the Paris election of 1869. Based on the policy outlined by Jules Simon in *La Politique Radicale*, it came to serve as the basis of most subsequent Radical manifestoes. French texts quoted in J. Reinach: *Discours et Plaidoyeurs politiques* (3 Vols., 1881); E. Ollivier: *L'Empire Libéral* (1895-1915, Vol. XI); and J. P. T. Bury: *Gambetta and the National Defence* (1936).

1. *The 'Cahiers' of the Electors:*

In the name of universal suffrage, basis of every political and social organization, let us instruct our Deputy to re-affirm the principles of Radical democracy and to demand with vigour: the most radical application of universal suffrage, both for the election of mayors and municipal councillors, with no local differentiation, and for the election of Deputies; re-partitioning of constituencies according to the actual number of electors entitled to vote and not according to the number of electors on the register; individual liberty to be in future protected by the law and not left at the mercy of arbitrary administrators; repeal of the Law of General Security; suppression of Article 75 of the Constitution of the Year VIII, and the direct responsibility of all *fonctionnaires*; trial by jury for every kind of political offence; complete freedom of the Press unrestricted by stamp-duty and caution-money; suppression of licensing of printers and publishers; freedom of meeting without let or hindrance, with liberty to discuss all religious, philosophical, political and social affairs; repeal of Article 291 of the Penal Code; full and complete freedom of association; suppression of the ecclesiastical budget and separation of Church and State; free, compulsory, secular primary education with competitive examinations for children of greatest intelligence for admission to higher education, which shall likewise be free; suppression of town dues, suppression of high salaries and pluralities, and modification of our system of taxation; appointment of all public *fonctionnaires* by election; suppression of standing armies, the cause of ruin to the nation's finances and business, a source of hatred between peoples and of distrust at home; abolition of privileges and monopolies, which we define in these words: 'A bonus to idleness'; economic reforms are connected with the social problem, the solution of which—although subordinate to political change—must be constantly studied and sought in the name of the principles of justice and social equality. Indeed this principle alone, put into general application, can cause social antagonism to disappear and give complete reality to our slogan: Liberty, Equality, Fraternity!

2. *The reply of Gambetta*:

Citizen Electors—I accept this mandate.

On these conditions I shall be especially proud to represent you because this election will have been conducted in conformity with the true principles of universal suffrage. The electors will have freely chosen their candidate. The electors will have determined the political programme of their delegate. This method seems to me at once right and in line with the traditions of the early days of the French Revolution.

I therefore in my turn adhere freely to the declaration of principles and the rightful claims which you commission me to press at the tribune.

With you, I think that there is no other sovereign but the people, and that universal suffrage, the instrument of this sovereignty, has no value and basis and carries no obligation, unless it be radically free.

The most urgent reform must therefore be to free universal suffrage from every tutelage, every shackle, every pressure, every corruption.

With you, I think that universal suffrage, once made the

master, would suffice to sweep away all the things which your programme demands, and to establish all the freedoms, all the institutions which we are seeking to bring about.

With you, I think that France, the home of indestructible democracy, will know liberty, peace, order, justice, material prosperity and moral greatness only through the triumph of the principles of the French Revolution.

With you, I think that a legal and loyal democracy is the political system *par excellence* which achieves most promptly and certainly the moral and material emancipation of the greatest number, and best ensures social equality in laws, actions and customs.

But—with you also—I consider that the progressive achievement of these reforms depends absolutely on the political regime and on political reforms, and it is for me axiomatic in these matters that the form involves and determines the substance.

It is, furthermore, this sequence and order of priority which our fathers have indicated and fixed in the profound and comprehensive slogan beyond which there is no safety: Liberty, Equality, Fraternity. We are thus in mutual agreement. Our contract is completed. I am at once your delegate and your trustee.

I go further than signifying agreement. I give you my vow: I swear obedience to this present contract and fidelity to the sovereign people.

(B) *The Programme of the Front Populaire*

(Adopted as a common election programme by the ten organizations in the *Rassemblement Populaire*, and issued on 11 January 1936. In the elections of 26 April [and the second ballot of 3 May] it was supported as a 'minimum' programme by the Communist Party. But both the Communists and the C.G.T.—although participants in the framing of the programme—refused M. Blum's invitation to enter his 'Popular Front' Government. The other eight participating bodies were the *Ligue des Droits de l'Homme, Comité de vigilance des intellectuels anti-fascistes, Comité mondial contre le Fascisme et la guerre, Mouvement d'action Combattante*, the Radical Party, the Socialist Party, the Socialist-

APPENDIX II

Republican Union, and the C.G.T.U. (Communist Trade Union Federation).

I. *Defence of Freedom.*

1. A general amnesty.
2. Measures against the Fascist Leagues:
    (*a*) The effective disarmament and dissolution of all semi-military formations, in accordance with the law.
    (*b*) The enforcement of legal measures in cases of incitement to murder or any attempt against the safety of the State.
3. Measures for the cleansing of public life, especially by forbidding Deputies to combine their parliamentary functions with certain other forms of activity.
4. The Press:
    (*a*) The repeal of the laws and decrees restricting freedom of opinion.
    (*b*) Reform of the Press by the following legislative measures:
        (i) Measures effectively repressing libel and blackmail.
        (ii) Measures which will guarantee the normal means of existence to newspapers, and compel publication of their financial resources.
        (iii) Measures ending the private monopoly of commercial advertising and the scandals of financial advertising, and preventing the formation of newspaper trusts.
    (*c*) Organization by the State of wireless broadcasts with a view to assuring the accuracy of wireless news and the equality of political and social organizations in relation to radio.
5. Trade Union Liberties:
    (*a*) Application and observance of trade union freedom for all.
    (*b*) Recognition of women's labour rights.
6. Education and freedom of conscience:
    (*a*) Measures safeguarding the development of public

education, by the necessary grants and by reforms such as the raising of the age for compulsory education to fourteen and, in secondary education, the proper selection of pupils as an essential accompaniment of grants.

(b) Measures guaranteeing to all concerned, pupils and teachers, perfect freedom of conscience, particularly by ensuring the neutrality of education, its non-religious character, and the civic rights of teachers.

7. Colonies: formation of a Parliamentary committee of inquiry into the political, economic and cultural situation in France's territories overseas, especially French North Africa and Indo-China.

II. *Defence of Peace.*

1. Appeal to the people, and especially the working classes, for collaboration in the maintenance and organization of peace.

2. International collaboration within the framework of the League of Nations for collective security, by defining the aggressor and by joint application of sanctions in cases of aggression.

3. Ceaseless endeavour to pass from armed peace to disarmed peace, first by a convention of limitation, and then by the general, simultaneous and effectively controlled reduction of armaments.

4. Nationalization of war industries and suppression of private trade in armaments.

5. Repudiation of secret diplomacy; international action and public negotiation to bring back to Geneva the states which have left it, without weakening the essential principles of the League of Nations, which are the principles of collective security and indivisible peace.

6. Greater flexibility in the procedure provided by the League of Nations' Covenant for the peaceful adjustment of treaties which have become dangerous to the peace of the world.

7. Extension of the system of pacts open to all nations, par-

ticularly in Eastern Europe, on the lines of the Franco-Soviet Pact.

III. *Economic Demands.*

1. Restoration of purchasing power destroyed or reduced by the crisis.
    (*a*) Against unemployment and the crisis in industry.
        (i) Establishment of a national unemployment fund.
        (ii) Reduction of the working week without reduction of the weekly wage.
        (iii) Bringing young workers into employment by establishing a system of adequate pensions for aged workers.
        (iv) Rapid execution of a public works programme, both urban and rural, linking local investments with schemes financed by the State and local authorities.
    (*b*) Against the agricultural and commercial crisis.
        (i) Revaluation of agricultural produce, combined with measures against speculation and high prices, in order to reduce the gap between wholesale and retail prices.
        (ii) Establishment of a National Grain Board (*Office du Blé*) to abolish the tribute levied by speculators against both the producer and the consumer.
        (iii) Strengthening of agricultural co-operatives, and supply of fertilizers at cost prices by the National Boards for Nitrogen and Potash, control and certification of sales of superphosphates and other fertilizers, extension of agricultural credits, reduction of leasehold rents.
        (iv) Suspension of distraints and regulation of debt repayments.
        (v) Pending the complete and earliest possible removal of all unjust measures imposed by the economy decrees, immediate abolition of measures affecting those groups whose conditions of

life have been most severely endangered by these decrees.

2. Against the robbery of investors and for the better organization of credit:

(*a*) Regulation of banking business. Regulation of balance sheets issued by banks and joint-stock companies. Further regulation of the powers of directors of joint-stock companies.

(*b*) State officials who have retired or are on the reserve-list to be prohibited from joining the board of directors of a joint-stock company.

(*c*) In order to remove credit and investment from the control of the economic oligarchy, the Bank of France must cease to be a private concern, and 'The Bank of France' must become 'France's Bank.' The Council of Regents of the Bank of France must be abolished: the powers of the Governor of the Bank of France must be increased, under the permanent control of a council composed of representatives of Parliament, of the executive authority, and of the main organized forces of labour and of industrial, commercial and agricultural activity. The capital of the Bank must be converted into debentures, with measures to safeguard the interests of small shareholders.

IV. *Financial Purification.*

1. Control of the trade in armaments, in conjunction with the nationalization of armaments industries. Prevention of waste in the civil and military departments.

2. Establishment of a War Pensions Fund.

3. Democratic reform of the system of taxation so as to relax the fiscal burden blocking economic recovery, and raising revenue by measures against large fortunes. Rapid steepening of income tax on incomes above 75,000 francs a year; reorganization of death duties; special taxes on monopoly profits, but in such a way as to have no effects on retail prices. Measures against tax evasions, in connexion with transferable ('bearer') securities.

APPENDIX II

4. Control of export of capital, and punishment of evasion by rigorous measures, including confiscation of property concealed abroad or of its equivalent value in France.

(C) *The Programme of the National Council of Resistance.*

(The organized resistance movements united under the *Conseil national de Résistance* drew up a programme of action on 16 March 1944. The first half concerned the course of immediate action; the second, printed below, concerned measures to be taken after liberation to secure 'a more just social order'. This second half, which came to be known as the 'Resistance Charter', was adopted by all major political parties before the general elections of October 1945, and therefore became the basis of general policy in the first stages of the Fourth Republic.

It offers striking comparison with Gambetta's Belleville Manifesto and the Popular Front Programme, printed above. See Chapters IV, V and VI for further discussion of the significance of these three documents.)

The representatives of Resistance proclaim that they have decided to remain united after liberation:

1. In order to establish the provisional government of the Republic formed by General de Gaulle to defend the political and economic independence of the nation, to re-establish France in her power and greatness, and to enable her to fulfil her universal mission.

2. In order to see that traitors are punished, and that action be taken against all those, in the realm of administration and professional life, who have come to terms with the enemy or have been actively associated with the policy of collaborationist governments:

3. In order to ensure confiscation of the property of traitors and traffickers in the black market; the taxation of profits of war and gains made to the detriment of the nation during the occupation, the confiscation of all enemy property, including shares acquired since the armistice by the Axis governments and their nationals in French colonial enterprises of every kind and constitution of these shares into an inalienable national patrimony;

4. In order to ensure the establishment of the widest democracy, by the restoration of universal suffrage, complete freedom of thought, of conscience and of expression; freedom of the Press, its honour and independence of the State, the power of wealth and of foreign influences; freedom of association, of meeting, of demonstration; inviolability of the home, and secrecy of correspondence; respect for the human person and the absolute equality of all citizens before the law.

Economic Reforms:

1. The setting up of a true economic and social democracy, entailing the eviction of the great economic and financial feudalities;

2. The rational organization of an economy which will assure the subordination of private interests to the general interest, and freed from professional dictatorship set up in the image of the Fascist States;

3. Intensification of national production along lines determined by the State after consultation with the representatives of all elements in production:

4. Return to the nation of the great monopolies in the means of production, the sources of energy, mineral wealth, insurance companies and the large banks;

5. The development and maintenance of co-operatives for the production, buying and selling of agricultural and industrial goods;

6. Right of access in the framework of business to the functions of management and administration for workers possessing the necessary qualifications, and participation of the workers in the direction of economic life:

Social Reforms:

1. The right to work and leisure, particularly by the restoration and amelioration of labour-contracts;

2. A considerable readjustment of wages and a guaranteed level of wages and salaries, and measures ensuring security for every worker and his family;

3. A guaranteed national purchasing-power by a policy promoting stability of currency;

4. Restoration, in its traditional freedom, of independent trade-unionism, endowed with extensive powers in the organization of economic and social life;

5. A complete plan of social security, designed to ensure for all citizens the means of subsistence in all cases where they cannot earn their own living, and with control over it assured for representatives of beneficiaries and of the State;

6. Security of employment, regulation of conditions of hiring and firing, restoration of workshop-delegates;

7. Raising and securing of the standard of living for workers on the land by a policy of remunerative agricultural prices; and generalizing, whilst improving, the experiment of the *Office du Blé* by social legislation according agricultural wage-earners the same rights as industrial wage-earners, by a system of insurance against the hazards of farming, by the establishment of a just law of rent and *métayage*, by facilities for young peasant families to acquire property, and by organizing a scheme for farm-equipment:

8. Old-age pensions for workers, compensation for accidents, and allocation of grants and allowances to the victims of Fascist terror (*Colonial and Educational Reforms are also mentioned*). Thus will be founded a new Republic which will sweep away the regime of base reaction instituted by Vichy, which will give democratic and popular institutions the efficiency of which they were deprived by the corruption and treachery which preceded capitulation. Thus will become possible a democracy combining effective control exercised by popular representatives with continuity of action in government.

APPENDIX III

THE FRANCO-GERMAN ARMISTICE CONVENTION, 1940

(Signed by Colonel-General Keitel, Chief of the German High Command, and General Huntziger, President of the French Delegation, on 22 June 1940, in the Forest of Compiègne.)

1. The French Government proclaims the cessation of hostilities against the German Empire in France, in the French possessions, the colonies, the protectorates and the mandated territories, as well as on the sea. It orders those French units encircled by German troops immediately to lay down their arms.

2. In order to assure the protection of the interests of the German Reich, French territory will be occupied by German troops to the north and to the west of a line drawn on the attached map.[1] The occupation of the territories which are to be occupied and which are not yet in German hands will start as soon as the Convention has been signed.

3. In those regions of France occupied by the Germans, the Reich is to exercise all the rights of an occupying power. The French Government undertakes to assist in all ways the carrying-out of orders made for the execution of these rights and to have them put into force with the help of the French administration. Consequently the French Government is immediately to notify the authorities and public services of the occupied territories that they will have to conform to the decisions of the German military commanders and to collaborate faithfully with them.

The German Government intends to limit the occupation of

[1] This line, starting to the east of the Franco-Swiss frontier near Geneva, ran through Dôle, Paray-le-Monial and Bourges to some twenty kilometres east of Tours: thence it ran southwards about twenty kilometres east of the Tours-Angoulême-Libourne railway, and on to the Spanish frontier, west of Pau.

the west coast of France, after the cessation of hostilities with England, to the minimum extent which may be necessary.

The Seat of the French Government. The French Government is free to establish itself in a town of its own choice in unoccupied territory, or, if it so desires, to establish itself in Paris. In this case the German Government will give to the French Government and to the central administrations all facilities for putting into force the administration from Paris of occupied and unoccupied territory.

4. The French armed forces on land, sea, and in the air are to be disarmed and demobilized within a period later to be determined. This measure is not to be applied to those units which are necessary for the maintenance of internal order. Their numbers and their armament will be fixed by Germany and Italy. The French units to be found in the territories which are to be occupied by Germany must be brought back as quickly as possible into the territories which will not be occupied and are to be similarly liberated. Before setting out, these troops will lay down their arms and equipment on the exact spot where they happen to be at the moment of the entering into force of this Convention. They will be responsible for the handing over in good condition of these arms and of this material into the hands of the German troops.

5. As guarantee that the Armistice will be observed, France will deliver in good condition all the guns, anti-tank guns, military aeroplanes, anti-aircraft guns, infantry armament, transport equipment and munitions of the French units which were fighting against Germany, and which happen to be, at the moment of the entering into force of the present Convention, in the territory which is not to be occupied by Germany. The extent of these deliveries will be fixed by the German Armistice Commission.

6. The remainder of the armaments, war material, and munitions of all kinds in the unoccupied region of France will be stored and put in safe custody under German or Italian control, with the exception of that which is to be left at the disposition of authorized French units. The German High Command reserves for itself the right in this matter to take all the

necessary measures to prevent the incorrect usage of these stocks. The manufacture of new war material is immediately to cease in unoccupied territory.

7. In the territories which are to be occupied, all the ground and coastal fortifications with their armaments, munitions, material, stocks, and installations of all sorts are to be handed over in perfect condition. The plans of these fortifications, as well as those of the fortifications already taken by the German troops, must similarly be handed over. The exact situation of mines, mine-fields on land, etc., must be supplied to the German High Command. These obstructions must be removed by French forces at the request of the German authorities.

8. With the exception of that part which will be left to the French Government for the protection of its interests in its colonial empire, the French war fleet must be assembled in those ports which will later be designated. It will there be demobilized and disarmed under German or Italian control. The designation of the ports will be made according to the home bases of these ships in peace-time.

The German Government solemnly declares to the French Government that it has no intention of using for the purposes of war the French Fleet which will be found in the ports put under German control with, however, the exception of the units which will be necessary to guard the coasts and to remove mines. Moreover, the German Government solemnly and expressly declares that it does not intend to make any unreasonable claims on the French Fleet at the time of the conclusion of the peace. With the exception of that part of the French Fleet (it will be fixed later) which is to defend French interests in her colonial empire, all the warships to be found outside France must be brought back to France.

9. The French High Command must give to the German High Command precise directions concerning all the mines laid by France, all the minefields near to ports or off the coasts, and all defensive positions. If the German High Command so requests, the French forces must themselves remove the mines.

10. The French Government agrees not to undertake any hostile action whatsoever against the Reich with any part of

APPENDIX III

the armed forces left at its disposition. Similarly the French Government will prevent members of the armed forces from leaving the country, as well as the transportation of arms, war material of any sort, warships and aeroplanes, to England or to any other foreign country whatsoever. The French Government will forbid French subjects from fighting against the Reich in the armies of the countries which are still at war with the latter. French subjects who do not conform to this law will be treated by German troops as *francs-tireurs*.

11. Merchant ships of all classes, comprising coastal small craft or those used in the ports which are in the hands of the French, must not until further notice put to sea. The recommencement of commercial navigation will be subject to the approval of the German Government or to that of the Italian Government. The French merchant ships which are outside French ports will receive from the French Government the order to return to France, or, if that is not possible, to enter neutral ports. All German merchant ships which have been captured and are in French ports are to be handed over intact on the demand of the German authorities.

12. All aircraft which are on French soil will be forthwith forbidden to take off. Any machine which takes off without German authorization will be considered as hostile and treated as such by the German Air Force. The aerodromes and installations of the air force which are in the unoccupied zone will be put under German or Italian control. Their being rendered useless may be demanded.

The French Government is bound to put at the disposition of the German authorities all foreign aircraft which are on unoccupied territory, or at least to prevent them from leaving. These aeroplanes are to be handed over to the German forces.

13. The French Government undertakes to see to it that in the territories which are to be occupied by the German troops all the buildings, all the installations and stocks for the army are delivered intact to the German troops.

Moreover, it is to ensure that the ports, industrial installations, and shipbuilding yards are left as they are and that they be neither damaged nor destroyed. The same clause applies equally to the ways and means of communication, and in particular to the railways, roads and canals, to the telegraphic and telephonic networks, to maritime signalling devices, and to means of guiding ships off the coasts. The French Government similarly undertakes, on the decision of the German High Command, to put in hand all the reconditioning which will be necessary. They will see that there is in occupied territory the necessary personnel and rolling stock of sufficient quantity for means of transport, and in the same proportion as for a normal peace-time period.

14. With regard to the French broadcasting stations, a restriction on transmitting will immediately be put into force. The recommencement of wireless transmission in unoccupied territory will become the subject of a separate agreement.

15. The French Government binds itself to assure across unoccupied territory the transit of goods between the German Empire and Italy to the extent required by the German Government.

16. The French Government, in agreement with the German authorities, will undertake the repatriation of the population in the occupied regions.

17. The French Government binds itself to prevent all transport of securities and foodstuffs from territory which is to be occupied into unoccupied territory or abroad. The measures concerning these securities and foodstuffs are to be taken in agreement with the German Government. However, the German Government will take into consideration the vital needs of the population of the unoccupied regions.

18. The cost of maintaining German troops in French territory falls on the French Government.

19. All German military and all German civilian prisoners who are actually in the hands of the French, including persons arrested or condemned, who have been put into prison and tried for an act carried out in the interests of the German Empire, must be at once handed over to the German troops. The French Government is obliged to hand over on demand all the Germans who are either in France or in French possessions,

colonies, protectorates, and mandated territories who are demanded by name by the German Government.

The French Government binds itself to prevent German prisoners of war and civilian prisoners from being transferred from French possessions into foreign countries. A list of prisoners will be supplied who have been transported outside France, as well as of prisoners of war who are incapable of being moved owing to illness or wounds. The care of German prisoners of war who are either ill or wounded will be taken in hand by the German High Command.

20. The French military who are prisoners of war of the Germans will remain prisoners until the conclusion of a peace.

21. The French Government guarantees to keep in good condition and to hand over intact all chattels and securities which according to the treaty are to be put at the disposition of Germany, and which it is forbidden to transfer out of the country. The French Government is responsible for all destruction, damage, or removals of property which go contrary to the spirit of the Convention.

22. The execution of the Armistice Convention is regulated and controlled by a German Armistice Commission which will carry out its duties according to the instructions of the German High Command. In addition this Commission will carry out the duties of assuring the necessary concordance between the Convention and the Franco-Italian Armistice Convention. In order to represent French interests and to receive its executive orders from the German Armistice Commission, the French Government will send a delegation to the offices of the German Armistice Commission.

23. The present Armistice Convention will come into force as soon as the French Government has made with the Italian Government an agreement on the cessation of hostilities.[1] Hostilities will cease six hours after the time on which the Italian Government has made known to the Government of

[1] An Armistice Convention in substantially similar terms, with additional provisions for demilitarized zones between French and Italian territories in North Africa, was signed by General Huntziger and Marshal Badoglio on 24 June 1940 in Rome.

the Reich the conclusion of this agreement. The Government of the Reich will make this time known to the French Government by means of wireless.

24. The Armistice Convention will remain in force until the conclusion of a peace treaty. It can be denounced at any moment and with immediate effect by the German Government if the French Government does not fulfil the obligations which it has assumed under this Convention.

This Armistice Convention has been signed in the Forest of Compiègne on the 22nd June 1940 at 18 hours 50 German summer time.

HUNTZIGER
KEITEL

BIBLIOGRAPHY

This list of some 300 books is not exhaustive, but includes most of the books referred to in footnotes. For the convenience of the reader books in English and in French are listed separately, and wherever an English translation is known to exist it has been given instead of the French edition. They are grouped under five headings:

I. The general historical background of republican democracy and the foundation of the Third Republic.

II. The general history and political system of the Third Republic.

III. The social and economic forces at work in modern France.

IV. Military and foreign affairs.

V. The Fourth Republic (including the interlude of the Vichy and Provisional Governments).

I. *Historical Background and Foundations*

A. *English.*

Brabant, F. H. *The Beginning of the Third Republic in France (February–September 1871).* Macmillan, 1940.
Bury, J. P. T. *France, 1814–1940.* Methuen, 1949. *Gambetta and the National Defence.* Longmans, 1936.
Charvet, P. E. *France.* Benn, 1954.
Cobban, A. *Rousseau and the Modern State.* Allen & Unwin, 1934.
Fisher, H. A. L. *Bonapartism.* Oxford University Press, 1908.
Jellinek, F. *The Paris Commune of 1871.* Gollancz, 1937.
Martin, K. *French Liberal Thought in the Eighteenth Century.* Benn, 1929.
Plamenatz, J. *The Revolutionary Movement in France, 1815–1871.* Longmans, 1952.
Ruggiero, G. de. *European Liberalism.* Oxford University Press, 1927.
Soltau, R. *French Political Thought in the Nineteenth Century.* Benn, 1931.
Spitzer, A. B. *The Revolutionary Theories of Louis Auguste Blanqui.* Columbia University Press, 1957.
Stannard, H. *Gambetta.* Methuen, 1921.
Thomson, D. *The Democratic Ideal in France and England.* Cambridge University Press, 1940.
Woodward, E. L. *French Revolutions.* Oxford University Press, 1934.

B. *French.*

Barbé, M. *Étude Historique des Idées sur la Souveraineté en France de 1815 à 1848.* 1904.

Bayet, A. et Albert, F. *Les Écrivains Politiques du XIXe siècle.* 1935.
Bertrand, A. *Les Origines de la Troisième République.* 1911.
Blanc, L. *L'Organisation du Travail.* 1840.
Bouniols, G. (Ed.). *Thiers au Pouvoir, 1871–3.* 1921.
Broglie, Duc de. *Mémoires,* in *Revue des Deux Mondes.* 1929.
Chanlaine, P. *Gambetta, Père de la République.* 1932.
Chastenet, J. *Histoire de la Troisième République.* 6 vols. 1952–.
Chesnelong, C. *L'Avènement de la République.* 1934. *Le Gouvernement de M. Thiers.* 1932. *La Campagne Monarchique d'Octobre, 1873.* 1895.
Dominique, P. *La Commune.* 1930. *Marianne et les Prétendants.* 1934.
Dreyfus, R. *Le Gouvernement de M. Thiers.* 1930.
Faguet, E. *Mgr. Dupanloup: un Grand Evêque.* 1914.
Falloux, Comte de. *Mémoires d'un Royaliste.* 3 vols. 1926.
Freycinet, C. de. *Souvenirs, 1848–93.* 2 vols. 1912–13.
Gambetta, L. *Lettres, 1868–82.* Ed. D. Halévy et E. Pillias. 1938.
Halévy, D. *La Fin des Notables.* 1930. *La République des Ducs.* 1937. *Pour l'Étude de la Troisième République.* 1937.
Lacombe, C. *Journal Politique.* 2 vols. 1907.
Lecomte, G. *Thiers.* 1933.
Lissagaray, P. *Histoire de la Commune de 1871.* 1896.
Malo, H. *Thiers, 1797–1877.* 1932.
Margueritte, P. et V. *La Commune.* 1903.
Meaux, Vicomte de. *Souvenirs Politiques.* 1905.
Napoléon, L. *Des Idées Napoléoniennes.* 1840.
Prévost-Paradol, L. F. *La France Nouvelle.* 1868.
Reclus, M. *M. Thiers.* 1929. *L'Avènement de la République, 1871–5.* 1900.
Richard, M. *Le Bonapartisme sous la République.* 1883.
Roux, Marquis de. *Origines et Fondation de la Troisième République.* 1933.
Thibaudet, A. *Les Idées Politiques de la France.* 1932.
Thiers, A. *Notes et Souvenirs, 1870–3.* 1903.
Weill, G. *Histoire du Parti Républicain en France, 1814–70.* 1928.

II. *General History and Political System*

A. *English.*

Anderson, W. (Ed.). *Local Government in Europe.* Appleton-Century Company, 1939.
Brogan, D. W. *The Development of Modern France, 1870–1939.* Hamish Hamilton, 1940.
Bruun, G. *Clemenceau.* Harvard University Press, 1943.
Campbell, P. *French Electoral Systems and Elections, 1789–1957.* Faber, 1958.
Chapman, B. *Introduction to French Local Government.* Allen & Unwin, 1953. *The Prefects and Provincial France.* Allen & Unwin, 1955.
Chapman, G. *The Dreyfus Case: A Reassessment.* Hart-Davis, 1955.

BIBLIOGRAPHY

Daniels, H. G. *The Framework of France*. Nisbet, 1937.
Daudet, L. *Clemenceau*. William Hodge, 1940.
Dreyfus, P. *Dreyfus: His Life and Letters*. Hutchinson, 1937.
Gooch, R. K. *The French Parliamentary Committee System*. Appleton-Century Company, 1935. *Regionalism in France*. Appleton-Century Company, 1931.
Haig, R. H. *The Public Finances of Post-War France*. Columbia University Press, 1929.
Hale, R. W. *Democratic France*. Coward-McCann, 1941.
Jèze, C. and Truchy, H. *The War Finance of France*. Yale University Press, 1927.
Middleton, W. L. *The French Political System*. Benn, 1932.
Pickles, D. M. *The French Political Scene*. Nelson, 1938.
Poincaré, R. *How France is Governed*. Fisher Unwin, 1913.
Renouvin, P. *The Forms of War Government in France*. Yale University Press, 1927.
Rogers, L. *The French Parliamentary System*. Columbia University Press, 1929.
Scott, J. A. *Republican Ideas and the Liberal Tradition in France, 1870–1914*. Columbia University Press, 1951.
Sharp, W. R. *The French Civil Service*. Macmillan, 1931.
Sieghart, M. *Government by Decree*. Stevens, 1950.
Soltau, R. *French Parties and Politics*. Oxford University Press, 1930.
Vaucher, P. *Post-War France*. Oxford University Press, 1934.
Werth, A. *France in Ferment*. Jarrolds, 1934. *The Destiny of France*. Hamish Hamilton, 1937. *The Twilight of France, 1933–40*. Hamish Hamilton, 1942.
White, L. D. (Ed.). *The Civil Service in the Modern State*. University of Chicago Press, 1930.

B. *French.*

'Alain'. *Éléments d'une Doctrine Radicale*. 1925. *Les Propos d'Alain*. 2 vols. 1920. *Propos de Politique*. 1934.
Bainville, J. *La Troisième République*. 1935.
Barthélemy, J. *Le Gouvernement de la France*. 1939.
Bayet, A. *Le Radicalisme*. 1932.
Berl, E. *La Politique et les Partis*. 1932.
Blum, L. *Souvenirs de l'Affaire*. 1935. *La Réforme Gouvernementale*. 1936. *Radicalisme et Socialisme*. 4th edn. 1936.
Bourgin, G., Carrère, J. et Guérin, A. *Manuel des Partis Politiques en France*. 1928.
Capitant, R. *La Réforme du Parlementarisme*. 1934.
Charensol, G. *L'Affaire Dreyfus et la Troisième République*. 1930.
Chastenet, J. *La France de M. Fallières*. 1949.
Clemenceau, G. *Sur la Démocratie*. 1930. *Au Soir de la Pensée*. 2 vols. 1930.

Coblentz, P. *Georges Mandel.* 1946.
Corcos, F. *Catéchisme des Partis Politiques.* 1932.
Dansette, A. *Les Affaires de Panama.* 1934. *L'Affaire Wilson et la Chute du Président Grévy.* 1936. *Le Boulangisme, 1886–90.* 1938.
Debû-Bridel, J. *L'Agonie de la Troisième République, 1929–1939.* 1948.
Deslandres, M. *Histoire Constitutionnelle de la France:* Vol. III. *L'Avènement de la Troisième République—La Constitution de 1875.* 1937.
Duguit, L., Monnier, H., Bonnard, R. *Les Constitutions et les Principales Lois Politiques de la France depuis 1789.* Latest edn. 1953.
Dutrait-Crozon, H. *Précis de l'Affaire Dreyfus.* 1924.
Duverger, M. *L'Influence des Systèmes Électoraux sur la Vie Politique,* 1950.
Esmein, A. *Éléments de Droit Constitutionnel Français et Comparé.* 2 vols. 1928.
Fabre-Luce, A. *Le Secret de la République.* 1938.
Flandin, P-E. *Politique Française, 1919–1940.* 1947.
Giraud, E. *La Crise de la Démocratie et le Renforcement du Pouvoir Exécutif.* 1938.
Goguel, F. *La Politique des Partis sous la Troisième République, 1871–1939.* 2 vols. 1946. *Géographie des Élections françaises.* 1951.
Gouault, J. *Comment la France est devenue républicaine.* 1954.
Halévy, D. *Apologie pour Notre Passé.* 1910. *La Décadence de la Liberté.* 1931. *La République des Comités.* 1934.
Hanotaux, G. *Histoire de la France Contemporaine, 1870–1900.* 4 vols. 1908.
Jacques, L. E. *Les Partis Politiques sous la Troisième République.* 1913.
Jaurès, J. *Les Preuves.* 1898.
Jouvenel, R. de. *La République des Camarades.* 1934.
Lavisse, E. (Ed.). *Histoire de France Contemporaine depuis la Révolution jusqu'à la Paix de 1919.* Vols. VII, VIII, IX cover the period.
Leroy, A. *Le Droit des Fonctionnaires.* 1906.
Martet, J. *M. Clemenceau peint par lui-même.* 1929.
Milhaud, A. *Histoire du Radicalisme.* 1951.
Paul-Boncour, J. *Entre deux Guerres.* 3 vols. 1945–6.
Persil, R. *Alexandre Millerand.* 1949.
Poincaré, R. *Au Service de la France.* 4 vols. 1926.
Rambaud, A. *Jules Ferry.* 1903.
Reclus, M. *La Troisième République de 1870 à 1918.* 1945. *Jules Ferry.* 1947. *Grandeur de 'la Troisième'. De Gambetta à Poincaré.* 1948.
Reinach, J. *Histoire de l'Affaire Dreyfus.* 6 vols. 1901–11.
Siegfried, A. *Tableau Politique de la France de l'Ouest sous la Troisième République.* 1908. *Tableau des Partis en France.* 1930.
Sorel, G. *La Révolution Dreyfusienne.* 1911.
Soulier, A. *L'Instabilité Ministérielle sous la Troisième République, 1871–1938.* 1939.
Tardieu, A. *L'Heure de la Décision.* 1934. *Métier Parlementaire.* 1937.

Thibaudet, A. *La République des Professeurs*. 1927. *Trente Ans de Vie Française*. 4 vols. 1919–21.
Trotabas, L. *Constitution et Gouvernement de la France*. 2nd edn. 1933.
Weil, B. *L'Affaire Dreyfus*. 1930.
Zévaès, A. *L'Affaire Dreyfus*. 1931. *Histoire de la Troisième République*. 1938.
Zola, E. *La Vérité en Marche*. 1901.

III. *Social and Economic Forces*

A. *English.*

Blum, L. *Léon Blum before his Judges*. Labour Book Service, 1943.
Bodley, J. E. C. *France*. Macmillan, 1899. *The Church in France*. Macmillan, 1906.
Buisson, F. and Farrington, E. E. *French Educational Ideals of To-day*. Harrap, 1920.
Clapham, Sir J. H. *The Economic Development of France and Germany, 1815–1914*. Cambridge University Press, 1921.
Clark, F. I. *The Position of Women in Contemporary France*. P. S. King, 1937.
Clough, S. B. *France: A History of National Economics, 1789–1939*. Scribner's, New York, 1939.
Ehrmann, H. W. *French Labor From Popular Front to Liberation*. Oxford University Press, 1947.
Einzig, P. *France's Crisis*. Macmillan, 1934.
Fontaine, A. *French Industry during the War*. Yale University Press, 1927.
Fraser, G. and Thadee, N. *Léon Blum, Man and Statesman*. Gollancz, 1937.
Guérard, A. *The France of To-morrow*. Harvard University Press, 1942.
Hayes, C. H. *France: A Nation of Patriots*. Columbia University Press, 1930.
Howe, S. E. *Lyautey of Morocco*. Hodder & Stoughton, 1931.
Hunter, N. *Peasantry and the Crisis in France*. Gollancz, 1938.
Jackson, J. H. *Jean Jaurès*. Allen & Unwin, 1943. *Clemenceau and the Third Republic*. Hodder & Stoughton, 1946.
Kuczynski, J. *A Short History of Labour Conditions in France, 1700 to the present day*. F. Muller, 1946.
Levine, L. *Syndicalism in France*. Columbia University Press, 1912.
Lévy, L. *France is a Democracy*. Gollancz, 1943.
Lorwin, V. L. *The French Labor Movement*. Harvard University Press, 1954.
Maillaud, P. *France*. Oxford University Press, 1942.
Maurois, A. *Lyautey*. John Lane, 1931.
Micaud, C. A. *The French Right and Nazi Germany, 1933–9*. Duke University Press, 1943.

Moon, P. T. *The Labor Problem and the Social Catholic Movement in France*. Macmillan, New York, 1921.

Ogburn, W. F. and Jaffé, W. *The Economic Development of Post-War France*. Columbia University Press, 1929.

Peel, Hon. G. *The Economic Policy of France*. Macmillan, 1937.

Phillips, C. S. *The Church in France, 1848–1907*. S.P.C.K., 1936.

Priestley, H. I. *France Overseas*. Appleton-Century Company, 1938.

Ritchie, R. L. G. (Ed.). *France: A Companion to French Studies*. Methuen, 1937; revised edn. 1951.

Roberts, S. H. *History of French Colonial Policy*. 2 vols. P. S. King, 1928.

Rogers, J. H. *The Process of Inflation in France*. Columbia University Press, 1929.

Saposs, D. J. *The Labour Movement in Post-War France*. Columbia University Press, 1931.

Simpson, W. J. S. *Religious Thought in France in the Nineteenth Century*. Allen & Unwin, 1935.

Thorez, M. *France To-day and the People's Front*. Gollancz, 1936.

Tissier, P. *I Worked with Laval*. Harrap, 1942.

B. *French.*

Annuaire de la Noblesse de France.

Barrès, M. *Les Déracinés*. 1897. *Mes Cahiers*. 1929.

Benda, J. *La Trahison des Clercs*. 1927.

Burrand, R. *La Vie Quotidienne en France de 1870 à 1900*. 1947.

Dansette, A. *Histoire Religieuse de la France Contemporaine*. 2 vols. 1951.

Dauphin-Meunier, A. *La Banque de France*. 1936.

Debidour, A. *Histoire des Rapports de l'Église et de l'État en France*. 1898. *L'Église Catholique et l'État sous la Troisième République*. 2 vols. 1906.

Dolléans, E. *Histoire du Mouvement Ouvrier, 1830 à nos jours*. 3 vols. 1947–53.

Fourcade, J. *La République de la Province*. 1936.

France, A. *L'Île des Pingouins*. 1908.

Frédérix, P. *État des Forces en France*. 1935.

Giraudoux, J. *Pleins Pouvoirs*. 1939.

Guéhenno, J. *Jeunesse de la France*. 1936.

Guérin, P. *Le Problème Français*. 1939.

Halévy, D. *Péguy et les Cahiers de la Quinzaine*. 1941.

Hoog, G. *Histoire du Catholicisme Social en France, 1871–1931*. 1946.

Jouhaux, L. *La C.G.T.* 1937.

Lachapelle, G. *Les Finances de la Troisième République*. 1937.

Lantoine, A. *Histoire de la Franc-Maçonnerie Française*. 1925.

Lecanuet, E. *L'Église de France sous la Troisième République, 1870–94*. 2 vols. 1910.

Louis, P. *Histoire du Socialisme en France*. 1925. Revised edn. 1946.

Manevy, R. *Histoire de la Presse, 1914–1939*. 1945.

Maurras, C. *Enquête sur la Monarchie, 1900–1909*. 1911.

BIBLIOGRAPHY

Michel, A. G. *La Dictature de la Franc-Maçonnerie sur la France.* 1924.
Miéville, H. L. *La Pensée de Maurice Barrès.* 1934.
Mirkine-Guetzévitch, B. (Ed.). *L'Œuvre de la Troisième République.* 1945.
Montreuil, J. *Histoire du Mouvement Ouvrier en France.* 1947.
Mun, Comte A. de. *Ma Vocation Sociale.* 1926.
Péguy, C. *Notre Jeunesse.* 1916.
Pelloutier, F. *Histoire des Bourses du Travail.* 1921.
Piou, J. *Le Comte Albert de Mun.* 1925.
Richard, C. *L'Enseignement en France.* 1925.
Seippel, P. *Les Deux Frances.* 1905.
d'Uzès, Duchesse. *Souvenirs de la Duchesse d'Uzès.* 1939.

IV. Military and Foreign Affairs

A. *English.*

Bloch, M. *Strange Defeat.* Oxford University Press, 1949.
Carroll, E. M. *French Public Opinion and Foreign Affairs, 1870–1914.* Appleton-Century Company, 1931.
Challener, R. D. *The French Theory of the Nation in Arms, 1866–1939.* Columbia University Press, 1955.
Draper, T. *The Six Weeks' War.* Methuen, 1946.
France and Britain: A Report by a Chatham House Study Group. R.I.I.A., 1945.
Gaulle, C. de. *War Memoirs: The Call to Honour, 1940–2.* 2 vols. Collins, 1955. (Eng. trans. of first volume of *Mémoires de Guerre.*)
Howard, J. E. *Parliament and Foreign Policy in France.* Cresset Press, 1948.
Jordan, W. M. *Great-Britain, France and the German Problem, 1918–39.* R.I.I.A. Oxford University Press, 1943.
Keith, A. B. *Speeches and Documents on International Affairs, 1918–37.* 2 vols. Oxford University Press, 1938.
King, J. C. *Generals and Politicians.* University of California Press, 1951.
Lorraine, J. *Behind the Battle of France.* Oxford University Press, 1943.
McCallum, R. B. *England and France, 1939–43.* Hamish Hamilton, 1944.
McKay, D. C. *The United States and France.* Harvard University Press, 1951.
Maurois, A. *The Battle of France.* John Lane, 1940. *Why France Fell.* John Lane, 1940.
d'Ormesson, W. *France.* Longmans, 1939.
Reynaud, P. *In the Thick of the Fight, 1930–45.* Cassell, 1955. (Abridged Eng. trans. of *Au coeur de la mêlée,* 1951.)
Schumann, F. L. *War and Diplomacy in the French Republic.* McGraw Hill, 1931.
Spears, Sir E. L. *Assignment to Catastrophe.* 2 vols. Heinemann, 1954.

Waterfield, G. *What Happened to France*. John Murray, 1940.
Weygand, General M. *Recalled to Service: The Memoirs of General Maxime Weygand*. Eng. trans. Heinemann, 1952.
Werth, A. *France and Munich*. Hamish Hamilton, 1939. *The Last Days of Paris*. Hamish Hamilton, 1940.
Wolfers, A. *Britain and France between the Two Wars*. Harcourt, Brace and Company, 1940.

B. *French.*

Allard, P. *Le Quai d'Orsay*. 1938.
Beau de Loménie, E. *La Mort de la Troisième République*. 1951. *Les Responsabilités des Dynasties bourgeoises*. 3 vols. Vol. II. *de MacMahon à Poincaré*, 1947.
Brinon, F. de. *France-Allemagne, 1918–34*. 1934.
Documents Diplomatiques. 1914. *Le Livre Jaune Français*. 1939.
Foch, F. *Mémoires*. 1930.
Gaulle, C. de. *Vers L'Armée de Métier*. 1934. *La France et son Armée*. 1939. *Le Fil de l'Épée*. 2nd edn. 1944.
Gohier, U. *L'Armée contre la Nation*. 1899.
Jaurès, J. *L'Armée Nouvelle*. 2nd edn. 1915.
Kammerer, A. *La Vérité sur l'Armistice*. 1944.
Serre, C. (*Rapporteur*). *Événements survenus en France de 1933 à 1945: Témoignages et Documents*. 9 vols. 1947.
Tardieu, A. *La Paix*. 1921.

V. *The Fourth Republic*
(*including Vichy and Provisional Governments*)

A. *English.*

Baudouin, P. *The Private Diaries of Paul Baudouin*. Eyre & Spottiswoode, 1948.
Earle, E. M. (Ed.). *Modern France: Problems of the Third and Fourth Republics*. Princeton University Press, 1951.
Edelman, M. *France: The Birth of the Fourth Republic*. Penguin Books, 1944.
Einaudi, M., Domenach, J-M., Garosci, A. *Communism in Western Europe*. Cornell University Press, 1951.
Farmer, P. *Vichy, Political Dilemma*. Oxford University Press, 1955.
Fortune, G. and W. *Hitler Divided France*. Macmillan, 1943.
Gavin, C. *Liberated France*. Cape, 1955.
Goguel, F. *France Under the Fourth Republic*. Cornell University Press, Oxford University Press, 1952.
Kernan, T. *Report on France*. Lane, 1942.
Langer, W. L. *Our Vichy Gamble*. Knopf, 1947.
Leahy, Admiral W. D. *I Was There*. Gollancz, 1950.

Lidderdale, D. W. S. *The Parliament of France*. Hansard Society, 1951; 2nd rev. edn. 1954.
Lüthy, H. *The State of France*. Secker & Warburg, 1955.
Matthews, R. *The Death of the Fourth Republic*. Eyre & Spottiswoode, 1954.
Mendès-France, P. *The Pursuit of Freedom*. Longmans, 1956.
Pickles, D. M. *France Between the Republics*. Contact Publications, 1946. *France: The Fourth Republic*. Methuen, 1955. *French Politics: The First Years of the Fourth Republic*. R.I.I.A., 1953.
Pierre-Gosset, R. *Algiers, 1941–1943: A Temporary Expedient*. Cape, 1945.
Schoenbrun, D. *As France Goes*. Gollancz, 1957.
Survey of International Affairs, 1939–1946: Hitler's Europe, ed. Toynbee, A. and V. M., 1954. *Documents on International Affairs, 1939–1946*. Vol. II. *Hitler's Europe*, ed. Carlyle, M., 1954. Oxford University Press for R.I.I.A.
Taylor, O. R. *The Fourth Republic of France: Constitution and Political Parties*. R.I.I.A., 1951.
Thomson, D. *Two Frenchmen: Pierre Laval and Charles de Gaulle*. Cresset Press, 1951.
Tissier, P. *The Government of Vichy*. Harrap, 1942.
Werth, A. *France, 1940–1955*. Hale, 1956. *The Strange History of Pierre Mendès-France and the Great Conflict over French North Africa*. Barrie, 1957.
Williams, P. *Politics in Post-War France: Parties and the Constitution of the Fourth Republic*. Longmans, 1954.
Wright, G. *The Reshaping of French Democracy*. Methuen, 1950.

B. *French.*

Aron, Robert. *Histoire de Vichy*. 1954.
Auriol, V. *Hier–Demain*. 2 vols. 1945.
Blocq-Mascart, M. *Chroniques de la Résistance*. 1945.
Blum, L. *L'Œuvre de Léon Blum*. 3 vols. Vol. I, *1940–5*. 1955.
Bouthillier, Y. *Le Drame de Vichy*. 2 vols. 1950–1.
Caillaux, J. *Mes Mémoires*. 3 vols. 1947.
Charles-Roux, F. *Cinq Mois Tragiques aux Affaires Étrangères, 21 Mai–1 Novembre, 1940*. 1949.
Decoux, Admiral. *A la Barre de l'Indochine (1940–5)*. 1949.
Debû-Bridel, J. *Les Partis contre Charles de Gaulle*. 1948.
Duverger, M. *Manuel de Droit Constitutionnel et de Science Politique*. 1948.
Encyclopédie Politique de la France et du Monde (ed. Chevallier, J. J. *et. al.*). 4 vols. 1950–1. Vol. I by F. Goguel.
Fauvet, J. *Les Forces Politiques en France*. 1951. *La France Déchirée*. 1958.
Fernet, Vice-Admiral. *Aux Côtés du Maréchal Pétain: Souvenirs 1940–4*. 1943.

Gard, M. M. du. *La Chronique de Vichy, 1940–4.* 1948. *La Carte Impériale: Histoire de la France d'Outre-Mer, 1940–5.* 1949.
Gaulle, C. de. *Discours et Messages du Général de Gaulle.* 2 vols. 1940–2. *Mémoires de Guerre.* 3 vols. 1954–9
Guy-Grand, G. *Au Seuil de la IVe République.* 1946.
Lassaigne, L. *Constitution de la République Française et Lois Organiques.* 1947.
Lebrun, A. *Témoignage.* 1946.
Mallet, A. *Pierre Laval.* 2 vols. 1955.
Marabuto, P. *Les Partis Politiques et les Mouvements Sociaux sous la Quatrième République.* 1948.
Mirkine-Guetzévitch, B. *La Quatrième République.* 1946.
Muselier, Vice-Admiral. *De Gaulle contre le Gaullisme.* 1946.
Noguères, L. *Le Véritable Procès du Maréchal Pétain.* 1958.
Pétain, Philippe. *Quatre Années au Pouvoir.* 1949. *Le Procès du Maréchal Pétain.* 1945.
'Pertinax'. *Les Fossoyeurs.* 2 vols. 1943.
Prélot, M. *Précis de Droit Constitutionnel.* 1948.
Priouret, R. A. *La République des Partis.* 1947.
Rossi, A. *Physiologie du Parti Communiste Français.* 1949.
Théry, J. *Le Gouvernement de la Quatrième République.* 1951.

INDEX

Action française, 29, 63, 73, 117, 141–2, 149, 157, 177, 195–6, 216, 220

Administration, 16, 55–8, 60–3, 87–8, 94, 97–8, 105, 110, 113, 118, 141, 147, 161, 164–8, 175–9, 208–10, 221–3

'Alain', 52, 73, 117, 133

Algeria, 56, 98, 126, 137, 164, 223, 231, 253–5, *see also* Colonies

Alsace and Lorraine, 40, 147, 149, 214

Anarchism, 17, 23, 25, 28, 46, 117, 122, 125

Anti-clericalism, 61n., 72, 104–5, 113, 121, 128, 139, 141–4, 149, 161, *see also* Separation of Church and State

Anti-semitism, 157–8, 161, 195, 222, 223, 225, *see also* Dreyfus

Aristocracy, 11, 43, 64–6, 71, 73, 91, 102

Armistice, 1940: 211–14, Appendix III

Army, 73, 79, 88, 106, 113, 128–30, 135, 139, 141, 147, 150–63, 167, 170–4, 179–80, 206, 208–9, 211–19, 254

Artisans, 31, 42, 45, 67–8, 103, 106, *see also* Working Classes

d'Aumale, Duc, 80–1, 153

Auriol, V., 237, 241

Babeuf, F. N., 19–20, 25, 132

Banks, 69–70, 105, 199, *see also* Financial Oligarchy *and* Appendix II

Barrès, M., 123–4, 149–50, 157

Barthou, L., 73, 180, 195, 205

Baudouin, P., 213n., 216, 221–2

Belleville Manifesto, 119–21, 234, *see also* Appendix II (A)

Bidault, G., 231, 240

Bismarck, Prince, 9, 25–6, 77, 84, 127, 137, 139, 147–8, 154, 163

Blanc, L., 21–3, 26, 32, 43, 132

Blanqui, A,. 25, 132

Bloc National, 151, 186, 188, 202

Blum, L., 50–1, 56, 71, 73, 108, 123, 151, 188–9, 199, 208, 224, 241

Bonald, L. de, 28, 35, 157

Bonapartism, 15–16, 30, 32–4, 37, 46, 55, 64–5, 76, 80, 83–8, 92, 94, 102, 116–17, 119–20, 154, 156, 162, 171, 195, *see also* Napoleon I *and* Napoleon III

Bordeaux, 56, 76, 214; Bordeaux Assembly, 84, 91, 93, 96, 118; Bordeaux Pact, 77–9, 83, 151

Boulangism, 63, 84, 102, 124, 130, 152–7, 162, 170, 177, 195

Bourgès-Maunoury, M., 246

Briand, A., 73, 108, 112, 152, 175, 188, 203–5

Brinon, F. de, 71, 201

Broglie, Duc de, 84, 86–8, 90, 97, 102

Cagoulards, 63, 183, 218

Caillaux, J., 152, 192

Camelots du Roi, 63, 142, 190, 195

INDEX

Capitalist organizations: Comité des Forges, 69, 71: Confédération Général de la Production Française, 69, 70, 199; *see also* Financial Oligarchy *and* Banks

Carnot, A., 104, 187

Centre, 87, 93, 104–6, 114, 119, 232, 241, 245, 253, 259

Chamber of Deputies, 13, 33, 39, 58–9, 64, 70–1, Chapter III *passim*, 118, 148, 164–5, 178, 184–5, 188, 189n., 190–1, 204, 232

Chambers of Commerce, 55, 56

Chambord, Comte de, 14, 61, 80–4, 87, 136

Charles X, 13, 28–9, 80

Chautemps, C., 189

Church, Roman Catholic, 11, 15, 19, 28–9, 34–5, 65–6, 71–3, 81, 87, 89, 103–4, 106, 113, 125–9, 135–6, 139–47, 152, 157–8, 161, 165, 170–2, 175, 177, 182, 184, *see also* Anti-clericalism, Papacy, Separation of Church and State

Cissey, General, 88–90

Clemenceau, G., 73, 106, 128, 130–1, 146, 149, 151, 153, 155, 159, 161, 163, 174, 176, 178, 187, 194, 202–3, 205

Collaborators, 217–9; splinter groups, 229; post-war persecution of, 232

Colonies, 66, 126, 130, 135, 137, 139, 149–50, 160, 163–9, 172, 216, 230, 251, *see also* Algiers *and* Lyautey, Marshal

Combes, E., 35, 106, 125, 128, 141–3

Commune, 26, 41, 44–6, 60, 88, 93, 97, 100, 103, 140, 147; Commune of 1793, 18, 25; Commune of 1871, 19, 24–7, 46, 76–7, 131–2

Communism, 18, 22–4, 46–7, 49, 67, 73, 104, 108–9, 114, 120, 128, 130–2, 150–1, 171, 177, 186, 192, 195, 197, 202, 212, 218, 233, 236, 244–5, 248, 250; First International, 26, 47, 51; Second and Third Internationals, 108, 150

Conseil d'État, 17, 59, 60, 63, 99–101

Conseil national du Crédit, 235

Conservatism, 28–30, 40, 42–4, 56, 71, 73, 75–6, 82–3, 87, 90, 92–5, 101, 104–5, 107, 121, 124, 133, 171, 176, 182, 191–2, 195, 221–2, *see also* Right Wing, Traditionalism

Constituent Assemblies (1945–6), 232, 237

Constitution: of Third Republic, 40, 45, 50, 55, 65, Chapter III *passim*, 118, 168–70, 209–10; Constitutional Laws, Chapter III *passim*, Appendix I, *see also* Laws, President, Senate, Chamber of Deputies: of Vichy Government, 220–1, of Fourth Republic, 237–42; Appendix I (J); *see also* National Assembly, President, etc.

Croix de Feu, 34, 63, 73, 142, 195–7

Czechoslovakia, 206–7, 209

Daladier, E., 107, 152, 197–8, 206, 208, 210, 212, 224

Darlan, Admiral, 89, 208, 217, 221, 231

Darnand, J., 160, 218, 228

Daudet, L., 123, 196

INDEX

Déat, M., 108, 218, 229
Decentralization, 98n., 100n., 116–19, 122, 165
Delcassé, T., 112, 130, 205
Départements, 44, 97–8, 118, 185
Déroulède, P., 162, 177
Doriot, J., 177, 218, 228, 229
Doumer, P., 166, 188
Doumergue, G., 188, 197
Dreyfus, A., 38n., 50, 53, 63, 72–3, 84, 103, 105, 117, 124–5, 129, 141, 142, 149, 152, 157–9, 161–2, 168, 179, 183, 195–6, 209
Dupanloup, Mgr., 29, 34, 81, 82

Economic reconstruction, 233
Education, 57–9, 73n., 120, 126, 128, 143–7, 149, 170, 172, 223, 252
Electoral machinery: Suffrage, 13, 17, 31, 40–4, 52n., 89, 93, 95, 97, 100, 119, 165, 184–5, 191, 232, 239; Proportional representation, 185, 186n., 242–3; *Scrutin uninominal*, 93–4, 117–18, 185; *Scrutin de liste*, 94, 117, 155, 185–6; *Deuxième tour*, 93, 95n., 185–6; Elections, 39–40, 43, 58, 64, 89–90, 93–4, 97, 107n., 108, 110n., 186n., 187n., 232, 237, 243–6
Étatisme, 18, 25, 33, 46, 60, 62, 117, 122, 126, 131, 155, 160, 167
European Defence Community, 251, 253

Fascism, 71, 73, 117, 134, 177, 196–9, 201, 204, 220, 222–3
Ferry, J., 73, 95, 106, 128, 144–5, 149, 153, 165–6, 187

Financial oligarchy, 66–71, 73, 102, 104, 106, 125, 133, 157, 182, 193–4, 197
Flandin, P. E., 70, 104, 197, 217
Fonctionnaires, see Administration
Foreign Policy, 59, 72n., 111–12, 130, 147–54, 200–10, 251–2
Fourier, C., 20, 21, 25
Fourth Republic, Chapter VII *passim*; constitution, 237–42; electoral system, 242–5; political groupings, 244–7, 250; social balance, 247–9; economic reconstruction, 249–50; political divisions, 252–3; causes of collapse, 257–9
France, A., 68, 73, 161
Franco-Soviet Pact, 195, 205, 207
Free French movement, 230–1
Freemasonry, 56, 106, 141
French Committee of National Liberation, 231
French National Committee, 230
Freycinet, C. de, 91, 153

Gaillard, F., 252, 253
Gambetta, L., 25, 27, 33, 37, 39–41, 44n., 73, 76, 79, 88–9, 92n., 101–2, 104–5, 116, 118–21, 128, 130, 140, 148, 151, 153, 177, 234
Gaulle, General de, 77, 98, 150, 211–12, 230–3, 238, 244, 254, 255
Germany, 26, 32, 45, 68, 71–2, 84, 105, 117, 127, 130, 134–8, 147–50, 154, 158, 160, 163, 165, 181, 183–4, 186, 190, 193–9, 201–9, 211–14, 216–19, 224, 226–7, 251
Giraud, General, 98, 216, 231

INDEX

Great Britain, 60, 68, 136, 138, 163, 165, 170, 172, 176, 200–9, 213, 230; Political system, 10–11, 17, 32, 48, 75, 93, 96, 100, 104, 114, 126–7, 132, 139, 174
Grévy, J., 73, 101–2, 154, 164, 187
Guesde, J., 19, 47, 159
Guizot, F., 31–2, 36

Henriot, P., 218
Herriot, E., 58, 73, 107, 123, 188, 241
Hervé, G., 177
Hitler, A., 19, 71, 195, 198, 213, 220

Individualism, 42, 52n., 105–9, 115, 117, 122, 124–6, 130–1, 133, 159, 229, 235
Industrialism, 41, 45, 66, 103, 134, 138, 173, 182, 184, 249
Internationalism, 134, 150, 204
Interpellation, 85, 110
Italy, 26, 32, 127, 134–9, 163, 196, 201, 205, 220

Jacobinism, 11, 19, 20–1, 25, 33, 37n., 105–6, 177, *see also* Radicalism *and* Revolutionary Ideas
Jaurès, J., 19, 36, 47, 49–50, 73, 104, 108, 146, 151, 161–2, 177, 180, 185
Jeunesses Patriotes, 73, 195
Jouhaux, L., 199

Labour organizations: *Confédération Générale du Travail*, 48–51, 72, 108, 172, 174–9, 182, 197–9, 222, 248; *Confédération Générale des Travailleurs Chrétiens*, 51; *Confédération Générale du Travail Unitaire*, 108, 197; Labour Congresses, 47–50; Matignon Agreement, 199; Syndicalism, 46–9, 73, 108, 120, 174
Lamartine, A. de, 32–3, 36
Lamennais, F. de, 34–5
Laval, P., 51, 58, 84, 89, 151, 160, 190, 195, 197, 201, 205, 211, 214–19, 221, 225–30; Germany demands French labour, 226–7
Laws: Law of Associations, 143, 178; Law of the Mayors, 88, 97; Law on the Organization of the Public Powers, Appendix I (I); Law of the Septennate, 88; *Loi Falloux*, 35, 140, 144; *Loi Rivet*, 78–9, 85; *Loi des Trente*, 85; *Loi Tréveneuc*, 98, 228; Wallon Amendment, 89–90, 215
League of Nations, 105, 198, 200–5
Lebrun, A., 214
Left Wing, 31, 38n., 42–3, 83, 86–7, 90, 92, 105, 108–9, 114, 125, 129–31, 133, 147–8, 150, 154, 176–7, 184–5, 194, 197, 204, 212, 222, 233; *Bloc des Gauches*, 72, 142, 150, 168, 183; *Cartel des Gauches*, 50, 151, 186, 188, 203; *Front Populaire*, 50, 56, 108, 132, 151, 176, 183, 198–9, *see also* Socialism
Légion Française des Combattants, 222, 228, 229
Lenin, 18, 108
Liberalism, 30–4, 37, 43, 94, 104–5, 112, 117–20, 121n., 127, 139

INDEX

Liberation, post-war, 232–3, 249
Ligue de la Patrie Française, 149
Ligue des Droits de l'Homme, 131
Ligue des Patriotes, 153, 155, 195
Little Entente, 203, 205–6
Louis XIV, 11, 123, 127
Louis XVI, 12, 119
Louis Philippe, 13, 32, 80, 164
Lyautey, Marshal, 61–2, 163, 166–7

Macmahon, Marshal, 63–4, 86–8, 94, 101, 139, 164, 187
Maginot Line, 184, 200, 208n., 209
Maistre, J. de, 28–9, 35, 151
Marie, A., 241
Marin, L., 104, 151
Marx, K., 23–4, 26
Massu, Gén., 254
Maurras, C., 29, 73, 123–4, 141, 148, 157, 196, 216, 222, 223
Mayors, 88, 97–8, 147
Mendès-France, P., 245, 252–3
Middle classes, 31, 43, 53–65, 68, 71, 73, 91, 102–7, 125, 160–1, 176–7, 182, 196, 248–9
Militarism, 16, 49, 61, 72, 102, 105, 113, 120–1, 124, 129–34, 152, 156–7, 160–2, 170–1
Millerand, E. A., 47, 49–50, 188
Ministerial responsibility, 13, 15–16, 31–2, 79, 85–6, 92, 110, 112, 113, 119, 236
Moch, J., 240
Mollet, G., 246, 252, 253
Monarchism, 14, 28–30, 34, 39, 59, 61, 63–4, 71, 75–87, 90–3, 97, 101, 106, 112–13, 116, 129, 136, 152–6, 162, 171, 195; Legitimism, 14, 28, 36, 61, 65, 80–2, 87, 102, 118; Orleanism, 13–14, 32–3, 61, 65, 80–2, 102, 131

Monnet Plan, 234–5
Mouvement Républicain Populaire, 128, 233, 240, 244–5, 250, 253
Mun, Comte Albert de, 62, 141

Napoleon I, 13, 32–3, 54–5, 59, 69, 97, 140–3, *see also* Bonapartism
Napoleon III, 9, 15, 17, 68, 77, 84, *see also* Bonapartism
National Assembly, 12–16, 25, 33, 39, 43, 64, 76–80, 83–93, 101, 136, 148, 211, 214, 220, 237, 239, 241
Nationalism, 123–6, 130, 134, 146, 148–9, 153, 157, 167, 177, 183, 195, 204

Pacifism, 129, 131, 149–50, 177, 212
Painlevé, P., 120, 185
Papacy, 29, 127, 134–6, 139–43, *see also* Church and Separation of Church and State
Paris, 25–7, 37, 45–7, 56, 76–7, 98, 107, 131, 136, 155, 159, 174, 183, 196
Paris, Comte de, 14, 61, 80–2
Peasant Proprietorship, 31, 41–2, 51, 105, 122, 172
Peasantry, 32–3, 39–46, 50–3, 64, 73, 103–6, 176, 182, 191–3, 222, 247–8
Péguy, C., 124–5, 133, 149–50
Pétain, Marshal, 29, 51, 63, 88, 132, 177, 208, 211, 213–21
Pflimlin, P., 254, 255
Pinay, A., 245, 251
Plebiscites, 15, 31, 33, 101, 120, 156n.

Pléven, René, 253
Poincaré, R., 73, 98, 149, 185, 187–8, 202–5
Poland, 203–7
Police, 88, 196, 209
Population, 45–6, 138, 164, 172, 179, 181–2, 249
Poujadists, 240, 245, 246
President, 14–15, 64, Chapter III *passim*, 187–9, 191, 214, 215, 220, 238, 241
Press, 17–18, 22, 30–1, 34, 67–8, 71, 72n., 84, 87, 108, 119–20, 123, 126, 142, 159, 175, 195, 198–9, 209, 222
Prévost-Paradol, L. A., 43, 118–19, 189n.
Proudhon, P. J., 22, 23, 26
Provisional Government 37, 77, 109, 121, 125, 128, 133, 150–1, 184, 233–6, App. I (I) and II (C)

Queuille, H., 241, 242, 245, 252

Radicalism, 32, 36–7, 42–3, 46, 51–2, 58, 73n., 79, 91, 93–4, 101–8, 112, 116–17, 119–21, 130, 140–1, 145, 171, 174–8, 186, 197, 245–6, 250
Ramadier, P., 241, 244
Rassemblement du Peuple Français, 243, 244–5, 250
Referendum, 101, 189n.
Renan, E., 73, 131
Republicanism, 15, 37–41, 44, 46, 58, 65, 72–105, 107n., 110n., 114, 120, 124, 128–31, 139, 141, 153, 156, 232–7, 256
Resistance, 128, 130, 132, Chapter VI *passim*; National Council of Resistance, 231; Charter, 234, Appendix II (C)
Revanche, 148–9, 153–4, 157, 163
Revolutionary Ideas, 10–13, 16, 23, 25, 36, 41–2, 57, 103, 112, 116, 127, 133, 143, 146, 222–3, 233, *see also* Jacobinism
Revolutionary tradition, Chapter I *passim*, 42, 46, 50, 52–3, 88, 103, 105, 112, 114, 116, 123, 132–3, 170, 198, 222, 233, 238
Reynaud, P., 104, 151, 210, 211, 213, 241
Rhineland, 183, 198, 200, 203, 205, 208–9
Right Wing, 31, 38n., 67, 82, 87, 90, 104, 113–14, 125, 129, 130, 151, 154, 157, 177, 184–6, 194–197, 202, 204, 212, 220, 222, 230; *see also Bloc National*; Bonapartism; *Légion Française des Combattants*; Monarchism; *Rassemblement du Peuple Français*
Riom Trials, 207, 224
Rocque, Colonel de la, 34, 195–6
Rouher, E., 84
Rousseau, J. J., 11, 14, 18, 20, 21, 25, 122, 126, 128, 204
Ruhr, 49, 193, 203
Russia, 10, 18, 71, 152, 172, 186, 194, 195, 201, 203, 205, 207–8, 218, 220, 231

Salan, Gén., 254
Saint-Simon, C-H de, 20–2, 25
Schuman, R., 240, 251
Second Empire, 15, 17, 22, 29, 37, 41, 84, 118–19, 124, 131, 140, 148
Second Republic, 13–14, 17–18, 22, 33, 35, 76, 118, 131–2

Sedan, 9, 18, 25, 33, 37, 119, 156, 179, 180
Senate, 15, 17, 44, 58, 64, 70, Chapter III *passim*, 118, 164, 184–6, 189n., 190–1, 204, 239
Separation of Church and State, 30, 34, 72, 120, 127, 129, 141–3, 163, 172, *see also* Anti-clericalism *and* Church
Separation of Powers, 14, 36, 54, 58, 86, 101, 117, 118n.
Sieyès, Abbé de, 11, 57
Socialism, 18–27, 30–3, 43, 47–51, 55, 72–3, 93, 104, 107–8, 114, 117, 121, 125, 128–32, 141, 145, 150, 162, 171–8, 182, 186, 192, 197, *see also* Labour organizations *and* Left Wing
Sorel, G., 46, 73, 131, 174
Sovereignty of the People, 11–12, 25, 31–2, 43, 132, 191
Spain, 200, 205
Stavisky, S., 183, 196, 209
Switzerland, 139, 170, 180

Tardieu, A., 104, 188, 189n.
Thiers, 18, 25–7, 32–3, 36–7, 40, 64, 75–88, 93, 97, 99, 105, 116–19, 147, 151, 187, 220, 221
Thomas, A., 152

Thorez, M., 108, 151
Trade Unionism, *see* Labour organizations
Traditionalism, 11, 36, 52, 122–3, 216–20, 222

Union, French, Appendix I (J)
U.S.A., 67, 206–7, 218; Political System, 10, 41, 54, 61, 75, 93, 104, 115, 139, 170, 188, 220, 231
U.S.S.R., *see* Russia

Vichy Government, 29, 40, 60, 63, 122, 130, 160, 168, 199, 208, 211–12, 214–25, 233, 238

Waldeck-Rousseau, R., 162
War of 1870, 15, 138; of 1914, 73, 108, 128; of 1939, 168, 183–4, 200, 206–10, Chapter VI *passim*
Weygand, General, 69, 213, 216, 221
Working classes, 26, 31, 39, 43, 45–53, 109, 125, 161, 174–6, 182, 194, 196, *see also* Artisans

Zola, E., 73, 159, 161